14 DAY BOOK
This book is due on or before
the latest date stamped below

WITHDRAWN

CALIFORNIA STATE UNIVERSITY, NORTHRIDGE LIBRARY

D0930168

Big Players and the Economic Theory of Expectations

Also by Roger Koppl

SUBJECTIVISM AND ECONOMIC ANALYSIS: Essays in Memory of
Ludwig M. Lachmann (*edited with Gary Mongiori*)

Big Players and the Economic Theory of Expectations

Roger Koppl
Professor of Economics and Finance
Fairleigh Dickinson University
Madison, New Jersey

© Roger Koppl 2002

All rights reserved. No reproduction, copy or transmission of
this publication may be made without written permission.

No paragraph of this publication may be reproduced, copied or
transmitted save with written permission or in accordance with
the provisions of the Copyright, Designs and Patents Act 1988,
or under the terms of any licence permitting limited copying
issued by the Copyright Licensing Agency, 90 Tottenham Court
Road, London W1T 4LP.

Any person who does any unauthorized act in relation to this
publication may be liable to criminal prosecution and civil
claims for damages.

The author has asserted his right to be identified as the author
of this work in accordance with the Copyright, Designs and
Patents Act 1988.

First published 2002 by
PALGRAVE MACMILLAN
Houndmills, Basingstoke, Hampshire RG21 6XS and
175 Fifth Avenue, New York, N.Y. 10010
Companies and representatives throughout the world

PALGRAVE MACMILLAN is the new global academic imprint of the Palgrave
Macmillan division of St. Martin's Press LLC and of Palgrave Macmillan Ltd.
Macmillan® is a registered trademark in the United States, United Kingdom
and other countries. Palgrave is a registered trademark in the European
Union and other countries.

ISBN 0–333–67826–5

This book is printed on paper suitable for recycling and
made from fully managed and sustained forest sources.

A catalogue record for this book is available
from the British Library.

Library of Congress Cataloging-in-Publication Data
Koppl, Roger, 1957–
    Big players and the economic theory of expectations / Roger Koppl.
        p. cm.
    Includes bibliographical references and index.
    ISBN 0–333–67826–5
        1. Rational expectations (Economic theory) 2. Economic forecasting.
3. Business cycles. 4. Money market–Forecasting. 5. Stock price forecasting.
6. Economics–History–20th century. I. Title.
HB3722 .K66 2002
339'.01–dc21   2001060270

10   9   8   7   6   5   4   3   2   1
11 10 09 08 07 06 05 04 03 02

Printed and bound in Great Britain by
Antony Rowe Ltd, Chippenham, Wiltshire

To Maria, who brings joy

Contents

List of Figures

List of Tables

Preface

This book outlines a theory of expectations. In my theory, expectations depend on institutions. Markets, especially financial markets, are not "efficient always" or "efficient never." They are more or less efficient, depending on institutions.

Brisk competition and stable rules of market exchange create an evolutionary filter of profit and loss. This filter tends to produce market efficiency. When the operation of this filter is disrupted, by an activist central bank for example, market participants are thrown into ignorance and uncertainty. In financial markets, herding results. Expectations are more prescient in the institutional settings tending toward efficiency, less prescient otherwise.

My theory resolves a paradox, dogging any theory of expectations. To have testable content, it seems, the theory would have to predict the unpredictable thoughts of people. If I am right, however, a testable theory need not predict thoughts. The key to resolving the paradox is to recognize the dual nature of expectations as both thoughts and actions. Thoughts are hard to predict. But actions can be predicted if people are constrained by brisk competition. If my theory has value, it should be of interest to economists working in many areas, including macroeconomics and financial markets.

My theory of expectations leads to the theory of "Big Players." This theory will be of interest to economists studying financial markets and bubbles. Big Players, such as discretionary finance ministers, encourage herding and bubbles. The theory of Big Players has testable implications about when bubbles are more likely and when less. My approach to financial markets includes efficient markets as an important special case sometimes approximated by real markets.

The same basic approach can be adapted to explain instability in money demand. If my approach is about right, instability in money supply causes instability in money demand. If this claim is sustained in future studies, the theory of money demand requires significant amendment.

I test the theory of Big Players using three different statistical techniques. These techniques are applied to data from the "credit ruble" of Czarist Russia. The first technique is Benoit Mandelbrot's R/S analysis. The second is standard GARCH analysis. The third is a new technique devised by Nardone and me (Koppl and Nardone 2001). The new technique gives us a different way to think about volatility dynamics. There is some evidence that it may have advantages over GARCH analysis. The new technique is related to the complexity theory of the Santa Fe Institute.

My theory is a product of the "Austrian" tradition of Mises and Hayek. The Austrian tradition uses interpretive techniques. The interpretive tradition in social science is also known as the *Verstehen* or "understanding" tradition. The tradition can be traced from Wihelm Dilthey to Max Weber and beyond. I have relied on the interpretive theory of Alfred Schutz, who combined Weber's method of ideal types with Edmund Husserl's phenomenological philosophy. Schutz's theory was intended to give support to the economic theory of Ludwig von Mises and other members of the Austrian School. I argue that Schutz and Hayek were Misesian methodologists. This argument may be of interest to students of methodology and the history of economic thought. Those who admire evolutionary psychology may be interested in the evolutionary account of *Verstehen* given in Appendix 1 (p. 204).

If I am right to view expectations as both thoughts and actions, economists need a theory of choice that encompasses both the "objective" and "subjective" dimensions of human action. To this end, I propose a friendly amendment to the idea of "routines" proposed by Nelson and Winter (1982). My suggested concept of "language game" (defined in the text) incorporates both the subjective and objective dimensions of action. It may thus have some advantages over the earlier notion of routine. My use of the concept of language games lets us "systematically … account for [two central] features of human behaviour, its responsiveness to incentives *and* its rule-following nature" (Vanberg 1994, p. 16, emphasis in original). It also includes the social nature of action in our basic description of choice. Such an inclusion seems necessary if we are to have a theory of action suitable to a theory of expectations. (The same point could be made about the theory of ideology.)

I use interpretive, mathematical, and statistical methods. I have used methods we might loosely call "scientific" and methods we might loosely call "humanistic." Some apology is required for this unusual combination. Some readers comfortable with one set of methods will dislike the other. I have tried to make it possible for readers to skip the "humanistic" parts and concentrate on the "scientific" parts, or vice versa. Only Chapter 1 is required reading for all comers. Greater uniformity of method might have been desirable, but the nature of my subject requires me to use both "scientific" and "humanistic" methods.

Economics has a dual nature. Economics studies the systematic but unintended consequences of human action. Human actions have intended meanings; their unintended consequences do not. The intended meanings of human actors are subject to interpretation. We try to understand them somewhat in the way we try to understand a poem or the instructions on a tube of toothpaste. The systematic but unintended consequences of human action are not subject to the same sort of interpretation precisely because they are unintended. They have no intended meaning, only a regular pattern. The pattern is meaningless in the same sense that the regularities of astronomy are meaningless. Economics is partly interpretation of subjective meanings and partly analysis of objective patterns. The dual nature of the subject requires the use of both "scientific" and "humanistic" methods.

My attempt to solve some problems relating to expectations in economics has driven me to produce not only a theory of expectations, but also a research program in economics. It has methodological, theoretical, and empirical aspects. Further work is required in each area. This research program does not, of course, replace existing theories. If it has value, the program will complement the ongoing work of other economists. It may be especially relevant to economists working in the "emerging new orthodoxy" described in the Coda (p. 195). Trends in New Institutional Economics, Post Walrasian Economics, Constitutional Political Economy, Complexity Economics, and Austrian economics suggest the possibility of a common evolutionary theory that takes cognition and institutions seriously. I offer this book to my colleagues with the hope that it may contribute to such a common theory.

Roger Koppl

Acknowledgments

The author and publishers acknowledge with thanks permission from the following to reproduce copyright material: Kluwer Academic Publishers for material in Chapter 3, from Roger Koppl, "Schutz and Shackle: Two Views of Choice," *Review of Austrian Economics*, 14 (2/3): 181–191 (2001); Academic Press, for material in Chapters 7 and 8, from Roger Koppl and Leland B. Yeager. "Big Players and Herding in Asset Markets: The Case of the Russian Ruble," *Explorations in Economic History*, 3(3): 367–368 (1996); Barmarick Publications (UK), for material in Chapter 8, from John Broussard and Roger Koppl, "Explaining Volatility Dynamics: The Case of the Russian Ruble," *Managerial Finance*, 25(1): 49–63 (1999); Gordon & Breach Publishing, for material in Chapter 9, from Roger Koppl and Carlo Nardone, "The Angular Distribution of Asset Returns in Delay Space," *Discrete Dynamics in Nature and Society*, 6: 101–120 (2001).

Mie Augier provided useful comments and much encouragement and practical help. John Broussard was co-author to parts of Chapter 8 and gave me many useful comments. William Butos is co-author of several chapters in this book. Working with Bill has been an exciting intellectual journey for me. His encouragement has been unfailing. Catherine Gilanshah gets credit for most of Chapter 10. Richard Langlois is probably the author of more in this book than I realize or would care to know. He has been an important influence on me for many years. Maria Minniti made this book possible. She patiently endured many discussions and rants about it. She also gave me more love and attention than any husband deserves. Without her love and support, the book would not have mattered. Barkley Rosser was an important source of encouragement early on. I have profited from many discussions with him. Andy Schotter made an indirect contribution to this book many years ago through an act of kindness that allowed me to stay in graduate school and finish my professional training. I owe much to my teacher, Leland Yeager. He is a co-author of Chapter 8. With each passing year, I discover that he has shaped my thinking more profoundly than I had previously imagined. I thank all of these people for their contributions to my efforts. Many other people deserve my thanks for comments and discussions. A few of them are Scott Beaulier, Peter Boettke, Don Boudreaux, Joe Cobb, Tyler

Cowan, Ben Drew, Paula Drew, Fred Englander, Robert Greenfield, Stephen Horwitz, Gary Jaworski, Carsten Koch, Israel Kirzner, Thorbjørn Knudsen, Kristian Kriener, David Laidler, Uskali Maki, Gary Mongiovi, Larry Moss, Klaus Niehans, Karen Palasek, John Schiemann, George Selgin, Richard Wagner, and Burton Zwick. I was privileged to be a Visiting Professor at the Copenhagen Business School in the Spring semester of 2000. That visit was essential to the completion of this book. I thank Kristian Kriener and Hans Siggaard Jensen for their invitation and for arranging for my visit. For financial support, I thank the Copenhagen Business School, the Earhart Foundation, and Fairleigh Dickinson University.

ROGER KOPPL

Part I

Introduction

1
Introduction and Summary[1]

Expectations and economic theory

The need for a theory

The problem of expectations is one of the central issues of economic theory. Every human action aims at a more or less distant future. Thus, expectations guide all action. For this reason, expectations matter in any economic argument. John Maynard Keynes (1936) helped to make expectations a separate and vital problem of economic theory. He explained unemployment as a product of deficient foresight. No one knows the future. F. A. Hayek (1937) argued that a tendency toward equilibrium exists only if "the expectations of the people and particularly of the entrepreneurs ... become more and more correct" over time. (1937, p. 45). "The only trouble," Hayek lamented, "is that we are still pretty much in the dark about (a) the conditions under which this tendency is supposed to exist and (b) the nature of the process by which individual knowledge is changed" (1937, p. 45).

Much has been written about expectations since Hayek's lament. And yet we are still pretty much in the dark. Keynes (1936, 1937) outlined a theory of expectations. Shackle (1949, 1972) and others have developed Keynes' theory. It is rich in useful insights. I will draw on them in later chapters. But I will also argue that the fundamentals of the theory are deficient. The orthodox treatment takes a view exactly opposite to that of Keynes. With rational expectations, everyone knows the future. There is widespread dissatisfaction with the rational expectations hypothesis. Fundamental criticisms of it are widely accepted. But no clear replacement has yet come along. Fundamental work on learning and expectations has been done by a variety of very different authors. (A few of the more prominent examples are Arthur

1994a, 1994b, Bikhchandani *et al.* 1992, Binmore 1987, Choi 1993, Denzau and North 1994, and O'Driscoll and Rizzo 1996.) This work has not yet given us a complete theory with empirical implications.

Hayek identified a gap in our knowledge. In this book I propose a theory of expectations that helps to fill this gap. The theory explains the process by which individual knowledge is changed. My general theory leads to the theory of Big Players. The theory of Big Players identifies some of the conditions under which the tendency toward equilibrium exists. It has testable implications. My co-authors and I have conducted several tests. So far, the theory holds up. Like other efforts, my theory is incomplete. But it provides broad foundations for further work in the area, and I have drawn from it a reasonably broad set of empirical implications.

The meaning of "expectations"

The term "expectations" covers two different economic concepts. A theory of expectations should encompass both senses of the term. It is unfortunate that one word covers both concepts. But past usage dictates that both concepts identify "expectations."

In its first meaning, expectations are expectations. In its second meaning, expectations are "as-if" rationalizations. Consider an American crossing the street in London. He knows perfectly well that Londoners drive on the left and that he must look to the right when he steps into the street. But when he does step into the street, he looks to the left. In one sense, he expects cars to drive on the left. If you ask him, he will tell you Londoners drive on the left. In another sense, however, he expects cars to drive on the right. He acts by habit, and cars driving on the right shaped his habits. The expectation is implicit in the action. He acts *as if* he expects cars to drive on the right.

A second example develops the point. My example will be treated more carefully in later chapters. In a stable environment, stock prices approximate present values. Traders have "rational expectations." This claim does not imply that any one trader has good foresight. It means only that there is no systematic tendency for prices to overestimate or underestimate present values. Otherwise, unexploited profit opportunities would exist. Since profit opportunities are quickly exploited, stock prices are unbiased estimates of present values. The market acts *as if* the *representative agent* has rational expectations whether or not any real trader makes unbiased estimates of present values. In this case, an economist may not be interested in the thoughts of agents. He may be interested only in their actions and interactions.

An exogenous instability might corrupt the market process that keeps prices in line with present values. Traders will be aware of their uncertainty about the future. In their ignorance and uncertainty, they may imitate one another. They herd. The expectations of these uncertain traders are their thoughts about the future, namely the increased difficulty of forecasting. By assumption, the market no longer disciplines agents well. The economist must take some interest in the thoughts of agents.

The as-if expectations of the representative agent do not refer to the cognitive processes of real people. Such expectations are "acognitive." The expectations invoked in a theory of herding refer to the cognitive processes of real people. Such expectations are "cognitive." In all markets, whether "efficient" or not, both types of expectations exist. Both can be studied. Their relative importance, however, is not always the same. When the market discipline of profit and loss is severe, cognitive expectations may not have much influence on the overall behavior of the market. Acognitive expectations, and the processes that shape them, may be more important. When the market discipline of profit and loss breaks down, acognitive expectations may be of less interest. The mental processes shaping cognitive expectations may grow in explanatory importance.

The example of the American pedestrian in London shows that cognitive and acognitive expectations may be inconsistent. But this is not the general case. They are probably consistent most of the time. In either case, they will have a kind of coherence. A coherent story accounts for both types and for their degree of consistency. We can understand why the American pedestrian has conflicting cognitive and acognitive expectations.

Cognitive expectations are our ideas about the future. They are "subjective." The "long-term expectations" of the *General Theory* are cognitive expectations. In this meaning, the economic concept of "expectation" is about the same as the common-sense meaning of "expectation." Cognitive expectations emerge from processes of learning.

Acognitive expectations are implicit in our actions. They are "objective." Rational expectations are acognitive, at least in some interpretations. In this meaning, the economic concept of "expectation" differs from the common-sense meaning of "expectation." Acognitive expectations emerge from natural selection.

It may seem odd to describe rational expectations as "acognitive." But defenses along these lines are common. Begg (1982), for example, invokes "economic Darwinism" (p. 63). He warns us not to take the model "too literally" (p. 30). We are "proceeding 'as if' individuals" were very clever (p. 30). But the notion of rational expectations as cognitive is still quite common. For example, Sargent (1993) interprets rational expectations as "describing the outcome of a process in which people have optimally *chosen* their perceptions" (p. 7, emphasis in original). The failure to clearly distinguish cognitive and acognitive expectations has contributed to confusion over the correct interpretation of rational expectations.

A theory of expectations should encompass both types of expectations. It should include a theory of cognitive expectations and a theory of acognitive expectations. Any economic argument should be consistent with both theories. It should provide a reasonable account of both cognitive and acognitive expectations. In this sense, there should be coherence between them.

Distinguishing the two meanings of "expectations" has consequences

Distinguishing the two meanings of "expectations" in economics has consequences. The distinction leads us to recognize very different types of analyses that are both important to a theory of expectations. The first uses the "humanistic" notion of "*Verstehen.*" The second uses the "scientific" notion of "natural selection." One must bring "humanistic" and "scientific" elements under one theoretical umbrella. A body of thought is "humanistic" if it rejects any reduction of human action to simpler non-human elements. In this sense, it may be said to respect the autonomy and dignity of man. A body of thought is "scientific" if it includes law-like generalizations.

The theory of cognitive expectations is closely related to theories of learning and to cognitive psychology. My principle sources in this regard are Alfred Schutz's *The Phenomenology of the Social World* (1932) and F. A. Hayek's *The Sensory Order* (1952a). Schutz's work is not an exercise in cognitive psychology. Like cognitive psychology, however, it provides a description of "shared mental models" (Denzau and North 1994) and of learning. Hayek and Schutz offer something missing in many accounts of cognitive psychology, namely, "*Verstehen.*" *Verstehen*, or "understanding," is the human ability to grasp what other people have in mind. (See Appendix 1.) We are skilled at guessing meanings even though the evidence is always inadequate to choose among competing possibilities. The *Verstehen* tradition is an important source of theories of interpersonal understanding. A theory of cognitive expectations must include a theory of interpersonal understanding.

Schutz's work was originally meant to defend the "Austrian" version of neoclassical economics (Prendergast 1986) and was a fundamental influence on Fritz Machlup (Koppl 2000a, Langlois and Koppl 1991).[2] Schutz's analysis of "anonymity" is fundamental to the theory of cognitive expectations. Hayek's work addressed a traditional problem in philosophy, namely the mind–body problem. His solution led him to a cognitive psychology with useful implications for economics. Because Hayek was first and foremost an economist, his theory of mind should be of special interest to economists who recognize the need for a cognitive element in economic theory.

In the right institutional context, the filter of profit and loss will select acognitive expectations that are highly adapted to the economic environment. Economic expectations will be relatively prescient. In some of these cases, the assumption of rational maximizing may be appropriate. In other contexts, however, natural selection does not yield approximations to optimal actions. Economic expectations will be less prescient. In such cases, the assumption of rational maximizing is inappropriate. The evolutionary environment determines the degree of "rationality" of outcomes and the prescience of expectations. Expectations will be more prescient in some environments than in others. My sources for the analysis of economic evolution include Alchian (1950), Hayek (1967a, 1967b, 1973), Langlois (1986b), Menger (1871, 1883), Schumpeter (1934), Adam Smith (1937), and Max Weber (1927).

A stable economic environment with atomistic competition tends to produce rational outcomes and prescient expectations. Lack of stability or atomism produces ignorance and uncertainty. Economic expectations grow less reliable. My empirical results address one way in which atomism may be reduced, namely, by the presence of a "Big Player." The presence of Big Players tends to produce "Keynesian" behavior in financial markets. This behavior includes herding. Stability and atomism encourages a more "neoclassical" result. The theory of Big Players draws on Keynes (1936) and others influenced by him, such as Scharfstein and Stein (1990). But it views quite differently the ignorance and uncertainty that produce herding. In Keynes' theory, ignorance and uncertainty are irremediable; herding is a consequence of liquidity. In my theory, ignorance, uncertainty, and herding are remediable consequences of the institutional environment of financial markets. They are always present in some degree, but policies and institutions influence them greatly.

A preview of some useful foundations for the theory

My theory brings together seemingly very disparate elements. It includes a theory of cognitive expectations and a theory of acognitive expectations. It includes "neoclassical" models of efficient financial markets and "Keynesian" models of herding. To bring all these elements together coherently, it is convenient to abandon the "neoclassical" model of utility maximization in favor of a version of rule following. In Chapter 5 I propose viewing any social action as a skilled performance subject to the publicly known rules of some *language game*. (Compare Koppl and Langlois, 1994, pp. 81–82.) A "language game" is "a set of rules about how to talk, think, and act in different situations" (Koppl and Langlois, 1994, p. 82).[3] The language-games framework is a semantic convention that I believe may be useful for economists. It includes neoclassical maximizing as an important special case.

The rules of a language game may be viewed from three perspectives. First, they tell us what to think. This perspective gives us the agent-theory of the language game. Second, they tell us what to say. This perspective gives us the agent-rhetoric of the language game. Third, they tell us what to do. This perspective gives us the agent-practice of a language game.

The "subjective" theory of cognitive expectations studies the agent-theories of operative language games. The "objective" theory of acognitive expectations studies the agent-practices of operative language games. The value of the language-games framework is precisely that it allows us to distinguish, within one unifying framework, the objective and subjective dimensions of human action. Furthermore, it can correlate them with the rhetoric used by economic actors. McCloskey and Klamer (1995) argue that we should view economic actors as "rhetors." A theory of agent-rhetoric is vital to the economic theory of ideology (Koppl and Langlois 1994).

The role of expectations in economics as a social science[4]

The theory of expectations I propose in this book grew out of an attempt to understand the problem of expectations as Ludwig Lachmann saw it. Lachmann first stated the problem of expectations that I have taken up. In his essay on "The Role of Expectations in Economics as a Social Science" (1943). Lachmann drew our attention to the need for a theory of expectations in which each person's actions are animated by the spontaneous activity of a free human mind. I will call the problem of building a radically subjectivist theory of expectations the "Lachmann problem."

It is not obvious how the Lachmann problem can be solved. How can I let the agents of my model be free and still predict anything – even within the model! We should take Lachmann's radical subjectivism seriously. But if we do, we seem to fall into the horrible pit of open possibility with no ladder upon which to get out. This, we have been told, is nihilism.

I think there is a way out. We can combine the radical subjectivist's attention to human thoughts with a more "objective" understanding of the evolution of rule-governed action. Doing so may permit us to correlate observable market conditions with certain properties of economic expectations. It may help us to learn when expectations will be more prescient and when less. It may help us learn when markets are driven mostly by fundamentals and when they are more subject to fad and fashion. This solution has been sketched above.

In his essay "The Role of Expectations in Economics as a Social Science" (1943), Lachmann mapped out a position from which he never deviated. It is this same position, for instance, that he adopted in an important essay for the *Journal of Economic Literature*, "From Mises to Shackle: An Essay on Austrian Economics and the Kaleidic Society" (Lachmann 1976). Lachmann called for a theory of expectations that goes beyond the efforts proposed by mainstream economists.

The "modern theory" of the 1930s had brought the "introduction of expectations" into economics (1943, p. 65). Some, Keynes among them, had treated expectations as "data." Others had proposed to treat them as "variables it is our task to explain" (Schumpeter 1939, vol. I, p. 55 as quoted in Lachmann 1943, p. 66). Lachmann rejected both ways of treating expectations.

We cannot regard expectations as mere "data," as given to us. We must ask "why they are what they are" (1943, p. 65). We are, indeed, "compelled" to seek out a "causal explanation" of economic expectations (1943, p. 65). Expectations, after all, are on a "somewhat different plane" (1943, p. 66) from the distribution of mineral deposits or the public's preferences between movie directors. The distribution of expectations, unlike that of mineral deposits, is "largely the result of the experience of economic processes" (1943, p. 66).

But neither can we regard expectations as variables to be inferred from the "business situation." Different interpreting minds will draw different inferences from the same "objective" data. Thus, "there will be as many 'business situations' as there are different interpretations of the same facts, and they will all exist alongside each other" (1943, p. 67).

Here we come to the dark heart of Lachmann's ideas on expectations. Expectations are not constant, or even changing, data imping-
ing, as it were, from outside the economic process. They are
interpretations. But interpretations differ in ways that defy prediction:
"The absence of a uniform relationship between a set of observable
events which might be described as a *situation* on the one hand, and
expectations on the other hand, is thus seen to be the crux of the
matter" (1943, p. 67, emphasis in original). We are thus obliged to
view expectations as "economically indeterminate" (1943, p. 67). For
Lachmann, "it cannot be emphasized too strongly" that attempts to
test empirical hypotheses with historical data will be "quite useless" if
they are "confined to the study of [the] relations between objective
facts and expectations" (1943, p. 68). The best we can do is to render
expectations "intelligible" by seeing in them a plan based on an interpretation of the facts of experience (1943, pp. 68–73). (I will come to a
somewhat more optimistic conclusion.)

For Lachmann, "it is by reducing 'action' to 'plan' that we 'understand' the actions of individuals" (1943, p. 69). He infers from this that
"it is the *subjective* nature of beliefs which imparts indeterminateness to
expectations" but "it is their *mental* nature which renders them capable
of explanation" (1943, p. 73, emphasis in original). He draws the further
conclusion that economists must (in 1943) expand beyond "the subjectivism of wants" to embrace "the subjectivism of interpretation" (1943,
p. 73). I take this to be the same position expressed in 1976 as the invitation to "extend" subjectivism from Mises to Shackle, from the subjectivism of "tastes" to the subjectivism of "expectations" (1976, p. 58). The
theory of expectations whose absence Lachmann calls our attention to
must embrace the "subjectivism of interpretation" (1943, p. 69). He later
spoke of the "subjectivism of active minds." "The mental activity of
ordering and formulating ends allocating means to them, making and
revising plans, determining when action has been successful, all these
are its forms of expression" (Lachmann, 1990, p. 37).

Lachmann has put a hard task indeed to economists. Expectations
are to be neither data nor variables. They are to be endogenous, but
not functionally related to observable facts. Rather than functional
relations, we are to see in expectations subjective interpretations of
facts whose meaning for future action is always more or less obscure.

A theory that satisfies Lachmann's call for a subjectivism of interpretations must satisfy three criteria. First, it must give expectations a
place within economic theory. Second, the theory must be subjective
in a strong sense: expectations are produced by active minds, each of

which is more or less unique. Finally, expectations must be endogenous to the market process.

The hard thing is to satisfy the second and third criteria simultaneously. Expectations may be right or wrong. Market efficiency depends crucially on the accuracy of economic expectations. If one doubts that markets tend to coordinate action, one may be inclined to think that expectations are formed through an essentially psychological process as in Keynes' Chapter 12. Greater faith in the market may incline one to think that expectations are indeed "rational" in a sense close to that of Lucas and Muth. But as I indicated earlier, both the New Classical and Old Keynesian approaches to expectations require one to choose in advance one's modeling strategy. One must decide *a priori* whether to represent expectations as "rational" and coordinative or as "psychological" and disequilibrating. The trick, I think, is to represent endogenously formed expectations in a way that skirts the unsatisfactory choice between *faith* and *doubt* in the coordinative prowess of markets. If we are stuck with an *a priori* choice between faith and doubt, an essential question of our discipline is not empirical or logical, but purely ideological. If the Lachmann problem can be solved, perhaps we can avoid this ideologically charged choice.

Outline of the theory

As I indicated above, I distinguish two kinds of expectations. Cognitive expectations are individual thoughts about the future. Acognitive expectations are propensities to act. I rely mostly on Alfred Schutz for my treatment of cognitive expectations. I rely mostly on F.A. Hayek for my treatment of acognitive expectations.

Schutz and the Lachmann problem

Schutz made a detailed study of how meanings are produced and distributed in society. He showed that we think in stereotypes. He called them "typifications." These typifications are always somewhat empty caricatures of the reality they represent. Some of them, however, are closer to reality than others. Some of our typifications of other people are very detailed. They contained many psychological particulars. Your typification of a loved one contains a rich psychological portrait of a unique individual. It is very "concrete." Other typifications are quite empty. Your typification of a "bus driver" does not represent any particular person. It contains a very thin psychological portrait. It is highly "anonymous."

Anonymous types help us to form reliable expectations. I explain how in Chapter 6, where I discuss "Anonymity and Reflexivity." In the right situation, that of "closed reflexivity," anonymity helps us form reliable expectations. You can reliably expect a bus driver to show up at the bus stop at the customary time and follow the customary route. You cannot reliably predict what unique individuals will do. No one expected Alexander to cut the Gordian knot.

The use of anonymous types helps economic actors make reliable predictions. Something similar may be said of economic theorists. Social scientists may be able to predict confidently the results of processes whose descriptions are given using only personal types of high anonymity. But when the description of a social process requires the use of some personal type(s) of low anonymity, the predictions of social science are more or less unreliable. This point is illustrated by three propositions discussed by Fritz Machlup (1936) in a paper intended to convey some of Schutz's ideas to an audience of economists (the quoted passage has been discussed in Langlois 1986a and Langlois and Koppl 1991):

> Statement (1): "If, because of an abundant crop, the output of wheat is much increased, the price of wheat will fall."
> Statement (2): "If, because of increased wage-rates and decreased interest rates, capital becomes relatively cheaper than labor, new labor-saving devices will be invented."
> Statement (3): "If, because of heavy withdrawals of foreign deposits, the banks are in danger of insolvency, the Central Bank Authorities will extend the necessary credit." (Machlup 1936, p. 64)

The first statement is more reliable than the second and the second is more reliable than the third. Why? As we go down from the first statement, we reach ideal types of lower anonymity. Machlup explained that:

> the causal relations such as stated in (2) and (3) are derived from types of human conduct of a lesser generality or anonymity. To make a statement about the actions of bank authorities (such as (3)) calls for reasoning in a stratum of behavior conceptions of much less anonymous types of actors. We have to know or imagine the acting persons much more intimately. (Machlup 1936, p. 64)

That greater intimacy implies a greater chance that the actor will surprise us by acting out of character. (Later in this chapter I will discuss what Langlois calls the "system constraint" and its role in determining when to use anonymous types.) We cannot be sure the central bank authorities will extend the necessary credit. It is a good guess they will, but they may surprise us with an act of monetary restraint. We can be much more confident in the coming reduction of wheat prices. We can rely on an anonymous typification of the wheat farmer. We need non-anonymous typifications of the central bank's high officials.

Schutz's concept of anonymity helps us to understand how social order is achieved in spite of the subjectivism of active minds. We can cooperate with anonymous others precisely because of their anonymity. Typifications of high anonymity are thin descriptions of robotic creatures. We know that each real person is unique. But we rely on stereotyped pictures of anonymous others. To the extent that we can rely on anonymous typifications of others, we can ignore the idiosyncrasies of our fellow actors. Concrete and anonymous typifications of other people are different. The difference matters. It helps us to solve the Lachmann problem.

The Lachmann problem is the need to have a theory of expectations that builds on the idea that each person's actions are animated by the spontaneous activity of a free human mind. The personal and interpretive quality of (cognitive) expectations spells trouble for any theory of expectations. We seem to require a detailed psychological portrait of each economic actor if we are to say anything at all about the market process. Moreover, each actor seems to require the same sort of psychological detail in his mental portrait of each of his fellow actors.

Schutz's discussion of anonymity shows that we do not always need to rely on a psychologically rich picture of economic actors. Both economic actors and economists may sometimes forgo thick description in favor of thin description. When the observer or his subject requires reference to concrete typifications, we may not be able to say much about expectations. In that case, the results of the market process will be hard to predict.

In other words, the Lachmann problem is more acute in some contexts, less acute in others. When it is most acute, the market process will be hard to fathom and economic theory of limited predictive value. When the Lachmann problem is least acute, the market process will be more transparent and economic theory will have greater predictive value.

Hayek and the Lachmann problem

I have argued that sometimes thin description is good enough. The trick is to know when. On this point Schutz is silent. I think it is fair to say that "radical subjectivism" has so far failed to tell us much about when economic actors might get along with anonymous types.

Perhaps we should not be surprised if radical subjectivism has not told us when thin description is enough. A radically subjectivist account would have to run in terms of the thoughts of economic actors. What we want to know is when those thoughts employ non-anonymous types. But a radically subjectivist account would have to begin with the thoughts of the agent. It is hard to see how a pure subjectivist could get beyond the circular claim that agents use thin description when they use thin description. What we seem to require is a set of "objective" conditions under which the "subjective" thoughts of agents may be represented as employing only anonymous types.[5] Similarly, we need a set of objective conditions under which our own thinking as scientific observers may employ only anonymous types.

Consider again Machlup's three statements. Statement (1) said that "If, because of an abundant crop, the output of wheat is much increased, the price of wheat will fall." What is it that lets our reasoning be guided by anonymous types in this case? Why is a thin description enough? As Langlois and I have argued, it is the "system constraint" (Langlois and Koppl 1991, p. 92). The system constraint is the constraint imposed on individual action by the larger institutional system within which the action takes place. Imagine we have one or a few idiosyncratic wheat farmers or wheat traders. They may act foolishly or arbitrarily. These few oddballs cannot reverse the tide of events. If they try, they risk losses and banishment from the market. The large number of competitors involved and the discipline of profit and loss ensure that we may safely ignore any idiosyncrasies of behavior in the wheat market. Thin description will do for economic observers.

Now consider the positions of participants in the wheat market. If they are operating under a tight system constraint, their actions will be driven into approximate conformity with the underlying situational logic. Those whose actions stray too far from this logic will suffer losses that, if uncorrected, will drive them from the market. A tight system constraint produces a relatively high correspondence between action and circumstance. Under such conditions, we may represent the thoughts of agents as expressing the same correspondence; agents act as if they had prescient expectations. The condition that lets us represent agents in this as-if way is the tight system constraint. But this is also the condition that lets observers rely exclusively on anonymous types. When the system constraint is tight, economic actors forgo thick description in favor of thin description.

The market's evolutionary selection mechanism sometimes keeps anticipations in line, but sometimes does not. I identify two conditions that promote prescient expectations. The first is that the rules of the game of market competition are stable. The second is that competition is atomistic.

The rules of the game are stable when changes in them are small and infrequent. The rules that count here are both formal and informal. Indeed, the only formal rules that count are those that are enforced at least some of the time. Human habits are constantly changing piece-meal. Thus, perfect stability is impossible. But we can often say that the rules of the game are more stable in this market, less stable in that one.

Competition is atomistic when it is rivalrous. When each supplier considers his own actions to have an insignificant impact on the overall market, when there is little "rival consciousness" (Machlup 1952), then competition is atomistic in the relevant sense.

Under the conditions of stability and atomism, I will argue, evolutionary selection mechanisms of the sort Hayek analyzed will produce relatively high levels of economic efficiency. Stable evolutionary environments produce prescient expectations in the social world, goodness of fit in the biological world.

The evolutionary and Hayekian considerations of the present section may not seem to fit well with the phenomenological and Schutzian considerations of the previous section. In the Hayekian view, expectations are (mostly) dispositions to act. The Schutzian framework takes expectations to be thoughts. It is not immediately obvious that these are consistent perspectives. Some definitions may help to clarify the issues.

Fitting cognitive and acognitive expectations together

The "expectations" of economic theory are often acognitive expectations. We say that creditors "expect" zero inflation if they do not insist on an inflation premium. This "expectation" may be nothing more than the conformity to old habits and ways of doing business. Conceivably, some creditors might even have cognitive expectations of inflation. If they don't understand the effect of inflation on purchasing power, they won't ask for an inflation premium. The case imagined is not purely hypothetical. In 1997, an important Italian labor leader expressed concern over the government's low inflation target. Such low inflation, he objected, would reduce the purchasing power of workers' wages.

One must be able to give a reasonable account of the cognitive expectations animating the actions of economic agents. This is a kind of test. If your model requires that we imagine agents acting on unreasonable cognitive expectations, the model is unreasonable. If the cognitive expectations at work are reasonable, the model passes the test.

Acognitive expectations and cognitive expectations are distinct objects. On narrow logical grounds, any combination of them is possible. But it seems reasonable to suppose the two typically fit together. A theory of acognitive expectations without a correlated theory of cognitive expectations is tenuous. We may wonder if any plausible cognitive expectations could correlate with the posited dispositions. Rational expectations, for example, are an assumption about acognitive expectations. Traders act on average as if they had the true model in mind. The assumption is reasonable in some circumstances. But it is not reasonable to assume rational expectations when the implied cognitive expectations entail, say, superhuman powers of calculation.

A theory of cognitive expectations without a correlated theory of acognitive expectations is also dubious, and for a parallel reason. Without the latter we cannot be sure the posited cognitive expectations would really come to prevail. Expectations are, as Lachmann insisted, endogenous to the market process. If we do not correlate our understanding of cognitive expectations with a story of the emergence of acognitive expectations, we have to doubt that the imagined cognitive expectations would really survive the test of market competition. An example may clarify some of the issues. My example will also bring us to some falsifiable implications of my theory of expectations.

Big Players

Consider the operation of a modern asset market. Traders must anticipate future values at least passably well if they are not to be forced out of the game by losses. Profits will encourage those with unusually good foresight to keep at it. An evolutionary selection mechanism works to keep anticipations more or less in line with underlying asset values. If the filter works well, prices will stay close to fundamental values. If the filter works badly, prices may wander freely. Whether the filter works well or not is an empirical question.

Efficient market theories predict that market prices will reflect all available information. (Different kinds of efficiency correspond to different assumptions about what information is available.) An important implication of such theories (together with a few subsidiary assumptions) is that the past changes in an asset's price give no evidence about the direction of future changes. In consequence, (and ignoring some complications about payouts) the expected value of an asset's price in any period is simply its price in the previous period. This property of the return series defines a "martingale." (A random walk is a special case of a martingale in which the higher moments are not expected to change over time. Statistical dependence in higher moments, as with GARCH models, does not violate the efficient markets hypothesis. See LeRoy 1989 for a review of basic issues.)

The statistical evidence for the efficiency of asset markets is strong enough to have persuaded many serious and competent judges. Others doubt. There are many apparent counter-examples. Some evidence suggests that observable market conditions help determine how efficient asset markets are. I review that evidence below and discuss it at greater length in later chapters. The degree of efficiency may be an endogenous variable.

According to the theory of "Big Players" discussed in Chapter 7, the order-giving properties of the filter of profit and loss are corrupted when "Big Players" derange markets. Yeager and I define a Big Player as "anyone who habitually exercises discretionary power to influence the market while himself remaining wholly or largely immune from the discipline of profit and loss" (Koppl and Yeager 1996, p. 368). An interventionist finance minister is our paradigm of a Big Player. But a Big Player may be any actor who combines three things: namely, the power to influence some market, a degree of immunity from competition, and use of discretion in the exercise of his power. Big Players corrupt economic expectations. In financial markets they encourage herding.

The point of the Big Players theory can be put in Schutzian terms. It is a matter of cognitive expectations. Big Players divert each trader's attention from underlying conditions of supply and demand towards the personality of the Big Player. It is hard to know what a Big Player will do. Market participants must base their expectations on a picture of the market in which a highly non-anonymous ideal type is prominent. But this picture is always more or less dubious. Thus, the overall reliability and prescience of economic expectations is reduced. In financial markets, traders come to have less confidence in their own expectations and relatively more confidence in the opinions of others. The importance of the non-anonymous type and the ignorance and uncertainty traders feel regarding the Big Player encourage them to follow the trend. Big Players encourage herding in financial markets.

The point of the Big Players theory may also be put in Hayekian evolutionary terms. The presence of Big Players destabilizes the evolutionary environment. Some actors in the market will have dispositions to act in ways that roughly correspond to the best available guess about the future. These are "fit dispositions." Others will have dispositions to act in ways that are more distant from the underlying economic realities. These are "unfit dispositions." Big Players make fit dispositions less likely to bring profits, more likely to bring losses. They make unfit dispositions less likely to bring losses, more likely to bring profits. Big Players make luck count for more, skill count for less. The dispositions guiding action will be less fit when Big Players derange markets. The overall reliability of acognitive expectations will be lower in the presence of Big Players. In financial markets, the disposition to follow trends is less likely to bring losses. The disposition to respond to fundamentals is more likely to produce losses. Traders who survive market competition under Big Players will have a higher average propensity to herd. Big Players encourage herding in financial markets.

Big Players also encourage "contra-herding." Contra-herding is the tendency for one day's movement in an asset's price to be reversed the next day. When Big Players operate, it is hard to understand the meaning of a price change. Some will see a trend. Other will expect a "correction." Some will follow the trend. Others will be contrarians. Herding and contra-herding will produce bulls and bears who will struggle over the price of the asset.

In the Big Players theory cognitive and acognitive expectations fit together. This complementarity is a strength of the theory. Other theories lack this complementarity. Keynes's treatment of long-run expectations, for example, is about cognitive expectations. It is not clear, in his analysis, what institutional properties of financial markets encourage the perversities he identifies, and what properties discourage them. Keynes refers only to liquidity. Models with rational expectations refer, presumably, to acognitive expectations. They seem to imply that cognitive expectations are perfectly plastic, taking whatever form is needed to generate the predicted behavior. As Thomas Sargent has noted, rational expectations seem to imply that economic actors know with certainty the very structural parameters of the economy that econometricians can only estimate with uncertainty (Sargent 1993, p. 21). The examples of Keynes and rational expectations help to show that we should prefer economic arguments that combine and correlate plausible treatments of both cognitive and acognitive expectations.

Statistical evidence

Chapters 8–10 report on empirical tests of the Big Players theory. Chapter 8 discusses Koppl and Yeager (1996) and Broussard and Koppl (1999). Yeager and I studied an important episode in Russian monetary history using data collected by Yeager. Broussard and I applied a different statistical techniques to the same data. Chapter 9 discusses Koppl and Nardone (2001). Nardone and I propose a new set of statistical tools and apply them to Yeager's ruble data.

Chapter 10 discusses Gilanshah and Koppl (2001). Gilanshah and I studied U.S. money demand from 1950 to 1990. In each of these studies the results were consistent with the Big Player theory. The results tend to support the theory.

Koppl and Yeager (1996) identify an important episode in Russian monetary history. Leland Yeager discovered the episode in question. Yeager gathered the exchange rates analyzed by Koppl and Yeager, Koppl and Nardone, and Broussard and Koppl. From 1856 to 1897 Russia had a paper currency, the "credit ruble." The ruble was typically subject to frequent interventions from the office of the treasury minister. It was a dirty float. Nicolai Bunge was an exception. During his tenure as finance minister, the ruble was left to float freely. Bunge was a strict non-interventionist in the foreign-exchange market. His successor, Ivan Vyshnegradsky was an unusually vigorous interventionist. The period of these two finance ministers gives us an unusually clear case of a move from less to more Big Player influence. Figure 8.1 (p. 150) shows how the behavior of the ruble changed after Vyshnegradsky took office.

Yeager and I analyzed the data graphed in Figure 8.1. We used Mandelbrot's R/S analysis. (My reasons for preferring the "classical" R/S analysis to Lo's approach are given in Chapter 8.) R/S analysis can be used to test for herding (Ahmed *et al.* 1997, Kaen and Rosenman 1986). An increase in the "Hurst coefficient" indicates an increase in herding. The test indicates an increase in herding in the international market for rubles during Vyshnegradsky's tenure as finance minister.

Broussard and I fit a GARCH model to Yeager's ruble data. Figure 8.2 (p. 152) shows the price movements of the ruble under the two finance ministers. We show that GARCH effects are stronger under Vyshnegradsky than under Bunge. We argue that this result is evidence of both herding and contra-herding in the ruble. Recall that contra-herding is the tendency for one day's movement in an asset's price to be reversed the next day. Imagine an asset's price rises for some reason. If no Big Player troubles the market, the price hike may be interpreted as fully reflecting some recent news. If a Big Player is influencing the market, traders will be uncertain. Bulls and bears will react differently to the same event. If the bulls outweigh the bears, the next day's price movement will be in the same direction and may be of about the same size. If the bears outweigh the bulls, the next day's price movement will be in the opposite direction and may be of about the same size. Whether the bulls or the bears prevail, the next day's price may move by about the same amount. This implies statistical dependence in the second moment of the return series. GARCH effects grow stronger when Big Players induce herding and contra-herding.

Nardone and I find further evidence for herding and contra-herding. Following Crack and Ledoit (1996), we plot each day's return against the return of the previous day. Figure 9.1 (p. 165) shows the resulting "compass rose" pattern. The compass rose results from discreteness in the data. We devised a way to identify patterns in the compass rose other than those imposed by discreteness. We plot the number of points clustered about each ray against the angle of that ray. This gives us the "theta histogram" of Figure 9.3 (p. 169). A Monte Carlo technique lets us construct the theta histogram that would exist if returns were statistically independent. The resulting "bootstrapped histogram" may be compared to the "empirical histogram." Figures in Chapter 9 show the empirical and bootstrapped theta histograms for Bunge and for Vyshnegradsky. Statistical tests show that the null hypothesis of statistical independence cannot be rejected for the Bunge period. Statistical dependence is clearly present in the Vyshnegradsky period. This difference between the Bunge and Vyshnegradsky periods is evidence that Big Players encourage herding and contra-herding.

Gilanshah and I study U.S. money demand from 1950 to 1990. We argue that the money supply process was more subject to Big Player discretion after 1970 than before. We show that this difference implies more herding in money demand after 1970 than before. Herding can occur in the market for cash balances. A significant portion of money demand comes from firms. Firms often hire specialists in cash management. Cash managers may engage in herding if they follow the same set of professional advisors. Big Players encourage cash managers to follow the advice of outside experts.

An increase of herding in money demand will change the behavior of the residuals of an appropriately specified money demand equation. R/S analysis of the residuals should show an increase in the "Hurst coefficient" when herding increases. We show that precisely such an increase occurs after 1970. One reason for the recent instability of U.S. money demand is the recent instability of U.S. money supply.

The following chapters develop the argument of this chapter more carefully. Chapter 2 explains how the methodological ideas of Schutz and Hayek emerged from inter-war Vienna and the "Mises' Circle" in which they both participated. The seemingly very different theoretical systems of Schutz and Hayek emerged from the same set of problems and the same very small circle of scholars. Schutz and Hayek were friends in Vienna and remained in contact until Schutz's untimely death in 1960. The theories of these two Viennese authors are based on the same basic methodological position and are thus perfectly complementary.

Chapter 3 explains Schutz's phenomenological psychology and his important idea of anonymity. (Discussion of Schutz's theory of relevance is postponed until Chapter 6.) Schutz is known for combining the ideal type method of Max Weber with the phenomenological philosophy of Edmund Husserl. The result of Schutz's synthesis is an unusually clear – and useful – picture of human action in society and of the division of knowledge in society.

Chapter 4 discusses Hayek's theory of mind and his evolutionary economics. Hayek's evolutionary approach to the study of man owes much to Armen Alchian's famous essay on evolution (1950). It is also based, however, on an essay Hayek wrote in 1920 while still a university student. It combines elements from evolutionary biology with elements from the older Scottish Enlightenment tradition of social thought (Horwitz 1999). Hayek's theory helps us to understand how the "lifeworld" Schutz describes could come to be and to have a relatively high degree of coherence.

Chapter 5 develops the language-games framework upon which I build my theory. As I explain there, the idea of language games comes from Wittgenstein (1958a, 1958b). It is doubtful, however, that my theory is "Wittgensteinian." It has certainly been colored in some degree by his ideas. But I have not attempted to stay close to his views, and I have probably made arguments no Wittgensteinian would accept. The language-games framework provides room for both rule-following and the sort of directed cunning expressed by rational-choice models.

Chapter 6 presents the core elements of my theory of expectations. The theory might be described as "Austrian" because it relies heavily on Kirzner, Hayek, and Schutz. The concept of "language game" lets me reinterpret Kirzner's entrepreneur as both Schutzian interpreter and Hayekian learner. The formation and adaptation of expectations is then embodied in the entrepreneurial agent. Chapter 7 presents the theory of Big Players and applies it to financial markets. Chapters 8–10 are devoted to statistical tests, as indicated earlier. Closing remarks are in a Coda.

Part II
Methodology

2
The Misesian Context

Introduction

I have argued that synthesizing Alfred Schutz and F. A. Hayek will help us to solve the Lachmann problem. This may seem a difficult matter. Schutz and Hayek developed two seemingly different systems of social thought. The two systems, however, are consistent and complementary.

Alfred Schutz was a phenomenological sociologist. He was therefore a follower of the rationalist philosopher, Edmund Husserl. Like Husserl, Schutz emphasized subjective processes of meaning formation and interpretation. Hayek was an economist who adopted the very "naturalism" Husserl criticized as an "absurdity" (Husserl 1911, p. 81).[1] By "naturalism," Husserl meant every real thing is a part of "nature" and thus "unequivocally determined by rigid laws" (1911, p. 79).[2] Hayek (1952a) was even guilty of what Husserl called "the naturalizing of consciousness" (1911, p. 80). Hayek was an anti-Cartesian who identified himself with the Scottish Enlightenment (1994, p. 140). As a phenomenologist, Schutz formed part of a rationalist, continental tradition that was highly Cartesian in important respects. (One of Husserl's last works was entitled *Cartesian Meditations*.)

Schutz and Hayek might seem to inhabit quite different intellectual worlds. But both were followers of the economist Ludwig von Mises. Alfred Schutz and F. A. Hayek were Misesians. Each of them wrote important books defending the basic methodological position Mises articulated (Hayek 1952a, 1952b, Schutz 1932a). (This claim is argued below.) While each of them developed a methodological position that descends directly from Mises, they developed Mises' ideas in very different ways.

The interpretation of meanings was the essential element in Mises' methodology. Mises' account of such "understanding" was based on Henri Bergson's idea of intuition. Both Schutz and Hayek replaced this account with another. Schutz replaced Bergsonian intuition with Husserl's "phenomenological psychology." Hayek replaced Bergsonian intuition with the "meta-conscious" recognition of patterns that are too complex for the conscious mind. I argue below that phenomeno-logical psychology is perfectly consistent with Hayek's combinatorial account of understanding. If we recognize the Misesian character of each thinker's system, we can see how to integrate the two into a larger, unified system. This system lets us solve the Lachmann problem. It gives us foundations for a radically subjectivist theory of expectations. The differences in the ideas of Schutz and Hayek in philosophy and psychology turn out to pose no fundamental difficulty to the integration I propose.

In this chapter I will attempt to sketch the historical context within which the systems of Schutz and Hayek emerged. The key figure in this regard is their common friend and mentor, Ludwig von Mises.

The methodology of Ludwig von Mises

The Viennese context

Between the wars Ludwig von Mises was the leader of the Austrian school of economics (Prendergast, 1986, p. 6). Mises saw himself as the heir to the school's founder, Carl Menger (Lachmann 1981, pp. vi–vii). Menger's Aristotelian methodological position had been articulated in the course of the famous *methodenstreit* conducted with the German Historical School (Prendergast, 1986, p. 10). Mises felt that Menger's position needed to be rehabilitated as a part of the struggle against "historicism, empiricism, and irrationalism" (Mises, 1933a, p. xxiv; see also Lachmann, 1981, p. v). Mises worked out his position in a series of articles, which were collected together in 1933 under the title *Grundprobleme der Nationalökonomie* (*Epistemological Problems of Economics*).

The principal target of his critical attacks was the historicism of the German Historical School. But his arguments apply to many targets, including positivism. In his preface to the English translation of 1960, Mises leads with an attack on "unified science," positivism, and scien-tism. From that introduction, one would imagine the book to have been targeted at the "logical positivists" of the Vienna Circle. It seems Mises considered his arguments equally effective against both groups.

Lachmann's introduction to the English translation of Mises' book notes that Mises may have given too much attention to the "German historians and too little to logical positivism" (1981, p. vii). But he also notes that "at precisely this time Vienna had become the headquarters of logical positivism" and Mises' book "was a challenge to positivists and empiricists of almost every school" (1981, p. vii). Hayek was later to argue for an essential connection between historicism and positivism (1952b). In *Theory and History*, Mises includes a chapter ("The Challenge of Scientism") that explicitly attacks Otto Neurath, positivism, and behaviorism (Mises 1957, pp. 240–263). Prendergast reports that the Austrian school's methodology "had been severely weakened by the cumulative attacks of historicism, the Lausanne school of mathematical economics, and after 1928, logical empiricism" (1986, p. 8). It seems fair, then, to describe Mises' position as standing in opposition to both historicism and positivism.

On the one side were the logical positivists. The positivists of the "Vienna Circle" accepted the distinction between "*a priori*," and "*a posteriori*." They characterized the difference in their own way, however. Propositions *a priori* are true solely on account of the rules of grammar. An *a posteriori* proposition was meaningful only if it could be "verified." The meaning is the test and the test is a possible verification. The positivists insisted that "science" be "empirical" and their extreme brand of empiricism was verificationism. Attempted verifications of a proposition were to be "objective" procedures, fully explicit and public. No element of intuition was allowed to corrupt them. Meanings, according to the positivists, could not be observed nor, therefore, verified. (Chapters 2 and 3 of Caldwell 1982 are an excellent introduction to Viennese positivism.)

On the other side there was the German Historical School, the historicists. Mises' methodology was originally meant to defend theory against this group. Among the historicists, Max Weber had emerged as a towering figure, one whom Mises admired greatly and claimed as a friend. Weber explained that "interpretive sociology" uses "ideal types" to understand events. Weber's ideal-type methodology requires the analyst to refer to the "meaning" an action has to the actor. This is a thoroughgoing subjectivism. Weber's ideal-type method was arguably the leading form of subjectivism at the time Mises was working out his own position.

Mises developed his criticism of Max Weber in "Sociology and History" (Mises 1929). Weber (1962) had argued that the method of ideal types was the proper method of "interpretive sociology." The ideal type, in Mises interpretation, was a distillation from experience. Thus, Mises interpreted the ideal type as an historical construct. Mises thought Weber's ideal type could not be a tool of theory. Its exclusive use would make the social sciences historical sciences. Weber's writings were important within the Mises circle and his method of ideal types was greatly esteemed. But the self-conscious heirs to Carl Menger were bound to view economics as an "exact science." They were thus bound to reject any view that reduced economics to a branch of history.

It may be that Mises erred in his interpretation of Weber. Oakley thinks Mises "failed to give due emphasis to the extensive common ground with Weber" (1997, p. 185). Schutz argued that Mises' criticism was about right when applied to the early Weber, but that Weber's more mature position was not subject to Mises' criticism. Schutz also recognized, however, that Weber's exposition was ambiguous. We probably cannot hope for a definitive interpretation of Weber. In any event, what matters for our story is not the correct interpretation of Weber, but that given by Mises.

Mises (1929) criticized Weber for viewing "abstract economic theory" as one of "those syntheses which are generally termed 'ideas' of historical phenomena" (Weber as quoted in Mises 1929, pp. 75–76). In other words, Mises rejected Weber's supposed historicism. Mises agreed "completely" with Weber's argument that in causal explanations of a "cultural phenomenon" or "historical individual" any "laws" one might appeal to can serve only as the "*means* of investigation," not the "*end*" (1929, p. 97, emphasis in original). That is, the law may help us to grasp the particulars of the case, but no more. The researcher must in any event, Weber argued, strive to correctly impute "the culturally significant components of the phenomena, in their individuality, to their concrete cases" (Weber as cited in Mises 1929, p. 97). Mises' disagreement with Weber centered solely on the utility of general laws in such efforts. Weber had argued that the more general the law, the less useful it would be in historical applications. Mises denied this, insisting on both the universal applicability of economic laws and the immediate relevance of them in many important cases.

Mises' (1929) criticism of Weber is consistent with his argument in "Conception and Understanding" (1930). There, as we shall see, he denies that our "understanding" of concrete human events is rational or discursive. It is achieved instead through an epistemologically distinct act of intuition. In so saying, as we shall see, Mises was drawing on Bergson's philosophy of intuition. Mises (1929, p. 74) ties Bergson and Weber together, arguing that "In France Bergson and in Germany

Windelband, Rickert, and Max Weber ... sought to define logically the character of history and historical investigation and to demonstrate the inapplicability of the concepts and procedures of physics to history." In this, Mises thought, they had succeeded. The efforts of the "Southwest German School of New Criticism ... must constitute the foundation and starting point of all further investigations concerning the logic of history" (1929, p. 74). They had gotten straight the logical character of history and the difference between history and natural science. Their errors consist mostly in their ignorance of "the existence of sociology as a nomothetic science."

It is very important that Mises linked Bergson and Weber as correct expositors of the logic of history. Mises took Weber's method of ideal types to be correctly and irrevocably an historical method of research. This method of research, Mises thought, depended upon acts of intuition. Such acts differ necessarily and radically from discursive reasoning, from the "conception" of praxeology and other sciences.

In Weber's hands, Mises thought, the method of ideal types was the method of history. What we call "social science" was not science at all, but history. Though *"Wissenschaft,"* it was not nomological. For Weber and other members of the German historical school, the interpretation of meanings, *Verstehen*, was historical and not scientific. It was historical because the meaning of an act is specific to time and place. It required a special intuition to grasp meanings, an intuition that apprehends the particulars of the situation. Science, by contrast, uses no such intuition; it does not employ *Verstehen*. Science seeks general truths, not the particular truths reached by intuition.

Mises' methodology was a defense against both positivism and historicism. The historicists offered subjectivism without science. The positivists offered science without subjectivism. Mises wanted both science and subjectivism. He attempted to construct a scientific subjectivism.[3]

The elements of Mises' system

Hayek speaks of the "extreme rationalism" of Mises and laments that Mises never fully "emancipated himself" from the "rationalist–constructivist" position that "as a child of his time, he could not escape" (1981, pp. xxiii–xxiv). I think Hayek was quite right about this. But this argument overlooks something important in Mises, namely, the role of Bergsonian intuition as a theory of interpersonal understanding.[4]

To rehabilitate Menger's program, Mises needed to find a way out of both historicism and positivism. He had accepted, however, the historicists' argument that our intuitive understanding of meaning is particular and historical, not general. And he recognized that our *a priori* knowledge conveys no particulars about the world in which we live.[5] His solution lay in the distinction between "conception" and "understanding." It is my impression that Mises' distinction between conception and understanding has been given too little attention. The importance of the distinction is probably heightened by the fact that it has become alien to our current habits of thought.

In an essay originally published in 1930, Mises first drew his distinction between "conception" and "understanding." Conception is "discursive reasoning" whereas "understanding seeks the meaning of action in empathic intuition of a whole." Mises thought these two ways of learning about the world operate under quite different epistemological principles. Mises' famous rationalism applied only to conception. With conception, "strict logic rules;" where understanding enters "subjectivity begins." For Mises, "conception is reasoning; understanding is beholding" (Mises 1930, pp. 133–134). This distinction let Mises give to "understanding" the job of learning about the plans of others. Thus, we form our expectations about the actions of others through "understanding." Only "conception," which has no business inferring people's purposes, is subject to the strictures of rationalism.

This important distinction is repeated in Mises' later writings. In *Human Action* he refers to them as "two different epistemological procedures." Conception is "the mental tool of praxeology;" understanding is "the specific mental tool of history" (1966, p. 51). In *Human Action* the difference is framed largely in terms of the general and the specific. Conception is the "cognition of universals and categories" whereas understanding "refers to what is unique and individual."

In *Theory and History*, Mises credits "first Dilthey" and "then Windelbrand, Rickert, Max Weber, Croce, and Collingwood" with having "succeeded brilliantly in elucidating the epistemological features of the study of history" (1957, p. 308). Dilthey was not untouched by error (1957, p. 308) and drew on Hume and others (1957, p. 312). Dilthey's "chief contribution" was showing that understanding "was epistemologically and methodologically different from the natural sciences and therefore also from experimental psychology" (1957, p. 312).[6]

In *Human Action*, Mises explains that "[i]n the philosophy of Bergson this understanding is called an intuition." He then quotes Bergson's definition of this intuition as "the *sympathy* by which one is transported into the interior of an object in order to coincide with what there is unique and consequently inexpressible in it"[7] (1966, p. 49, emphasis in original).

The difference between conception and understanding coincides with the difference between science and history. "In the domain open to conception," Mises argued, "strict logic rules: one is able to prove and disprove; there is a point to conversing with others about what is 'true' and what is 'false' and to posing problems and discussing their solution" (1930, pp. 133–134). No such scientific disputes are possible with regard to understanding. "We are unable to impart to others any certain knowledge of what is intuitively foreknown and apprehended, of what has not been hardened in the forge of conceptual thought." With regard to understanding we cannot do better than to "bid others to follow and re-experience the complex whole we have experienced" (1930, p. 134).

These themes are also discussed in Mises' essay of 1933, "The Task and Scope of the Science of Human Action." "Science," Mises explains, "which is dependent both on discursive reasoning and on experience, does not present us with a unified picture of the world ... . We are unable to fathom life through reason, nor can we experience it through science. Reason and science," insists Mises, "deal only with isolated fragments detached from the living whole and thereby killed" (1933b, p. 44). It is not through science, but in living that "we experience the unity an indissoluble congenerousness of all life" (1933b, p. 45). Significantly, Mises goes on to join these remarks explicitly to Bergson. "It is true," he says, "as Bergson has seen with unsurpassed clarity, that between reality and the knowldge that science can convey to us there is an unbridgeable gulf" (1933b, p. 46). The results of the understanding do not give us scientific verities, but historical interpretations. "Understanding is precisely the method that the historical sciences (in the broadest sense of the term) employ in dealing with the unique, the non-repeatable, that is, in treating what is simply historical" (1933b, p. 12). Clearly, "this method can never lead to the discovery of empirical laws" (1933b, p. 12). It is through understanding that we can "grasp ... something that we are unable to bring under rules and explain through them" (1933b, p. 12).

In *Human Action* Mises declares praxeology and history to be the "two main branches of the sciences of human action" (1966, p. 30). The first branch, praxeology, "is not concerned with the changing content of acting, but with its pure form and its categorical structure." The second branch, history, is the "study of the accidental and environmental features of human action" (1966, p. 47). Praxeology gives "exact and precise knowledge of real things;" it is science and its method is "aprioristic reasoning," which is "purely conceptual and deductive" (1966, pp. 38–39). History uses "the knowledge provided by logic, mathematics, the natural sciences, and especially by praxeology." But it uses these sorts of knowledge only as "indispensable auxiliaries." The "specific task of history" requires the "specific method" which is "the *understanding*." And that specific task is "is the study of [the] value judgments" animating men's actions "and of the effects of the actions as far as they cannot be analyzed by the teachings of all other branches of knowledge" (1966, p. 49). Similar assertions can be found in Mises' *Theory and History*. (See also Butos 1997).

In this way, Mises was able to keep both "science" and "understanding" as essential elements of political economy. Mises' position had five features important to us here. They are loose apriorism, methodological dualism, understanding, methodological individualism, and economic law.

Loose apriorism

First, as we have seen, Mises was an apriorist. The core of his position, however, is a loose apriorism, not strict apriorism. In the strict sense, knowledge is "*a priori*" when it passes Kant's double test. "Necessity and strict universality, therefore, are infallible tests for distinguishing pure from empirical knowledge, and are inseparably connected with each other" (Kant 1787, p. 26 [section II of "Introduction"]). Loose apriorism is the claim that much of our scientific knowledge is not derived from experience or subject to direct empirical test. Knowledge that is "*a priori*" in the loose sense is similar to knowledge that is *a priori* in the strict sense. In both cases, the knowledge is general knowledge that organizes our more particular observations. In both cases, the knowledge cannot be shown wrong by a counter-example. An apparent counter-example is really just something outside the scope of application of the *a priori* knowledge. Lakatos' "hard core" is *a priori* in the loose sense, but not in the strict sense. Strict apriorism implies loose apriorism.

Today, many methodologists accept some form of loose apriorism. Perhaps most do. Lakatos is a good example. So is Kuhn. In the 1930s, however, loose apriorism was not so widely accepted. Nor was it clearly distinguished from strict apriorism. In the context of the times, Mises' apriorism was very advanced, and an improvement on prevailing views. Mises did not distinguish loose apriorism from strict apriorism. Many of his statements seem to defend strict apriorism. I believe it is fair to say, however, that the real core of Mises' apriorism is simply the independence from direct empirical test. Mises' loose apriorism is important and unambiguous. It is not entirely clear that he was truly a strict apriorist.

Consider Mises' treatment of the disutility of labor. Mises says the "disutility of labor is not of a categorical and aprioristic character ... But the real world is conditioned by the disutility of labor." Thus, "Only theorems based on the assumption that labor is a source of uneasiness are applicable for the comprehension of what is going on in this world." One might infer that our knowledge of labor economics is not *a priori*. "However, this reference to experience does not impair the aprioristic character of praxeology and economics" (1966, p. 65). It is not clear that the "aprioristic" knowledge obtained by assuming the disutility of labor meets the criteria of necessity and strict universality. Nor is it clear that it was meant to.

Mises argued for the existence of an *a priori* science of human action, "praxeology." But the philosophical status of praxeology is somewhat unclear. Kurrild-Klitgaard suggests that Mises may have "radicalized" his apriorism in later writings (2001, p. 139 n. 14). In 1933, Mises had "never fully articulated the epistemological basis of his apriorism, and in particular he did not tie these explicitly to any particular philosophical basis, not even that of Kant, despite adopting a number of Kantian concepts" (Kurrild-Klitgaard 2001, p. 127). Indeed, in his review of the book, Schutz laments that Mises "analyzes the character and methods of the social sciences in a fine manner even though he deliberately abstains from a discussion of the question of a general epistemology basic to the problems of the social sciences" (Schutz 1934: 92). (Kurrild-Klitgaard 2001, p. 127 directs our attention to this important quote from Schutz.) Even later when Mises paid more attention to the epistemological foundations of his "praxeology," the philosophical grounds of his argument remain obscure. Caldwell (1982, p. 121), Prychitko (1994), and others associate Mises with Kant or post Kantianism. But he does not cite Kant and the phrase "synthetic *a priori*" appears nowhere in his writings.

Even in his most strident expression his apriorism, Mises explicitly refuses to clarify epistemological status of the "*a priori*" truths of economics. "The question whether the judgements of praxeology are to be called analytic or synthetic and whether or not its procedure is to be qualified as 'merely' tautological are of verbal interest only" (p 1966, p. 44).

Fritz Machlup characterized the situation quite well. He was asked about Mises and apriorism in an interview conducted in about 1980. "Mises gave us his views on his *a priori* ideas and they were criticized by [Felix] Kaufmann, [Alfred] Schutz and others, but you see it isn't really necessary to criticize these terms ... You may call any model *a priori* because you can 'build' the model, according to your own specifications"

(Machlup 1980, p. 9). Citing the physicist Henry Margenau, Machlup went on to explain that "Construction is always *a priori*, even if you construe with some experience in mind. The domain of construction needs constructs and postulated relationships between constructs, but it is itself not the result of observation; it is *a priori*. So you don't have to take these distinctions so seriously as Mises himself did and as some of his followers do today" (1980, p. 9).

Methodological dualism

Mises defended methodological dualism. The method of "understanding" is distinct from anything employed in the physical sciences. Moreover, the pure *a priori* discipline of economics employs categories such as "preference" "exchange," and "purpose," which have no application in physical science. Mises carefully distinguished methodological and metaphysical dualism. "Methodological dualism," Mises explained, "refrains from any proposition concerning essences and metaphysical constructs." It simply accepts a basic fact, namely, that "we do not know how external events – physical, chemical and physiological – affect human thought" and action. It is an argument from ignorance. Our "ignorance splits the realm of knowledge into two separate fields, the realm of ... nature, and the realm of human thought and action" (Mises 1957, p. 1).[8]

Methodological dualism is not the doctrine that the social sciences are "deductive" and the natural sciences "inductive." It is the doctrine that "understanding" is a method of the social sciences, but not of the natural sciences.

Understanding

Mises advocated the method of "understanding" or "*verstehen.*" As we have seen, he thought Henri Bergson had properly characterized the nature of "understanding." He also thought that the "understanding" he advocated was essentially that of the historians, including Max Weber and other members of the German Historical School. Mises credits members of the German Historical School, including Max Weber, with providing "the clarification of the logical problems of the historical sciences." Although they did not realize that a "universally valid science of human action" existed, this fact "does not vitiate what they accomplished for the logic of the historical sciences." In particular, "they brought into relief the distinctive logical character of the historical sciences in connection with the doctrine of 'understanding'" (Mises 1933a, p. xviii). Mises fully accepted Weber's method of "ideal type" for history.

It is true that "understanding" played an essential role in Mises' thought. Thus the late Don Lavoie had grounds to place Mises and the Austrian school in the same "hermeneutical" tradition with Dilthey and Weber (1994, p. 54). Indeed, he greatly advanced Misesian interpretation by pointing out the fundamental identity between vital aspects of Mises' position and the views of Dilthey and other German historicists. This point seems to have been underplayed by those who have been scandalized by the association. If Lavoie erred in his attempted hermeneutical rehabilitation of Mises' methodology, it was not by recognizing the influence of Dilthey and others, but in attempting to "absorb" both objective conception and subjective understanding in a supposed intersubjective interpretation (1994). The failure of some to appreciate just what Mises had in mind with regard to "understanding" may have caused some confusion about Lavoie's argument.

Methodological individualism

Mises defended methodological individualism. In Mises' hands the concept meant simply that explanation of social causation should not bypass the individual acts through which that causality works. "Collective" entities exist and operate. But they operate through the agency of individual actors and individual actions. "A collective whole is a particular aspect of the actions of various individuals and as such a real thing determining the course of events" (1966, p. 43).

I use the term "methodological individualism" with some misgivings. It has come to hurt, not help communication. Methodological individualism is easily confused with ontological individualism, the doctrine that individuals are "prior" to society and have the properties they do "independently" of society. It is not clear what such a claim might really mean. In any event, methodological individualism and ontological individualism are not the same. Moreover, "methodological individualism" is often taken to mean *naïve* methodological individualism. Neither Mises, nor Schutz, nor Hayek argued for ontological individualism. All three held to sophisticated versions of methodological individualism that recognized society's role in shaping the individual.[9] (Langlois 1989 contains a good review of the issues.)

Economic law

Mises defended the existence of "universally valid economic theory" (1933a, p. xxiv). This theory provided laws that are analogous to the laws of physics. "Economics too can make predictions," Mises explains, "in the sense in which this ability is attributed to the natural sciences"

(1929, p. 118). "One must study the laws of human action and social cooperation as the physicist studies the laws of nature" (1966, p. 2). Examples include "what effect an increase in the quantity of money will have on its purchasing power ... what consequences price controls must have" (1929, p. 118), and "the future effects of a proposed change in currency legislation" (1933a, p. xx). Note that these are all examples of prediction within the realm of "catallactics," that is, the theory of markets (Mises, 1966, p. 232).

The standard view of Mises' methodology emphasizes his notorious apriorism with its supposed deductive method. (In this regard, Caldwell 1984 is representative.) It is true that Mises himself placed great deal of emphasis on apriorism. But I think that apriorism is not the really essential characteristic of Mises' position. His desire to put understanding and theory together is more important. Mises thought the historicists had correctly characterized the method of history. He also thought the Austrians were right to defend the existence of economic theory. (Mises considered himself heir to Menger.) There is a degree of tension between these two opinions. To resolve the tension, Mises appealed to the difference between conception and understanding. One, he argued, is the method of theory; the other is the method of history. Social science discusses human action. The concrete content of action is grasped through "understanding," not "conception." Thus, the work done by "conception" in the social sciences must be *a priori*. Conception gives us the form of action; understanding gives us the content of action.

If my interpretation is about right, then the continuing emphasis on Mises' use of a supposed deductive method is somewhat exaggerated. Deductive logic does not make a methodology Misesian. Any methodology that combines economic law and subjective understanding is close to Mises. A truly Misesian methodology combines the five elements I have listed above, namely, loose apriorism, methodological dualism, understanding, methodological individualism, and economic law. It is in this sense that both Schutz and Hayek were Misesian methodologists.

Mises' system has, I think, been underrated among economic methodologists. (Caldwell 1984 and Lavoie 1986 are exceptions.) As we shall see below, Schutz and Hayek both adopted fundamentally Misesian methodological positions. Each of these thinkers is recognized as a serious and important methodologist. Mises' student Fritz Machlup (1978) followed Mises and Schutz, and is recognized as a leading methodologist. (The widespread view that Machlup was a positivist is criticized in Langlois and Koppl 1991 and Koppl 2000a.) Thus, we should acknowledge Mises' methodology as an important scholarly achievement.

Mises' system, however, has difficulties. It probably cannot be sustained without the sorts of modifications proposed by Schutz and Hayek. There are at least four difficulties with Mises' position. First, and most importantly, it relies on Bergson's rather mysterious notion of intuition (Mises 1930, pp. 130–145; 1966, pp. 47–51, 881–882).In Bergson's philosophy, intuition is the intellectual faculty that allows one to "enter into" another object and "participate" in its "motion." The knowledge thus acquired is supposed to be a kind of completed infinity in which a "whole" is grasped (Mises 1930, pp. 133–134; 1966, p. 49; Bergson 1903b, pp. 159–162). It seems doubtful that such a grasping of completed infinities is really possible. Indeed, I doubt the idea has a clear meaning. At the same time it divides our acts of apprehension into two separate watertight compartments. In the compartment labeled "conception," everything is rational, analytical, and orderly. In the compartment labeled "understanding," we transcend reason and reach into the heart of things, discovering thereby such things as "the quality of values" (Mises 1930, p. 133). Such a sharp division probably does not exist in fact.

Second, Mises' solution leaves theory with very little to say. By placing all but the most completely empty and formal properties of action under the study of history, Mises conceded too much to the historicists. Mises' praxeology has less to say about human action than we might have hoped. Most of what we are accustomed to view as "theory" becomes "history." Mises' apriorism was cogently criticized by Hayek (1937). The theorems of catallactics all entail assumptions about expectations and knowledge. Such assumptions are empirical in nature, not *a priori*. But then Mises was wrong to claim that economic theory could address such questions as "what consequences price controls must have" (1929, p. 118).

Third, Mises exaggerates the difference between *a priori* and *a posteriori* and, therefore, the difference between theory and history. Any theory, any argument, has its *a priori* element. The general form of a theoretical argument is "If A, then B." The antecedent, A, is the argument's *a priori*. Some elements of the *a priori* will have been "tested," others are guesses. Still others are conventions and thus true merely on account of how we use language. Any element of this *a priori* can be criticized as not true or not useful. Thus the *a priori* is always present, but it is neither inviolable nor immune from criticism. (See Machlup 1978 on the difference between psychologically and logically prior and on other issues.) If Popper was more or less right to claim that science progresses by conjectures and refutations, then the *a priori* element in our reasoning may change over time in the wake of experience. Similarly, the difference between "theory" and "history" or "pure" and "applied" theory is a matter of degree.

Finally, and most importantly for us, Mises' system leaves no room for a theory of expectations. (Thus, Lachmann was right to criticize Mises for neglecting expectations.) Expectations are formed through the unfolding of the market process. They are a matter of entrepreneurial understanding. Thus, there is an essential extra-rational element to them. Given Mises' epistemology, a theory of expectations would have to be a matter of discursive reason. But we can have no discursive conception of acts of understanding except to recognize them as such. We can only "behold" entrepreneurial expectations through acts of understanding. Here conception cannot penetrate. Thus no "theory" of economic expectations is possible for Mises. In Mises' system, expectations are a matter of understanding. Expectations, for Mises, are ideas about the future of economic life. Thus, they are about the content of action, not its formal structure. Acts apprehending the content of action are acts of "understanding." They fall outside the purview of pure theory, which employs only "conception."

Schutz and Hayek

Schutz and Hayek both attempted to reform Mises' methodology. Hayek adopted a naturalistic attitude. Schutz adopted a phenomenological perspective. Both, however, remained Misesians. Both defended, in some way, loose apriorism, methodological dualism, understanding, methodological individualism, and economic law. Both defended, in other words, the fundamentals of Mises' methodology. Because of the differences in the foundations each thinker gave to his system, their methodologies seem quite far apart. As we shall see, they are not.

Both Hayek and Schutz replaced Mises' account of understanding with a different account. Schutz relied on Husserl's "phenomenological psychology." Hayek relied on his own innovative theory of mind, based on evolutionary biology. In both cases, however, the essence of the matter is replacing Mises' Bergsonian account of inter-subjective understanding with another account. And in both cases, the replacement produced a system free of the limits of Mises' original position. Considering the differences between them, it is surprising to find that the two systems are compatible and may be fitted together with little modification to either one. I will look first at differences in their ideas in philosophy and then at differences in their ideas in ideas in psychology.

Hayek and Husserl did not hold compatible philosophical positions. This would seem to doom any attempt to simply stitch together Hayek and Schutz. Schutz was, after all, a close follower of Husserl. Surprisingly, this difference makes no difference. In a famous "Appended Note" to *The Phenomenology of the Social World*, Schutz explained that he was engaged in an exercise in "phenomenological psychology," not "transcendental psychology." This means that Schutz was specifically avoiding as many philosophical commitments as possible. Schutz's kept his analysis of the "lifeworld" relatively close to the ground. He did not commit himself to any of Husserl's metaphysical doctrines, nor to Husserl's claim that we can ground our knowledge through transcendental phenomenology. It means, importantly, that Schutz never left the naturalistic attitude of common sense. He takes the existence of the lifeworld and of his fellow humanity as unproblematic.

Hayek's points of disagreement with phenomenological philosophy all concern transcendental phenomenology. Hayek was an anti-foundationalist, anti-rationalist, and anti-Cartesian. He could not accept, therefore, Husserl's attempt to ground all knowledge in a Cartesian meditation. But none of this speaks to the empirical accuracy of Schutz's analysis of the life world. There are no basic philosophical obstacles to integrating Schutz and Hayek.

Hayek and Schutz have consistent psychological theories. Langlois (1998) has argued that Schutz's psychology employs a variant of the "categorization–action system." The same may be said of Hayek. In each case, action is explained as a patterned response to a situation that the agent must "define" and respond to. In Hayek's case, such categorization is viewed externally and from, ultimately, an evolutionary perspective. With Schutz the categorization is viewed from within and described phenomenologically. Hayek looks from the outside. Schutz looks from the inside. Both are looking at the same object: the agent's definition of the situation. Hayek's account of "attention" in *The Sensory Order*, for instance, is very similar to Schutz's account of the "system of relevancies" that guides action. In psychology, too, there are no basic obstacles to integrating Schutz and Hayek.

3
Schutz[1]

Schutz is famous for his synthesis of Husserl and Weber. But as Christopher Prendergast notes, Schutz did not engage in "some abstract and unmotivated attempt to 'synthesize' Weber and Husserl" (1986, p. 1). Schutz's motive was to shore up the methodological defenses of the Austrian school of economics. Prendergast describes Schutz as "committed" to the "overall methodological standpoint" of the Austrian school (1986, p. 3). The "titular head" of the school was Ludwig von Mises (1986, p. 6). The seminar Mises ran from his office in the Austrian Chamber of Commerce was "the prime vehicle for forging and maintaining the distinctive theoretical, philosophical, and policy tradition of Austrian marginalism" (1986, p. 6). The Mises Circle was the main element of the "inner circle" of Schutz's audience (1986, p. 5). Schutz thought that Mises' methodology lacked a satisfactory theory of intersubjective understanding (1986, p. 11).

Schutz replaced Mises' Bergsonian theory of inter-subjective understanding with one based on Edmund Husserl's philosophy of "phenomenology." This replacement allowed Schutz to rehabilitate Weber's ideal type methodology. As we have seen, Mises accepted Weber's methodology of ideal types with regard to history. He also accepted Bergson's theory of inter-subjective understanding. If Bergson were rejected, Schutz would need to either accept Weber's theory of inter-subjective understanding or find another one. Weber's theory was unsuitable because it was not very clear.

Weber had claimed that the actor "attaches" meaning to his act. Schutz could not accept this formulation (1932a, p. 215). Moreover, many of Weber's most important concepts and distinctions were inadequately developed (Schutz 1932a, p. xxxi). They could not be accepted as is. Weber's "interpretive sociology" needed rehabilitation based on a closer analysis of basic concepts, especially "meaning."

Schutz's analysis of meaning led him to the view that all thinking requires ideal types. Most thinkers reserve the term "ideal type" for the constructs of social scientists. Schutz employed it for both scientific and common-sense interpretations of the social world. We think in stereotypes. Our own experiences are "meaningful" only when we reflect on them. But to reflect on them is to apply ideal types to them. The same holds for the interpretation of others. To interpret the "meaning" of another's action is to apply some set of typifications to them.

Schutz studied the knowledge people employ in their everyday action. He found that this knowledge is ideal-typical. We exist in an "intersubjective world." We can act in this world because we interpret it. Our interpretations arise from experiences, "our own or those handed down to us by parents or teachers" (1953, p. 7). These direct and indirect experiences give us a "scheme of reference" in the form of our "knowledge at hand" (1953, p. 7).

The "stock of knowledge at hand" with which we interpret the world tells us that the world is full of "more or less well circumscribed objects" having "more or less definite qualities" (1953, p. 8). Objects resist us and may be acted upon. These objects, Schutz tells us, are not perfectly self-contained and "insulated." They appear to us "from the outset," as existing "within a horizon of familiarity and pre-acquaintanceship" given by the knowledge currently "taken for granted until further notice" (1953, p. 8).

In everyday action, some knowledge is taken for granted at any time. This taken-for-granted knowledge is a collection of "pre-experiences" of the world. These "unquestioned pre-experiences" are not themselves real experiences. They are "from the outset, at hand as *typical*" (1953, p. 8, emphasis in original). They come "carrying open horizons of anticipated similar experiences" (1953, p. 8). Our experience of "the outer world" is not that of a disjointed collection of unrelated "sense-contents".[2] Through the stock of knowledge at hand, we experience the world as a more or less structured whole containing "mountains," "trees," "animals," "fellow-men," and so on (1953, p. 8).[3]

The world is known to us in its typicality. It is known to us as a system of types; typical objects, typical relationships among typical objects, typical problems and typical solutions to these typical problems (1953, pp. 13–14). Even the most familiar objects are known only in their typicality. Schutz calls these types "typifications." Typifications are the ideal types of everyday action. Today, the term "ideal types" is usually reserved for the typifications of scientific reason. A typification differs from an ideal type only because it need not meet the scientific standards of coherence and adequacy-to-purpose required of ideal types. Schutz, however, used the terms "typification" and "ideal type" interchangeably.

I might think about my "Barlow" pocket knife, currently out of view. In doing so I form a typification of its shape, of the rusted surface of its blades, and the feel of it in my hand. Withdrawing it from my pocket, I now confront it in a new setting, in this light, at this moment, feeling just the way I do right now. The shape, the rusted surface of the blades, and the feel of it in my hands are – right now in the midst of my direct experiencing of them – in some measure foreign to my typifications of them. This is because all lived experiences "are as such unique and irretrievable events" (Schutz 1953, p. 20). My typification of my pocket knife is a constellation of anticipations, a pre-experiencing "carrying open horizons of anticipated similar experiences." It is a picture, not the real thing.

A typification is more or less empty of particulars. Otherwise it would not be a typification, but a lived experience. The particulars of lived experience will be "filled in" when the anticipated and typified event is "actualized" in experience (Schutz 1959, p. 286).

Earlier, I said that to interpret the "meaning" of another's action is to apply some set of typifications to them. But it is a metaphor to say that we "apply" ideal types to our experiences. According to Husserl and, following him, Schutz, we attend to our experiences with a retrospective glance. I can't think about my experience except by thinking *back* on it. Even when I am thinking about events unfolding before me, I must look at what has just occurred if I am to have a conscious experience of it. By attending to experience, we become conscious of it. This is the importance of Franz Brentano's concept of the "intentionality of consciousness" for Schutz's system. Brentano taught that all consciousness is consciousness *of* something. An ideal type describes the something of which we are conscious when we are conscious of something. Husserl was Brentano's student (Natanson, 1973, p. xiii). Husserl followed Brentano's doctrine of intentionality. As a phenomenologist, Schutz followed it as well. To say that we "apply" an ideal type to our experience implies that we have a conscious experience and then bring in an ideal type. But in order that the experience be conscious, it must already be interpreted and thus classified by means of an ideal type. Thus, my statement that we "apply" an ideal type is metaphorical. Some elaboration may be in order.

Following Bergson and Husserl, Schutz identified a level of consciousness beneath this everyday level organized by our stock of knowledge (1932a, p. 47). This underlying level provides the material that is transformed by our typifications into meaningful experience. Bergson called this underlying level of consciousness "*durée*." At its deepest level, according to Schutz, meaning comes from reflecting on this inner flow.

We are not generally aware of the inner "stream of consciousness" (1932a, p. 47). But we can immerse ourselves in it. If we do so, we find that experiences do not come in discrete units. "If we simply live immersed in the flow of duration [*durée*], we encounter only undifferentiated experiences that melt into one another in a flowing continuum" (1932a, p. 51). Acts of attention pluck out elements from this flow. To pluck out elements in this way is, at the same time, to classify them by placing them into one or more of the typifications that organize our common-sense knowledge. The act of attention regards the experience as this or that type of thing. The elements plucked out of the stream of consciousness become "discrete" experiences. They are discrete because they are retained in the form of a typification. Attention can do all this only if the experience from which it plucks out elements has already flowed past. This attentional modification of experience operates on acts of consciousness. The *durée* is composed of such acts. Attention operates on completed acts of consciousness and thus only on past experience.[4] Thus, the realm of meaningful experience emerges from a "prephenomenal" (1932a, p. 56) realm of inner experience. "The reflective glance singles out an elapsed lived experience and constitutes it as meaningful" (1932a, p. 71). A lengthier quote from Schutz may illuminate the issue:

> Meaning does not lie *in* the experience. Rather, those experiences are meaningful which are grasped reflectively. The meaning is the *way* in which the Ego regards its experience. The meaning lies in the attitude of the Ego toward that part of its stream of consciousness which has already flowed by, toward its "elapsed duration." (1932a, pp. 69–70, emphasis in original)

The idea of a prepredicative realm of experience may seem to contradict fundamental elements of Hayek's theory of mind. In Chapter 4, I will report that Hayek showed all mental activity to be classificatory. In his system, the most elementary sensations are already the product of interpretation. Hayek's "naturalistic" argument may seem inconsistent with the existence of a "prepredicative" realm of undifferentiated experience. If so, then no very straightforward integration of Schutz and Hayek would be possible. I think, however, that the two views are consistent.

If there is a prepredicative flow of subjective experience as Bergson, Husserl, and Schutz describe, then it is composed of phenomenal elements, experiences. These experiences are not "meaningful" in Schutz's sense because they do not form a part of the common-sense knowledge of everyday acting. But they are perfectly "meaningful" in quite another sense. They are, Schutz explains, "psychic phenomena" such as "pain, sexual sensations ... joy, sorrow, [and] disgust" (Schutz 1932a, p. 53). All of these experiences, while "meaningless" in Schutz's sense, come from classifications performed on impulses occurring within the central nervous system. Employing a broader sense of "meaning," Natanson says, "Experience in its prepredicative givenness is richly endowed with meaning." He offers "familiarity" as "an example of the density of the prepredicative organization of experience" (1973, p. 15).

We can now understand why Schutz rejected Weber's claim that the actor "attaches" meaning to his act. This suggests the absurdity of an action that has no meaning or that has not yet been given a meaning. The actor intends the action. The act and its intension are not separate. I intend my buying as buying, my walking as walking, my joke telling as joke telling. In Schutz's words, "the meaning is merely the special way in which the subject attends to his lived experience; it is this which elevates the experience into an action." Thus, "the formula 'the actor attaches a meaning to his action' must be interpreted metaphorically" (1932a, p. 215).

Schutz used the terms "type," "ideal type," and "typification." One could use any of a number substitutes, including "stereotype," "construct," and "category." Whatever the label, all thinking entails ideal types.

Typifications fall around us in concentric rings, those near us are highly specific, and those farther away are more general, more empty. Thus, I have the typifications "my 'Barlow' knife," "pocket knife," "knife," "cutting instrument," "tool," "human artifact," and "object of the external world." It is the same with the typifications we have of other people.

If I think of an absent friend, I form a typification "of his personality and behavior based on my past experiences" of him (Schutz, 1953, p. 17). If I mail a letter, I form a typification of "unknown people called postmen" whose actions are "not quite intelligible to me" (1953, p. 17). But I think they will act in typical patterns that typically result in the letter arriving more or less promptly. "I understand 'Why France [in 1953] fears the rearmament of Germany'" even if I never met a Frenchman or German (1953, p. 17). I follow the rules of English grammar "in order to make myself understandable" (1953, p. 17). At the highest levels of abstraction, I see in any "artifact or utensil" a reference to its producer even if he is, for me, only a perfectly anonymous "fellow-man" who produced the thing for other perfectly anonymous "fellow-men" to use in ways and for ends unknown to me (1953, p. 17).

Ideal types are interpretations. Schutz makes no exception for direct experience, including direct experience of others. To think about one's direct experience, one must pull back from it and apply a retrospective glance to it (1932a, pp. 51–53). Walsh and Lehnert's translation of Schutz (1932a) does not include the following very important sentence: "Hence, the experience of a fellow-man in a We-relation is, strictly speaking, also 'mediate': I apprehend his conscious life by interpeting his bodily expressions as indications of subjectively meaningful processes" (Schutz, 1932b, p. 26).[5] This sentence gives direct expression to Schutz's repudiation of Mises' Bergsonian theory of inter-personal interpretation. While Schutz retained much from Bergson, including his analysis of "*durée*," he rejected the idea that we can "enter into" the lifestream of another. He thus rejected the basic idea in Mises' account of inter-subjective understanding.

This repudiation of Bergsonian intuition applies equally to common-sense and scientific interpretations of human action. A further consideration applies to social science. Because social science requires complete clarity of its concepts, the experience upon which it relies is always indirect. We can draw no scientific implications from our direct experience of another. Science "nowhere refers back to the face-to-face experience" (1932a, p. 223). No immediate intuitions enter science.[6]

Some of Schutz's language might seem to suggest more immediacy of understanding than Schutz in fact allowed. He says, for instance, that "whereas I can observe my own lived experiences only after they are over and done with, I can observe yours as they actually take place" (1932a, p. 102). This sounds close to the sort of "entering into" that Bergson and Mises argued for. But Schutz develops and qualifies the point at length (1932a, pp. 102–107). In the end he concludes that "[t]he very postulate of the comprehension of the intended meaning of the other person's lived experiences becomes unfulfillable" (1932a, p. 107). When we interpret the "meaning" of another's action, we impute some meaning to it. We classify the action according to some set of ideal types.

This view of interpretation exposes an important ambiguity in the idea of the "meaning" of another's action. I may interpret an action in a way that makes little or no reference to the meaning the actor himself may have intended. If I say that you have opened the door, I may not mean to imply that you tried to do so. Perhaps your foot brushed against it by chance. On the other hand, I might interpret an action in a way that makes direct reference to the inner experiences of the actor. The criminal is re-enacting, say, the abuses he suffered as a child. There is a kind of "inner" meaning and an "outer" meaning. This is the difference between the "objective" and the "subjective" meaning of an act.

Subjective meaning refers to the mental processes of the actor. "We speak, then, of the subjective meaning of the product if we have in view the meaning-context within which the product stands or stood in the mind of the producer. To know the subjective meaning of the product means that we are able to run over in our own minds in simultaneity or quasi-simultaneity the polythetic Acts which constituted the experience of the producer" (Schutz, 1932a, p. 133).

The subjective meaning tells us what went on in the actor's mind to produce the action. The objective meaning is the meaning as it exists independently of the thought processes of the actor. "Objective meaning, on the contrary, we can predicate only of the product as such, that is, of the already constituted meaning-context of the thing produced, whose actual production we meanwhile disregard" (Schutz, 1932a, pp. 133–134). For Schutz, "Objective meaning therefore consists only in a meaning-context within the mind of the interpreter, whereas subjective meaning refers beyond it to a meaning-context in the mind of the producer" (Schutz, 1932a, p. 134).

Schutz illustrates with the concept of "wood is being cut" (1932a, p. 110). That "wood is being cut" may mean "the ax slicing the tree and the wood splitting into bits." That would be an objective meaning. On the other hand there is "genuine understanding of the other person" (1932a, p. 111) in which "the center of attention is the woodcutter's own lived experiences as actor" (1932a, p. 110). We might ask what the cutter's project is and why he has chosen it.

The difference between objective and subjective meanings, however, is one only of degree. Between the extreme poles of the most private subjective meaning and "pure objective meaning there is a whole series of intermediate steps" (1932a, p. 136).

The meanings I may impute to the actions of my postman, for example, may be ordered from the more objective to the more subjective. No reference to his intentions need be made to "understand" that the flap of my mailbox is getting lifted through, somehow, the movements of the postman's hand. Very little insight into the act's meaning to him is needed to understand that the postman purposefully lifted the flap. More insight into the thoughts of the postman are required to infer that he his lifting the flap in order to insert letters, that he is delivering the mail. Further insight into his personal biography would be needed to go beyond this interpretation to the subjective meanings that tell me what keeps him at his job and what part this particular action plays in his overarching life plan. It may be impossible for me to reach the subjective meaning that tells the postman his fealty to duty gives honor to his father who died a noble death on the field of battle. This may be, in some sense, the "real" meaning of the act. But it is a subjective meaning inaccessible to me. The difference between subjective and objective meaning is a matter of degree.

Schutz's distinction between objective and subjective meaning matters. If he is right, then Mises' distinction between conception and understanding is untenable. However subjective or objective are the meanings one attempts to understand, the act of understanding does not change its epistemological character. In the case of the most perfectly objective understanding, it is clear that no element of "understanding" in Mises' sense occurs. That is, though we may rightly claim to "understand" the action, there is no question of being transported *à la* Bergson to the interior of the object of our understanding. But even when we turn to subjective meanings, Schutz teaches, we understand through "postulating certain motives" (1932a, p. 244). No Bergsonian transports occur. Are we to think that we go deeper into the object's interior when we understand more fully subjective meanings? No. Whenever we understand more or less subjective meanings, we are imputing such meanings to another. We are guessing. Some guesses are more probable than others. But all entail some doubt.

By identifying the distinction and the grades of objectivity present in subjective meanings, Schutz was able to make the highly parallel distinction between higher and lower degrees of "anonymity" of ideal types. Ideal types are more or less abstract representations of actors and actions. If the meaning imputed to the action of an agent is highly subjective, many details of that agent's motives, skills, biography, and so on will be required. Our ideal type of that agent will be filled with biographical and psychological particulars. If instead we are interested only in the more objective meanings of the action, then our picture of the actor can be largely devoid of particulars; it can be more thin. Our ideal type of that agent will be rather empty. The more empty is an ideal type of particulars, the more "anonymous" it is. The more filled with particulars, the more idiosyncratic and less anonymous.

Any interpretation of the actions of others contains some reference to the meaning the actor intended. Some interpretations, however, provide more detailed account of subjective meaning than others. Thus we can rank (personal) ideal types according to the completeness of the description of the actor's subjective meaning context. When we fill in only a few particulars, the ideal type is "anonymous." When we fill in many particulars, the ideal type is "concrete." We might say that the ideal type has a psychological programming. Anonymous types have very little psychological programming. Concrete (or "intimate") types have a rich psychological programming. This "programming," however, refers to subjective meaning contexts. It does not refer to particular actions the type might perform.

The social world is arrayed about me as a network of ideal types. Those closest to me include the ideal types of greatest intimacy. Those farther away are more anonymous. My ideal types of my loved ones are filled in with many particulars. Those of my colleagues are highly concrete, but less intimate than those of my family. My ideal types of say, my fellow voters, are rather anonymous, though I do imagine some subjective meaning context for their choices. Finally, at the highest level of anonymity is my ideal type of acting man as such, the fellow human who acts.

Schutz's analysis of common-sense knowledge includes a theory of relevance. I will discuss his theory of relevance in Chapter 6. Before moving from Schutz's analysis of common-sense knowledge to his analysis of the everyday choosing based on this knowledge, three clarifying remarks may be in order.

First, common-sense knowledge is not 'objective,' but subjective. There is no presumption that this knowledge is 'true,' 'scientific,' or even internally consistent. It may not even be particularly well-suited to the actor's purpose. (Bleeding with leeches is not a very good cure for most diseases.) Subjective knowledge is not fully clear and distinct. Everyday knowledge is a mixed bag of typifications often jumbled together "in a very incoherent and confused state" (Schutz 1943, p. 72). Some pieces are clear and distinct bits of knowledge. Others are vague. The linkages between the several parts of everyday knowledge are not well ordered or understood. "There are everywhere gaps, intermissions, discontinuities" (1943, p. 73).

Second, our knowledge is always in flux (1959, p. 284). The sheer rolling-on of lived experience modifies, enlarges and enriches our knowledge.

Finally, our knowledge is largely pre-given. Each of us "was already born into a social cosmos" (1943, p. 70). The typification "my pocket knife" is not mine and mine alone. It is uniquely my own only insofar as it differs from the typification "anyone's pocket knife." If we are in the same "in-group," then we share the typification "anyone's pocket knife" even if we have never met. The knowledge which is mine alone has its place within the (generally more general) knowledge shared by the members of my "in-group." Similarly, my knowledge, even those parts which are mine alone, is pre-given at the "moment" of choice.[7] In emphasizing the pre-giveness of everyday knowledge, Schutz ends up neglecting the role of novelty and creativity in everyday action, (see Koppl 2001).

Having looked at common-sense knowledge, we may now study Schutz's analysis of the everyday action based on it. Acting man chooses. The word "choose" differentiates "conduct" from "action." It distinguishes the mere doing of something, such as a habit or routine, from the realization of a plan, a "project."

Choosing for Schutz is a process of deliberation. Schutz often quoted Dewey's remark that deliberation is "a dramatic rehearsal in imagination of various competing possible lines of action ... It is an experiment in making various combinations of selected elements of habits and impulses to see what the resultant action would be like if it were entered upon" (quoted in Schutz 1951, p. 68). Schutz calls this rehearsing "projecting." A project is a plan, a potential course of action, which is imagined as bringing about a certain state of affairs.

A crucial feature of Schutz's treatment of "projecting" is its temporal structure. According to Schutz, "it is not the ongoing process of action, but the phantasied act as having been accomplished which is the starting point of all projecting" (1953, p. 20). Imagining the end of action to have been already achieved is "thinking in the future perfect tense" (1953, p. 20). According to Schutz, in all cases of deliberative choice, the chooser imagines ends before he considers means.

According to Schutz, we have available to us at any time an array of typifications that might be applied to the situation in which we find ourselves. When we adopt an end for action, we pick up one of these typifications (Schutz and Luckmann 1973, pp. 215–223). We employ, Schutz argues, the "knowledge at hand at the time of projecting" (1953, p. 20). This knowledge, in turn, emerges from the experience of past actions. "Consequently, all projecting involves the idealization of 'I-can-do-it-again,' i.e., the assumption that I may under typically similar circumstances act in a way typically similar to that in which I acted before in order to bring about a typically similar state of affairs" (1953, p. 20).

All that has been said of the ideal types of common sense may be applied to scientific ideal types as well. In particular, the interpretive sociologist uses ideal types of varying degrees of anonymity. What we call either "history" or "applied economics" entails the use of relatively concrete ideal types. "Theory" uses more anonymous types. The distinction, therefore, between theory and history is not the categorical one Mises imagined. We use the term "theory" for arguments and explanations that use only relatively anonymous types; we use the terms "history" and "applied theory" when relatively concrete types are used. Where one draws the line between "theory" and "history" is largely a matter of taste.

Schutz's system has the five characteristics of Mises' system listed earlier. First, it is aprioristic. The knowledge of social science is based "on conclusions of thought," Schutz maintained. "The original and fundamental scheme of science, the expressive scheme of its propositions, and the interpretive scheme of its explanations is, therefore, essentially that of *formal logic*" (1932a, p. 223, emphasis in original).

Second, Schutz was a methodological dualist. The methods of the social sciences differ from those of the natural sciences. The social sciences refer to subjective meaning, the natural sciences do not. The methods of phenomenological psychology, therefore, apply only in social science.

Third, Schutz defended "understanding." Indeed, *The Phenomenology of the Social World* is a detailed account of what inter-subjective understanding is (phenomenologically).

Fourth, Schutz defended methodological individualism. Interpretive sociology, for Schutz, attempts "to explain human actions" by asking "what model of an individual mind can be constructed" to "explain the observed facts" (Schutz 1953, p. 43).

Fifth, Schutz defended nomological theory. Schutz considers the "obvious objection" that "the existence of the so-called law-constructing (or nomothetic) social sciences contradicts our earlier assertion that all social sciences are type-constructing in nature" (Schutz 1932a, p. 242). He reproduces two lengthy passages of Mises "'Soziologie und Geschichte,'" an essay that "we have already quoted repeatedly" (1932a, pp. 242–243). In them, Mises criticizes Weber's ideal type methodology for failing to recognize that the fundamental laws of economics "are valid always and everywhere when the conditions presupposed by them are present" (Mises as quoted in Schutz 1932a, p. 243).[8] "No doubt Mises' criticism is valid against Weber's earliest formulations of the concept of ideal type" (1932a, p. 243). But the concept as rehabilitated by Schutz is immune to Mises' criticism. In particular, Schutz's concept permits both "empirical" and "eidetic" ideal types, "and by eidetic we mean 'derived from essential insight'" (1932a, p. 244).

This last remark alludes to Husserl's concepts of "essence" and "eidetic" (Husserl 1913, pp. 45–57). The substance of the idea is that the "eidetic" type need not refer to any empirical object or phenomenon. The type is constrained, however, to fit the logic necessary to it. The "miser" cannot be a chair; it must be a person. Similarly, the miser cannot spend freely. Free spending is inconsistent with the inner logic of miserliness. In Husserl's example, it is an empirical insight that "all 'real' bodies are heavy." It is an eidetic insight that "all material things are extended" (Husserl 1913, p. 54).[9] Thus, the empirical ideal type of "banker" may be "conservative," while the eidetic ideal type is not necessarily conservative.

Mises was right, Schutz argued, to criticize Weber's ideal type methodology. His criticism was "valid." But the methodology as rehabilitated by Schutz was immune to Mises' criticism. "Mises is right," Schutz explains, "when he criticizes Weber for interpreting the marginal utility theory in too narrow a fashion," mistaking it for the image of "an economy run entirely according to the calculations of entrepreneurs." Mises, "the most significant advocate of the *a priori* character of economics," was right to argue that "modern theoretical economics" starts from "the behavior of anyone and everyone ... Here, as Mises repeatedly emphasizes, is to be found the basis of the objectivism and objectivity of the propositions of catallactics. But this 'objectivity' of Mises is, therefore," Schutz avers, "the same as the concept of objectivity we ourselves put forward in our discussion of the objective and subjective contexts of meaning" (1932a, p. 245). The distinction between history and theory does not turn on the method by which knowledge is gained, either discursive reasoning or Bergsonian intuition, but the anonymity of the ideal type.

With Schutz's enlarged sense of ideal type, "even the examples cited by Mises – the economic principle, the basic laws of price formation, and so forth – are in our sense ideal types" (Schutz 1932a, p. 244). Thus, we can accept Mises' criticism of Weber while maintaining that economic theory uses "ideal types" in the Schutzian sense. "Mises' argument really turns out to be a defense against the intrusion of ideal types of too great concreteness and too little anonymity into econom-ics" (1932a, p. 244). Economic theory uses only highly anonymous ideal types, "and it is in this sense that economic principles are, in Mises' words, 'not a statement of what usually happens, but of what necessarily must happen'" (1932a, p. 245). Thus, economics is, for Schutz, "nomothetic."

Schutz's rehabilitation of Mises' position was successful in the sense that it is free of the deficiencies of Mises' system I listed earlier. First, I cited Mises' use of the Bergson's concept of intuition. Schutz, as we have seen, rejected Bergsonian intuition.

Second, I noted that Mises' distinction between theory and history leaves "theory" with very little to say about human action. Mises' claim that economics can predict such things as "what consequences price controls must have" (1933, p. 118) is inconsistent with his claim that "praxeology" describes only the form of action and not its content. In the language of Schutz, we may now say that in Mises' methodology, only the most completely anonymous ideal types are admitted in economic theory. But the sorts of predictions Mises thought economics to give require ideal types that are not completely anonymous. They are highly anonymous, but not perfectly anony-mous. With Schutz we can and should admit such imperfectly anony-mous types into economic theory.

Third, I noted that Mises methodology makes a theory of expectations impossible. As I have argued on another occasion, Schutz's concept of anonymity "lays the ground for a subjectivist theory of expectations" (Koppl 1997, p. 73). Economic actors cannot reliably predict the actions of relatively concrete ideal types. But if certain identifiable conditions prevail, economic actors can reliably predict the actions of anonymous types. The economist, therefore, can reliably predict the expectations of economic actors when he can imagine them to be themselves relying upon anonymous types in the formation of those expectations.

Finally, I noted that Mises exaggerates the difference between *a priori* and *a posteriori* and, therefore, the difference between theory and history. Schutz, as we have seen, recognized the movement from theory to history as a continuous one. Schutz's system gives us a Misesian methodology free of the defects characteristic of Mises' original system.

In standard economic theory, preferences are given. There is no more fundamental element in our description of the agent than prefer-ences. Schutz analysis, however, reveals that interpretation is prior to preference. His analysis builds on Husserl's distinction between "open" and "problematic" possibilities.

Our knowledge is in some degree vague and inadequate. It is a system of types. These types carry "open horizons." In other words, they are somewhat empty and can be filled in many ways. This open-ended quality of our typifications makes them "open possibilities" (Schutz 1951, p. 81). "All anticipation has the character of indeterminacy," Schutz explains, "and this general indeterminacy constitutes a frame of free variability; what falls within the frame is one element among other elements of possibly *nearer* determination, of which I merely know that they will fit in the frame but which are otherwise entirely undetermined. This is exactly the concept of open possibilities" (1951, p. 81, emphasis in original).

Contrasted to open possibilities are "problematic possibilities" (1951, pp. 79–82). Open possibilities do not imply the need to choose. Problematic possibilities do. Any typification or interpretation is an open possibility. When two interpretations come into conflict, then a choice must be made. Problematic possibilities arise and are resolved in the context of action. Deliberate choice is always choice between problematic possibilities.

I choose between, say, two projects, A and B. While deliberating, I waver between the two. I incline first to the one, and then to the other. But as I pass in my imagination between the two poles, the meaning of each alternative is changing. I consider A and incline toward it. I consider B and incline toward it. I then return, in my mind, to project A inclining again in that direction. But "the project to which I return is no longer the same as that which I dropped" (1951, p. 85) if only because I have grown older and view it, now, differently. I began by wavering between A and B. Later, I wavered between A' and B', and then A'' and B'', and so on. Finally, the "free action detaches itself" and falls "like too ripe a fruit" (1951, p. 86).

Once the choice is made, the problematic alternatives between which the agent wavered are finally constituted. They are fixed by the choice. "The sociologist's assumption that the actor in the social world starts with the definition of the situation is," Schutz explains, "equivalent to the methodological postulate, that the sociologist has to describe the observed social actions as if they occurred within a unified field of true alternatives, that is, of problematic and not of open possibilities." Similarly, the "so-called 'marginal principle,' so important for modern economics, can be interpreted as" the postulate that we view "subjects as if they had to choose between pregiven problematic possibilities" (1951, pp. 83–84). (Note that choice between "pregiven problematic possibilities" is not "real" choice.)

Thus, the agent's preferences do not exist prior to action. They are determined by the action and given only in action. Underlying these preferences are acts of interpretations and re-interpretation. These acts are temporally and logically prior to the final constitution of the actor's preferences. Interpretation precedes preference.

The view that interpretation precedes preference has something of a precedent in the Austrian tradition. Carl Menger defined "value" as "the importance that individual goods or quantities of goods attain for us because we are conscious of being dependent on command of them for the satisfaction of our needs" (1871, p. 115). This definition follows a lengthy discussion of how "economizers" plan their affairs and, while planning, estimate their "requirements" for various goods. In Menger, marginal utility is the product of prior planning that occurs in the context of scarcity. Menger did not have the idea of "*Verstehen.*" But there is a sense in which, for Menger too, interpretation precedes preference.

Schutz's system contains many strengths. I draw heavily on it in the following chapters. But I believe there is an important economic idea missing from Schutz's phenomenology of the social world. Schutz did not clearly recognize that human action may generate systematic, but unintended consequences. As Hayek argued, these unintended consequences are the subject matter of economics and other social sciences.

According to Schutz, "pure economics; is a perfect example of an objective meaning-complex about subjective meaning-complexes, in other words, of an objective meaning-configuration stipulating the typical and invariant subjective experiences of anyone who acts within an economic framework" (1932a, p. 245). This characterization of economics implies that any object of scientific inquiry within economics must have passed through the mind of some economic agent. It must already have been typified by that agent.

Schutz's characterization of economics excludes much of economic theory. The theory of general equilibrium, for example, identifies patterns in the price structure of a unified market economy. Real transactors will be perfectly aware of individual prices. But they will be unaware of the price structure described by general equilibrium theory. To analyze such unintended consequences, we must appeal to causal connections that are "mechanistic" in the sense that they are not intended by any of the actors whose actions nevertheless bring them about (Koppl 1992). Schutz's characterization of economics seems to exclude such causal mechanisms.

I admit that the situation is at least somewhat ambiguous. Schutz claims, for instance, that "even the examples cited by Mises – the economic principle, the basic laws of price formation, and so forth – are in our sense ideal types" (1932a, p. 244). Also, there is the following striking remark from Hayek (1988). "Thus one might describe economics (what I now prefer to call catallactics ...) as a metatheory, a theory about the theories people have developed to explain how most effectively to discover and use different means for diverse purposes" (1988, p. 98). Thus, one might attempt to argue that Hayek's unintended consequences fit perfectly within Schutz's framework of "constructs of the second order." In my opinion, however, unintended consequences do introduce a new element not addressed by a purely interpretive method. The leading theorist of unintended consequences is F. A. Hayek, to whom we now turn.

4
Hayek[1]

Like Schutz, Hayek was a Misesian methodologist. The view that Hayek was a Misesian methodologist is probably a minority opinion. In spite of the work of Caldwell (1988, 1992a, 1992b), the most common view may still be that of Hutchison (1984) who argued that Hayek abandoned Misesian methodology in 1937. "Hayek I" was a follower of Mises, Hutichson argues, and "Hayek II" was a follower of Popper.[2] Hutchison's views are based on a reading of Mises that differs from my own. In Hutchison's reading, the essential feature of Mises' methodology is strict apriorism. Hutchison's principal text is Mises (1962). If Kurrild-Klitgaard (2001) is right, however, Mises (1962) is a "radicalized" apriorism not present in the 1930s.

Mises' reaction to Hayek 1937 is revealing. The article, Hayek relates,

> was an attempt to persuade Mises himself that when he asserted that the market theory was a priori, he was wrong; that what was a priori was only the logic of individual action, but the moment you passed from this to the interaction of many people, you entered into the empirical field. Curiously enough, while Mises was very resentful of any criticism by his pupils and temporarily broke both with Machlup and Haberler because they had criticized him, he took my critique silently and even approved the article as if he had not been aware that it was a criticism of his own views. I cannot explain this. (Hayek 1994, p. 72)

In 1937, Hayek took his distance from Mises. But the distance may not have been as great as Hutchison holds. Mises seems to have seen it as a small distance or as no distance at all. In Chapter 2 I emphasized Mises' loose apriorism, rather than the passages suggesting a stronger apriorism. If I was right to do so, Hayek's 1937 article did not constitute a fundamental break with Misesian methodology. It might better be seen as a friendly amendment. As I will argue presently, even after 1937, Hayek defended loose apriorism.

Hayek's methodological views are developed with special care in two books published in 1952, *The Counter Revolution of Science* and *The Sensory Order*. These two books are closely related. Their arguments should be viewed as continuous and interdependent. The former reprints essays published in the 1940s. The latter brings to fruition a position Hayek developed in an unpublished essay from 1920. Together they map out a Misesian methodology of the social sciences.

The Counter Revolution of Science begins with a brief look at "The Influence of the Natural Sciences on the Social Sciences." This short chapter is followed by a longer chapter on "The Problem and the Method of the Natural Sciences." This second chapter is a kind of semi-popular treatment of many of the themes of *The Sensory Order*.[3] In particular, the chapter contains summary statements of important points made in the concluding chapter of *The Sensory Order*, "Philosophical Consequences." That same philosophical chapter of *The Sensory Order* contains three separate references to *The Counter Revolution of Science*. Another three references appear earlier in the book. *The Counter Revolution of Science* is the only work of Hayek cited in *The Sensory Order*. It seems fair to conclude that the two books are developing one continuous argument. Logically, *The Sensory Order* is volume 1; *The Counter Revolution of Science* is volume 2.[4]

Chronologically, the situation is more confused. Hayek wrote the essay that eventually became *The Sensory Order* in 1920. He reports that he "seriously resumed work" on it in 1946 (Hayek 1994, p. 125). Parts One and Two of *The Counter Revolution of Science* were published as essays between 1941 and 1944. Part Three was published in 1951. Hutchison's thesis is weakened by the fact that the basic ideas of *The Sensory Order* were in place in 1920. As I will note again below, Hayek tells us that the "basic idea" of the book "has often proved helpful in dealing with the problems of the methods of the social sciences" (1952a, p. v).

It is very significant, I think, that Hayek starts *The Counter Revolution of Science* where *The Sensory Order* leaves off. Hayek saw humanity as located between the extremes explored by natural and social science. The natural sciences move down from large observable phenomena to small causes that we can observe only indirectly. The social sciences move up from small observable causes to large consequences we can observe only indirectly:

> The place where the human individual stands in the order of things brings it about that in one direction what he perceives are the comparatively complex phenomena which he analyzes, while in the other direction what are given to him are elements from which those more complex phenomena are composed that he cannot observe as wholes. While the method of the natural sciences is in this sense, analytic, the method of the social sciences is better described as compositive or synthetic. (Hayek 1952b, pp. 66–67)

Hayek's opinion to this effect was nothing new in 1952. In a footnote to the passage cited above, Hayek quotes his own remark from 1935 that

> the position of man, midway between natural and social phenomena – of the one of which he is an effect and of the other a cause – brings it about that the essential basic facts which we need for the explanation of social phenomena are part of common experience, part of the stuff of our thinking. In the social sciences it is the elements of the complex phenomena which are known beyond the possibility of dispute. In the natural sciences they can only be at best surmised. (Hayek 1935, p. 11 as cited in Hayek 1952b, p. 66, n.3)

In the paragraph from which this quote is drawn, Hayek uses the phrase "complex phenomena" six times. It seems significant that he uses this phrase repeatedly in 1935.

A vivid example of the connection between the two books of 1952 is found early in *The Counter Revolution of Science*. Hayek explains that it is the procedure of natural science "to substitute for the classification of events which our senses provide a new one which groups together not what appears alike but what proves to behave in the same manner in similar circumstances" (1952b, p. 31). He notes that this view "may sound surprising" (1952b, 31). Indeed, at the time this was written philosophers tended to argue that natural science simply re-orders our sensory data. Who seriously argued that the sensory order was *displaced* by science? The answer is Hayek. In the concluding, philosophical chapter of *The Sensory Order*, Hayek says natural science consists in the "reclassification, or breaking up of the classes formed by the implicit relations which manifest themselves in our discrimination of sensory qualities, and the replacement of these classes by new classes defined by explicit relations" (1952a, p. 169).

The connection between *The Sensory Order* and *The Counter Revolution of Science* is important. The argument of *The Counter Revolution of Science* is easily recognized as Misesian. The book contains a famous footnote celebrating Mises for his consistent subjectivism. The note is attached to Hayek's statement that "it is probably no exaggeration to say that every important advance in economic theory during the last hundred years was a further step in the consistent application of subjectivism" (1952b, p. 52). *The Counter Revolution of Science* is a sustained argument against "scientism," which Hayek defines as the "slavish imitation of the method and language of [natural] Science" (1952b, p. 24).

By contrast, the argument of *The Sensory Order* may seem much less Misesian. It may even seem to be itself an example of "scientism." It contains favorable references to figures such as Ludwig von Bertalanffy and Norbert Weiner. Hayek claims that "with regard to purposiveness," machines such as anti-aircraft guns and automatic pilots "differ from a brain merely in degree and not in kind" (1952b, p. 126). He even affirms "the logical possibility that the knowledge of the principle on which the brain operates might enable us to build a machine fully reproducing the action of the brain and capable of predicting how the brain will act in different circumstances" (1952b, p. 189).

To contrast the two books in this way would be a mistake. *The Sensory Order* is every bit as subjectivist and Misesian as *The Counter Revolution of Science*. In the preface, Hayek informs us that the "basic idea" of the book, fully formed in 1920, "has often proved helpful in dealing with the problems of the methods of the social sciences" (1952b, p. v). He expresses relative indifference to the possibility that the more technical aspects of the book contain errors. "I am much more concerned about what would constitute an explanation of mental phenomena, than whether the details of this theory are entirely correct" (1952b, p. viii).

Hayek develops a theory of mind in *The Sensory Order*. Hayek's theory is meant to solve the mind–body problem. He is trying to understand how matter might give rise to mind on the assumption that there is no special mind substance floating around in our heads or anywhere else. More precisely put, Hayek tried to show "how the physiological impulses proceeding in the different parts of the central nervous system can become in such a manner differentiated from each other in their functional significance that their effects will differ from each other in the same way in which we know the effects of the different sensory qualities to differ from each other" (1952a, p. 1).

This is a relatively narrow problem that applies equally to human and animal intelligence. Hayek applies the solution, however, to all the higher forms of mental life (1952b, p. 146). Hayek had a "computational" theory of mind. Today's most prominent exponent of this type of theory is probably Danial Dennet. Some versions of the computational theory are reductionist and insensitive to the fact that all knowledge is contextual. As I explain below, Hayek's theory is anti-reductionist. It fully recognizes that all knowledge is contextual.

The sensory "qualities" Hayek refers to are "the different attributes or dimensions with regard to which we differentiate our responses to different stimuli" (1952b, p. 2). Human and animal behaviors reveal an order placed on external events. Indeed, they constitute this order. It is this order which Hayek calls the "sensory order." Science, on the other hand reveals (or constructs or posits) a different order. The mind–body problem is that of relating the two orders. If we posit a separate mind substance, then we have to imagine some sort of mysterious communication between unlike substances (mind and matter) as Descartes thought or, perhaps, a pre-existing harmony created by God as Leibniz thought. If we abandon the assumption that such a substance exists, we open the door to an evolutionary explanation of mind as matter in motion.

Hayek interprets the mind–body problem as one of relating the order of events presented by science, the "physical" order, to that of the senses, the "phenomenal" order (1952b, pp. 2–8). It is a matter of explaining how the physical order might generate the phenomenal order. The phenomenal order consists in the patterned responses of an organism to its environment. This environment is described as a physical order. For Hayek "psychology must start from stimuli defined in physical terms and proceed to show why and how the senses classify similar physical stimuli sometimes as alike and sometimes as different, and why different physical stimuli will sometimes appear as similar and sometimes as different" (1952b, pp. 7–8). The senses give us a natural and naïve picture of how the world works. Science replaces this picture with another one, less likely to disappoint our expectations. Theoretical psychology, Hayek contends, has the job of explaining how the world described by science could generate, as a part of it, organisms possessed of the more naïve picture from which this same scientific view departs.

The solution to which Hayek builds is that evolution generates central nervous systems whose internal operations constitute an imperfect model of the outside world (1952b, pp. 7 and 107–112). It is very much of the essence of Hayek's theory that minds are models of the world. One could almost say that to think is to manipulate a little world that mimics the big world. This way of expressing things, however, is not quite right. It raises impossible questions. What sort of homunculus is doing the manipulation? And does that homunculus have another little homunculus inside it? A better expression of the matter would be to say that to think is to have your actions governed by a mechanism whose internal structure and rules of operations constitute a model of the outside world.

If this view of things is right, the big world produces in the higher species a lot of little worlds more or less similar to the original. Putting it this way may help us to see from whence arise the logical limits of knowledge of which Hayek makes much. The physicist David Wolpert (1996) has made broadly similar arguments. Wolpert claims (rightly, I believe) to have proved that the Laplacian dream of a perfectly predictable universe is logically impossible. A modified version of Wolpert's argument is discussed in Appendix 4 (p. 212).

Hayek argues that the phenomenal order is generated by the central nervous system which, in turn, is a product of biological evolution. The central nervous system is made up of fibers that carry impulses. Some of these fibers, the "afferent fibers," carry impulses up from receptor sites to the brain. Others, the "efferent fibers," carry impulses back down to motor sites. Others still, the great majority, make up the brain. The consequences of a given set of impulses from the afferent fibers consists in the induced pattern of impulses running down the efferent fibers. What that induced pattern of impulses will be depends on what happens in the brain. Each of the incoming impulses induces some pattern of nerve firings within the brain. But what pattern of such firings a impulse will produce depends on what other impulses are coming in at the same time, on what others have just come in, and on the whole constellation of affairs within the brain.

An organism for which the induced constellation of efferent impulses bore no relationship to the incoming afferent impulses would not be responding to its environment. We would deny that it is thinking. An organism for which the induced constellation of efferent impulses bore a simple and invariable relationship to the incoming afferent impulses would be responding to its environment, but only in ways we call "mechanical." We would deny that it is thinking. We recognize an organism's behavior as governed by "mental" phenomena when the organism is responding to its environment, but in ways more complex than reflex action.

Natural selection has produced a set of rules that govern the brain's activity in response to incoming impulses. These rules translate afferent impulses into efferent impulses. When an organism happens to be governed by mental rules that give it "inclusive fitness," which is, roughly, differential reproductive success, those rules are passed on. The tendency of natural selection is to favor rules that better reflect the crucial elements of the organism's environment. Animals that know better when to run and when to fight have better chances. As long as the environment is so complex that errors are made, there is room for improvement in mental functioning. And improvement may imply a greater complexity of behavior, i.e. greater complexity of the rules governing mental behavior.

The tendency toward greater intelligence contends with other tendencies moving in other directions. A large cortex extracts a biological price. Other factors beside sophistication of behavior influence fitness. I do not know how great the element of chance has been in the emergence of intelligent life. The tendency toward greater intelligence has in fact resulted, however, in the emergence of the human and animal minds.

As Butos and I (1997a) have said, the simplest version of a central nervous system matching Hayek's description

> would put any impulse cluster into one of two boxes. We might think of one box as carrying the label "go right" and the other "go left." Biological evolution would tend to select, from among such simple organisms, those whose central nervous systems tended to say "go left" when more nourishing environments existed to the left and "go right" when more nourishing environments existed to the right. Natural selection would tend to favor those spontaneous variations that generated more complex responses ("go left then right") to environmental stimuli. Emergent species would, then, tend to have ever more receptor sites, ever more nerve fibers, ever larger brains, and, in consequence, ever more complex ways of classifying and responding to incoming signals.

The rules of mental activity have the effect of classifying the incoming impulses. The brain partitions the set of possible impulse clusters into equivalence classes according to rules about such things as what impulses are coinciding with what other impulses and what impulses follow what other impulses. In the early stages of the mind's evolution, the rules are simple ones inducing, say, motion toward light. In the later stages the level of complexity of the rules is so great that we find ourselves obliged to describe them in the mentalistic language of ends and means. The bird, we say, is "building a nest," or "feeding its young," or "courting." Even in the case of bird brains, we find ourselves driven to mentalistic language because of our inability to describe the precise environmental factors that induce each wiggle, chirp, and flap.

The rules of mental activity are, in Hayek's system, rules of classification. They effect a classification of the impulses clusters coming up the afferent fibers. The rules give us a taxonomy. It is this taxonomy of impulse clusters that constitutes the sensory order. To perceive, say, "green" is find a certain set of impulses classified by the central nervous system in the same way as others which induce the perception of "green." The experience of "green" is a property of the mind's taxonomic framework, not the external world. If evolution has done its job, however, the taxonomy giving us the experience of color will reflect something worth knowing about the outside world.

This view of the mind as taxonomic order follows from the motivating insight of Hayek's theory. According to Hayek, "we do not first have sensations which are then preserved by memory, but it is as a result of physiological memory that the physiological impulses are converted into sensations. The connexions between the physiological elements are thus the primary phenomenon which creates the mental phenomena" (1952a, p. 53). This view of the mind and its evolution implies that the mind is a model of the external world. The rules favored by natural selection would tend to be the ones reflecting useful information about the organism's environment. The central nervous system is a signal system. Some signals should imply fight, others should imply flight. The actions induced by the structure and function of the brain constitute the interpretation of the signals. Sometimes the brain says fight, sometimes it says flight. Those organisms who read the signals better will be more likely to have inclusive fitness; they will be fruitful and multiply. Thus evolution favors rules for the operation of the organism's central nervous system, i.e. the organism's mind, which render it a serviceable model or interpretation of its environment.

Hayek distinguishes two aspects of this interpretation. First, there is the part of it which is relatively stable and unresponsive to new stimuli. Second, there is the more fluid part that reflects immediate facts of the organism's environment. Hayek calls the first aspect "map" and the second "model." (See Hayek 1952a, pp. 107–118.) Some aspects of the mind's map are quite invariant for the individual. They are the product of evolution of the species and cannot be altered by the organism's personal experiences. Others are more variable products of the individual's experience. In any event, the map shows "the different *kinds* of stimuli" the organism might experience that "have acquired significance for it" through its personal and phylogenic history. The map is silent about "the particular environment in which the organism is placed at the moment" (1952a, p. 115, emphasis in original). That information is given by the model. The model is the organism's interpretation of its immediate environment.

Hayek's theory of mind is easily misunderstood. It does not say that each individual's mind is a product of his personal history only. Each mind is pre-programmed with a map that emerged from the biological history of the species. (It does not matter for our purposes how much of this map is in place at birth and how much unfolds as the organism matures.) All men and women share a common mental structure because we have a common biological history. (It is a detail for us that some sexual dimorphism of mental structure may exist. See Barkow *et al.*1992.) We have a common mental constitution. Our individual maps differ in their details because of differences in our personal and social histories – and, perhaps, other causes. The mind's map is variable, but not perfectly plastic. The stick in the water looks bent even though I know perfectly well it is not.

The biological origins of our common mental map help to explain why the rules of mental life are hierarchically organized. The elements of our common map that were put in place earliest in biological time will generally govern the largest number of mental events. They are probably the hardest to override with rules acquired later in biological time. However rarely or frequently old rules are overridden by new rules, there will be a temporal layering of rules, which implies some degree of hierarchy.

Hayek's theory of mind leads to two apriorisms, one of the physical sciences and one of the social sciences. I will discuss them in that order.

Our mental "map" is the product of biological evolution and personal history. For humans (and perhaps other species) it is also a product of our social history. At all these levels the map is a product of the environment that produced it. But at any one moment it is the interpretive framework and thus "*a priori.*" Hayek explicitly rejects "John Locke's famous fundamental maxim" that all our knowledge comes from the senses. Hayek affirms the existence of a rather Kantian *a priori* by saying "[a]ll that we can perceive is thus determined by the order of sensory qualities which provides the 'categories' in terms of which sense experience can alone take place" (1952a, p. 167).

Hayek acknowledges that we "possess 'knowledge' of the phenomenal world which ... must be true of all that we can experience through our senses. This does not mean, however, that this knowledge must also be true of the physical world" (1952a, p. 168). Past experience of the organism and of its species has produced an *a priori* that guides it and determines its perceptions. But it "does not always work, i.e., it does not always lead to valid predictions," and this fact "forces us to revise that classification" (1952a, p. 168). We learn. What we learn when we learn is a new *a priori* (1952a, p. 168).

Disappointed expectations lead us to reclassify data. But because the new classes we define are different from the sensory classes they replace, they are "defined by explicit relations" among members of the newly formed classes. We redefine water as that which puts out fire when we discover clear liquids that burn. A realistic example is the mechanical theory of heat. The theory that heat is a form of energy does not refer to human sensations of hot and cold. It does refer to measurements performed under the assumption that the energy of a closed system is conserved. Such measurements have established the existence of a constant "mechanical equivalent of heat." This equivalence identifies a regularity in the "explicit relations" among classes of events. It does not refer to feeling of warmth and coolness.

In science, the more we learn, the more complete is the tendency of classes of phenomena to be defined formally in terms of one another. As this process of formalization proceeds, the sensual element in our picture of the world recedes, "the greater becomes the part of our knowledge which is embodied in the definitions of the elements, and which therefore is necessarily true. At the same time the part of our knowledge which is subject to control by experience becomes correspondingly smaller" (1952a, p. 170). The *a priori* element grows. "Science," Hayek concludes, "tends necessarily toward an ultimate state in which all knowledge is embodied in the definitions of the objects with which it is concerned; and in which all true statements about these objects therefore are analytical or tautological and could not be disproved by any experience" (1952a, p. 171).

Hayek knew that he had been led by empiricist reasoning toward a highly aprioristic view of science and knowledge. "In so far as we have been led into opposition to some of the theses traditionally associated with empiricism, we have been led to their rejection not from an opposite point of view, but on the contrary, by a more consistent and radical application of its basic idea" (1952a, p. 172). The basic idea of empiricism is that all our knowledge is due to experience. Hayek's point is that "[p]recisesly because all our knowledge, including the initial order of our different sensory experiences of the world, is due to experience, it must contain elements which cannot be contradicted by experience" (1952a, p. 172).

Hayek's apriorism of the physical sciences might be labeled "Fabian apriorism." His apriorism of the social sciences is different, and quite close to that of Mises.

For the natural scientist, the "views people hold about the external world are ... always a stage to be overcome" (1952b, p. 39). The social scientist, Hayek argues, is in a very different position. He must consider "the fact that people perceive the world and each other through sensations and concepts which are organized in a mental structure common to all of them" (1952b, p. 39). He must recognize "the fact that man has a definite picture, and that the picture of all beings whom we recognize as thinking men and whom we can understand is to some extent alike" (1952b, p. 39). This fact "is a reality of great consequence" and the basis of social science (1952b, p. 39). Hayek's point is fundamentally the same as Schutz's point that the social world is a pre-interpreted reality.

In recognizing this fact and making it the foundation of social science, Hayek is accepting Mises' apriorism. This position is Hayek's apriorism of the social sciences. "We know ... that in his conscious decisions man classifies external stimuli in a way we know solely from our own subjective experience of this kind of classification" (1952b, p. 43). We assume the identity of mental structure, we "take it for granted," even though "no objective test" could confirm it (1952b, p. 43). "It would be impossible to explain or understand human action without making use of this knowledge" (1952b, pp. 43–44). Hayek claims that "all propositions of pure economic theory" fit the pattern of "a statement about the implications of certain human attitudes toward things and as such necessarily true irrespective of time and place" (1952b, p. 55). Pure theory is *a priori*. Hayek and Mises adopt the same aprioristic doctrine that "the [common] structure of men's minds ... provides us with the knowledge ... in terms of which we can alone describe and explain" social phenomena (1952b, p. 58).

Hayek's apriorism, however, differs from Mises' in one important respect. Hayek thought that most statements of economic theory contains more than the *a priori* component, which we have just seen him label "pure economic theory." They also contain "empirical statements" such as the claim that land is often a relatively specific factor of production. (Thus, the "law of rent" often applies to land.) Any empirical statement of this type "is an assertion that the conditions postulated" in an economic law "prevail" in a given time and place (1952b, p. 55). Hayek then cites his 1937 paper "Economics and Knowledge."

As far as I know, Hayek's apriorism of the social sciences is not directly expressed in *The Sensory Order*. But in connection with methodological dualism (to which we shall turn presently) Hayek does say that in social science "our starting point will always have to be our direct knowledge of the different kinds of mental events, which to us must remain irreducible entities" (1952a, p. 191). Moreover, Hayek notes that we "use our direct ('introspective') knowledge of mental events in order to 'understand,' and in some measure even predict, the results to which mental processes will lead in certain conditions" (1952a, p. 192). (I will use this quote again.)

Hayek also adopts Mises' methodological dualism. In *The Counter Revolution of Science*, Hayek says, "We know that people will react in the same way to external stimuli which according to all objective tests are different, and perhaps also that they will react in a completely different manner to a physically identical stimulus" (1952a, p. 43). This language parallels language of Mises that we have already quoted. Also, in *Theory and History*, Mises defends methodological dualism by noting that, "Identical external events result sometimes in different human responses, and different external events produce sometimes the same human response. We don't know why" (1957, p. 18). The language just quoted appears also in *The Sensory Order*. "[P]sychology must start from stimuli defined in physical terms and proceed to show why and how the senses classify similar physical stimuli sometimes as alike and sometimes as different, and why different physical stimuli will sometimes appear as similar and sometimes as different" (1952a, pp. 7–8).

As we have seen, Hayek's solution to this problem represents the mind as a classificatory apparatus. Hayek argues that a classificatory apparatus must be more complex than the objects it classifies with respect to the elements accounted for in the classification (1952a, pp. 184–188). Thus, he concludes, the mind cannot fully explain itself. The last paragraph of *The Sensory Order* is worth quoting in full:

> Our conclusion, therefore, must be that *to us* mind must remain forever a realm of its own which we can know only through directly experiencing it, but which we shall never be able fully to explain or to "reduce" to something else. Even though we may know that mental events of the kind which we experience can be produced by the same forces which operate in the rest of nature, we shall never

be able to say which are the particular physical events which "correspond" to a particular mental event. (1952a, p. 194, emphasis in original)

Hayek followed Mises in accepting the doctrine of understanding. Indeed, in *The Sensory Order*, he explicitly defends "*verstehende* psychology" (1952a, p. 192). We "use our direct ('introspective') knowledge of mental events in order to 'understand,' and in some measure even to predict, the results to which mental processes will lead in certain condtions" (1952a, p. 192). Chapter 3 of *The Counter Revolution of Science*, "The Subjective Character of the Data of the Social Sciences," is devoted to the idea of inter-subjective understanding. Hayek illustrates this with the case of an archaeologist trying to learn if a piece of stone was a manufactured tool or a product of nature. "There is no way of deciding this but by trying to understand the working of the mind of pre-historic man, of attempting to understand how he would have made such an implement" (1952b, p. 46).

In *The Sensory Order*, Hayek develops a kind of naturalistic theory of inter-subjective understanding. This theory follows from his general theory of mind. Any two humans share the same philogenic history and thus share the same basic mental structure. That structure consists in the patterned responses of the organism to the nervous impulses stimulated by the external world. But precisely because the mind is a finite classificatory apparatus, the rules governing its behavior are not explicitly knowable by it.

The point here is combinatorial. Consider a simple classificatory apparatus. We have, say, a machine designed to sort oranges into two boxes, "large" and "small." Any orange has only one diameter. The machine, however, recognizes two kinds of diameters, "large" and "small." Thus, with respect to diameter, the sorting machine is more complicated than the oranges it sorts. (See also Hayek 1952a, p. 188.) More generally, a classificatory apparatus must be more complex than the objects it classifies with the respect to the elements accounted for in the classification.

Imagine that the object to be classified might be described according to m attributes. These might be size, color, and weight. Imagine further that each of them may take on n values. These may be small, large, and medium; black, white, and gray; and light, heavy, and medium. Then the object may take on any of n^m values. It may be small, white, and heavy, or it might be large, white, and heavy, or any of (in this case) 25 other values. Thus the object described by m words can be so described only by a classificatory apparatus possessed of n^m categories. The classificatory apparatus must be more complex than that which it classifies (Hayek 1952a, pp. 186–187).

From this result it follows that the mind cannot fully explain itself. To explain itself, the mind would have to classify all possible mental events. The mind would therefore have to be more complex than itself, an absurdity. Thus our explanations of mental events are always only of the principle and never truly complete. The mind cannot fully explain itself. For this combinatorial reason, inter-subjective understanding is always a matter of "intuitive" grasping of "meanings." It is always a matter of "understanding." (Hayek 1952a, p. 192).

Hayek accepted Mises' methodological individualism. In *The Counter Revolution of Science*, Hayek distinguishes those of an actor's opinions that guide his actions from those which provide theories of such collectives as "capitalism" and "society." "That [the social scientist] consistently refrains from treating these pseudo-entities as facts, and that he systematically starts from the concepts which guide individuals in their actions and not from the results of their theorizing about their actions, is the characteristic feature of that methodological individualism which is closely connected with the subjectivism of the social sciences" (1952b, p. 64).

Finally, Hayek accepted Mises' claim that economics is nomothetic. In Hayek's work this idea is most characteristically expressed in the formula that economics studies the unintended consequences of human action. "If social phenomena showed no order except insofar as they were consciously designed, there would indeed be no room for theoretical sciences of society" (1952b, p. 69).

The Misesian character of *The Counter Revolution of Science* is further revealed by the many references to Mises it contains. It contains a famous footnote in which Hayek celebrates Mises' subjectivism. It is significant, I think, how sweeping the praise is. Subjectivism "is a development which has probably been carried out most consistently by Ludwig von Mises," Hayek notes. Moreover, "most peculiarities of his views ... trace to the fact that in the consistent development of the subjectivist approach he has for a long time moved ahead of his contemporaries." Hayek suggests that "all the characteristic features of his theories," including "what he calls his *a priorism*," and his criticism of central planning, "follow directly" from the "central thesis" of subjectivism (1952b, p. 52, n.7). The book contains several other direct references to Mises, including one approving of Mises' term "praxeology" (1952b, p. 45, n.3).

Hayek's rehabilitation of Mises' methodology was successful in the sense that it is free of the deficiencies of Mises' system that I listed earlier. First, I cited Mises' use of Bergson's concept of intuition. Hayek clearly rejected this theory of inter-subjective understanding in favor of his combinatorial theory.

Second, I noted that Mises' distinction between theory and history leaves "theory" with very little to say about human action. Hayek's clearest statements on this issue are to be found in his 1937 paper "Economics and Knowledge." But as we have seen, in *The Counter Revolution of Science* he argues that the statements of economic theory contain empirical statements to the effect that the postulated conditions of pure theory apply in a given case. Thus, Hayek was willing to admit such empirical content into economic theory.

Third, I noted that Mises' methodology makes a theory of expectations impossible. By admitting empirical claims into economic theory, Hayek created space for an economic theory of expectations. Butos and I (1993) have attempted to outline a Hayekian theory of expectations. This book expands on the theory and integrates with ideas from Schutz and others.

Finally, I noted that Mises exaggerates the difference between *a priori* and *a posteriori* and, therefore, the difference between theory and history. Hayek's willingness to include empirical content in economic theory breaks down Mises' exaggerated distinction between theory and history. *The Sensory Order* carries the philosophical implication that the distinction between *a priori* and *a posteriori* is fluid. As I noted earlier, for Hayek, the mind's structure "reflects some features of the external world, since it was shaped by the world." Our "*a priori*" knowledge is shaped by experience. Thus, Hayek's theory breaks down Mises' sharp distinction between *a priori* and *a posteriori*.

Part III
Theory

5
Language Games and Economic Theory

Introduction

The theory of expectations developed in Chapter 6 integrates many elements. It relies heavily on Schutz and Hayek. To integrate those elements coherently, it is convenient to abandon the "neoclassical" model of rational maximizing in favor of a rule-following model. In the rule-following framework I will propose, however, neoclassical models reappear as important special cases. The version of rule-following I will propose was originally proposed by Koppl and Langlois (1994). Any social action is a skilled performance subject to the publicly known rules of some *language game*. (Compare Koppl and Langlois, 1994, pp. 81–82.) A "language game" is "a set of rules about how to talk, think, and act in different situations" (Koppl and Langlois, 1994, p. 82).

The language-games framework is not a theory of economics. It is only a convention regarding the description of individual action. It may be called a "theory of action." But, like Mises' praxeology, it is not subject to direct empirical test. The language-games framework is not *true*; it is *useful*. Much of its utility consists in bringing objective and subjective meanings together within a coherent unifying framework.

Langlois and I used the term "social game." But we were inspired by Ludwig Wittgenstein's concept of "language game." We chose to use a different term because we did not want to make any claims about what Wittgenstein might have "really" meant. Like Langlois, I have come to prefer the original term, however, in spite of its dangers. Our idea derives directly from Wittgenstein, whether or not we have been true to his original meaning. The language-games framework is a semantic convention that I believe may be useful for economists. It serves this function or not, regardless how close my use is to Wittgenstein. Appendix 2 (p. 208) briefly considers some of the issues. It identifies some important ways in which my use of the concept deviates from Wittgenstein.

Language games

Action is a skilled performance subject to the publicly known rules of some language game. When you take an action, you have a purpose; you deploy means to achieve an end according to plan. Your means, ends, and plans are more or less familiar to you and those to whom your action is directed (Schutz 1953). They are familiar because they fit a pattern; they follow a rule. From this point of view, whenever you do something, you follow a set of rules. Each such set of rules is a language game. The language game is not the unfolding of actions and reactions; it is not the play. The language game is the set of rules governing action and reaction. The pattern the rules induce may be recognizable only through an "intuitive" grasping of meanings. Often, we recognize the pattern through an act of interpretation.

The rules of a language game are constraints, not marching orders. The rules of chess constrain us. Only certain moves are allowed. But the moves we make within the constraints are freely chosen. One's strategy is chosen through "instrumental rationality." Good players typically adopt rules of thumb, however, to guide their choices. Depending on the purposes of the analyst, these rules, too, may be thought of as a part of the operative set of language games governing play of the game. Heuristics constrain our choices just as surely as formal rules. But, like the formal rules, they leave room for free choices made within the constraints they create.

I said the rules of a language game are "publicly known." The public to whom the rules of a given language game are known may be wide or narrow. The rules of English grammar are known by a very large number of persons. Accounting rules are known only to a relatively small group of specialists. But the number of persons who might learn accounting has no particular limit. A group of friends may have formal or informal rituals of greeting, hierarchy, and so on. These rules serve their function only if they are known and applied only within the group. Indeed, a language game typically defines an "in group." Those in the group know the rules; outsiders do not. Thus, the rules of a language game are "publicly known" only to the members of the relevant in-group. The relevant in-group may be open, so that strangers and newcomers are easily admitted. "English speaker" and "New Yorker" are two examples. It may instead be closed. High-school cliques are famously closed in-groups.

Elevator etiquette is a language game. On an elevator one faces forward and watches the illuminated panel of numbers indicating the elevator's progress from floor to floor. One keeps still and makes little noise. This language game requires skill. A drunk may do the wrong thing. His skills as an elevator passenger have been diminished by alcohol. Many individuals follow the rules of elevator etiquette without realizing that they do so. They *know how* to follow the rules even though they do not *know that* they follow the rules. Even people who do not know that they follow the rules of elevator etiquette do know when the rules are broken. Should a rider sing loudly, or move about, or simply face the wrong way, it would make others uncomfortable. The oddball's fellow riders would probably get off as quickly as possible. The rules of elevator etiquette are enforced by social sanctions, in this case ostracism. One may have a momentary feeling of embarrassment after entering and elevator with two sets of doors. Which way to face? This momentary embarrassment comes from discovering that one lacks a rule to guide one through the unexpected contingency of an elevator with two exits.

Bargaining is a language game. Bargaining is governed by many very complex rules. One must know, for example, how close to stand, how much eye contact to make, whether to smile, when to feign anger, when to really be angry, and so on. Different persons possess the skill of bargaining in different degrees. Bargaining is thus a skilled performance subject to the publicly known rules of a language game.

Calculating a money profit is also a language game. It is governed by publicly known rules. Publicly traded corporations make calculations subject to the rules of generally accepted accounting practice. The private owner of a small business may calculate a profit by more idiosyncratic methods. But if he can be said to "calculate a profit" at all, then some publicly known rules apply. He must have a figure for cost and one for revenue. He must subtract the cost from the revenue according to the rules of arithmetic. If he does not follow the rules of arithmetic, we would not say that he is "calculating" a profit at all. The number arrived at would not be called a "profit." He might make a calculation mistake. But if his methods for performing the "subtraction" were sufficiently bizarre, we would not say that he has made an error in his arithmetic. We would say that he was not performing a "subtraction" at all. Similarly, if we thought his "cost" figure came from a numerological analysis of last night's baseball game, we might deny that his action was the calculating of a profit. If an action is to be interpreted as "calculating a profit," it must follow the publicly known rules that define the action. Thus even many actions that we might at first wish to think of as perfectly "private" are, in fact, subject to the publicly known rules of some language game.[1]

A language game is a set of rules. Whenever you do something, you follow the rules of some language game. As we have seen, Hayek considered both action and thought to be rule governed. I follow his definition of a rule as "a propensity or disposition to act or not to act in a certain manner, which will manifest itself in what we call a *practice* or custom" (1973, p. 75 emphasis in original). Ludwig Wittgenstein, too, links rules with customs. "To obey a rule, to make a report, to give an order, to play a game of chess, are *customs* (uses, institutions)" (Wittgenstein, 1958b, p. 81 emphasis in original). Hayek emphasizes the abstract quality of rules and recognizes that we know and can state only a small fraction of the "rules which govern both action and thought." He cites "fair play" as an example of a set of rules we know how to follow, but cannot fully articulate (Hayek, 1973, p. 76).

I have described action as a "skilled performance." An action is a performance because it is aimed at others. Even the things we do when all alone fit into broader plans that are in some degree aimed at others. (For this book, it probably doesn't matter if there is some sort of solitary action that cannot be thought of as a skilled performance. The social sciences concern social actions.) Since our actions are aimed at others, they must be understandable to others. They must fit a recognizable pattern. They must follow a rule. A performance is skilled because the actor must know how to follow the rules of the language game that defines the action. This know-how is skill. Children know how to follow the rules of grammar even though they do not know that they are following the rules. Many of the characteristic grammatical mistakes of children come from applying the general rule to an exceptional case. "I rided my tricycle." Skills are generally acquired through trial and error.

The rules defining a language game can be looked at from many perspectives. In our paper on ideology (1994), Langlois and I distinguished three, namely the *theory*, the *rhetoric*, and the *practice* of a language game.

Language games tell us how to think about things. They guide our thinking by employing certain categories and hierarchies in some realm of action. If we look at the rules of a language game from the point of view of their cognitive function, we have the *theory* of the language game. The theory of a language game is the "shared mental model" of Denzau and North (1994). Witch doctors act on the theory that evil spirits cause illness. The actions of a technical trader in financial markets are guided by the theory that the past movements of an asset's price reliably predict the direction of future movements. The actions of a fundamentalist are sometimes based on the theory that past earnings reliably predict future earnings. When we imagine several people playing a language game together, for example bargaining, then we can distinguish the theory animating each of the different players. In such cases we may speak of the *theories* of a language game. Sometimes the "theory" of a language game might be confused with a scientist's theory that uses the construct "language game." In such cases the term "agent-theory" eliminates the ambiguity.

The agent-theory plays a different role in the agent's life from the scientist's theory.[2] If I want to explain a race riot, I had better make reference to the agent-theory that men are divided into "races," that the racial categories into which they divide people are enduring, and that this concept of "race" is perfectly coherent and unambiguous. I must do so even if I think the concept of "race" is shifting, vague, and incoherent. I must do so even if I think the concept of race effects no sensible partition of humanity. The scientist's theory will not ignore the concept of "race." Nor will it naïvely accept the concept. It will contain a model of the rioter's race theory. The rioter will be represented as someone who employs the concept of race in judging himself and others. The scientific model does not contain the agent-model. It contains a scientific model of the agent-model. It is a construct of a construct. The rioter uses a construct of the first degree. The scientist uses a construct of the second degree (Schutz 1954, p. 59).

The theory of a language game is not necessarily an explanatory framework explicitly available to the agent. The theory of the language game is the set of typical thoughts typical agents have when playing the game. It is, in fact, the set of typical thoughts the typical agent must by definition have if he is playing a given language game. It is the meaning to the agent of his action and of the context of that action. It is the meaning of the language game for the agent. Within that meaning we can find an explanatory framework. The explanatory framework need not be explicitly available to the agent. It may be wholly implicit. In many instances, the observing scientist may be interested in that explanatory framework, explicit or implicit. In some cases the explanatory framework will be very coherent. In other cases it will be incoherent. But the subjective meaning of the language game is not identical to the explanatory framework contained in that subjective meaning.

Language games tell us how to talk about things. If we look at the rules of a language game from the perspective of their guidance of speech, we have the *rhetoric* of the language game. As with the theory of a language game, we may sometimes use the plural. We might speak of the *rhetorics* of a language game. The rhetoric must persuade. A voluntary exchange is an agreement. Agreement is reached through rhetorical acts. Entrepreneurs must persuade venture capitalists to invest. They must persuade potential customers of the superior benefits of their product or service. McCloskey and Klamer have noted the rhetorical nature of entrepreneurship (1995, p. 194). They estimate that "sweet talk," i.e. persuasion, is over 25 per cent of GDP (1995, p. 193).

After becoming Chairman of the Board of Governors of the Federal Reserve System, Alan Greenspan earned fame for the obscurity of his rhetoric. In the early years of his tenure as Fed chairman, his public remarks and Congressional testimony would be filled with long, winding sentences delivered with great solemnity and earnestness. The sentences were complicated and hard to follow. Each remark was an ellipsis wrapped in a prevarication inside an ambiguity. Careful study was required to see that none of his seemingly weighty remarks actually said anything. (Since making a very clear remark about "irrational exuberance" December 5, 1996, he has been less obscure.) If his intention was to leave the market alone, this rhetoric was probably the only one suitable to his purpose. His was a practiced obscurity designed to frustrate any attempt to impute meaning to his remarks and draw from that meaning inferences about Fed policy. The rules of Fed watching required Fed watchers to discover meaningful news in the Fed chairman's remarks. To minimize the unwanted influence of Fed watchers on market performance, Greenspan chose a rhetoric of obscurity.

Finally, language games tell us what to do. Looking at them from this perspective gives us the *practice* of a language game. In some cases one may speak of the *practices* of a language game. In some cases one may speak of the "agent-practice" of a language game. The observing scientist may describe a practice in language alien to the subjects playing the language game. The logic of marginal cost pricing might describe the practice of a competitive firm. The firm managers, however, are unlikely to say or think that they practice marginalism. This is one of the central points at issue in the Machlup–Lester debate reviewed below.

Consider Machlup's example of a "theory of overtaking" (1967). "Overtaking" means passing another vehicle on the public roads. A theory of overtaking would be designed to predict when overtaking will be more likely and when less. Such a theory would describe several variables the driver would respond to, such as the quality of the road surface and the speed of oncoming vehicles. Such a theory might reasonably include the concept of a "coefficient of friction." In the theory, drivers might even estimate this coefficient. But only a few real drivers will know what a coefficient of friction is. Fewer still will think of themselves as estimating it when deciding whether to pass. None will make a numerical calculation. The scientist's description of the practice of overtaking, however, might reasonably include numerical calculations of the coefficient of friction.

It is not true that a language game will have one set of rules defining its theory, a second and disjoint set defining its rhetoric, and so on. There is one set of rules that may be looked at from more than one point of view. The theory, rhetoric, and practice of a language game, then, are not perfectly distinct entities.

It may be useful to flesh out the idea of language games with a few more examples. The Machlup–Lester debate shows that a difference can exist between the theory and the practice of a language game. During the debate, Machlup criticized Hall and Hitch (1939).

Hall and Hitch had conducted interviews of business managers. In essence, they asked businessmen if they equated marginal cost and marginal revenue. The businessmen denied it. Many reported that they added a markup to average cost. Of course, they would explain, "they might charge less in periods of exceptionally depressed demand." Similarly, they might raise prices in periods of strong demand. Morevover, "the conventional addition for profit varies from firm to firm and even within firms for different products" (Hall and Hitch, 1939, p. 19 as cited in Machlup 1946, p. 180).

Hall and Hitch thought their study showed that marginalist reasoning simply didn't apply to the world. Had they been Popperians, they might have said that marginalism was "falsified." Machlup reached a very different conclusion. Hall and Hitch reported that their informants insisted that they priced at average cost plus a markup. But their reports showed that the markup fluctuated with demand. They behaved, in fact, just as marginalist theory predicted. The study showed "precisely what one should have expected to hear" (Machlup 1946, p. 180).

I think Machlup got it right. Hall and Hitch seem to have extracted from their informants the theory of the language game of price setting. Standard marginalist logic captures the practice of this same language game of price setting. The theory and the practice of a language game must have some sort of congruence. But they are distinct entities that may often be described with very different language. Similarly, the rhetoric and practice of a language game must have some sort of congruence. The theory, practice, and rhetoric must all fit somehow. The sort of congruence required depends on context. If the language game requires the actor to lie, for example, the congruence will be very indirect. The lie must serve, or seem to serve, the actor's purpose.

In the case of price setting, the actor's theory describes the practice reasonably faithfully. But you must study it carefully. The agent's self-description uses a language inappropriate to the scientific purposes of the observing economist. In other cases, the theory may not accurately describe the practice. People can think they are doing one thing when they are really doing another. Whether the agent's theory is true or false, the scientist's description of it may differ from the actor's description.

It is no accident that Machlup saw what Hall and Hitch had missed. Machlup was a self-conscious student of Alfred Schutz. As we have seen, Schutz distinguished the "constructs" of the actor from the social scientist's "second-order constructs." The businessman's construct was that of average-cost-plus-markup with certain adjustments and qualifications being made for "special" circumstances. Marginalism is the social scientist's construct; it is an interpretation of the actor's construct.

Schutz's distinction between first- and second-order constructs applies to both the theory and the practice of a language game. This fact reflects the fundamental continuity between the theory and practice of any language game. The theory and the practice both identify the meaning of the actions taken and of the context of those actions. They both identify the meaning of the language game. The agent-theory is a *relatively* subjective meaning of the action. It identifies relatively intimate and internal features of the actor's thoughts. The practice is a *relatively* objective meaning of the action. It makes less direct reference to the thoughts of the agent.

Both "neoclassical" economists and radical subjectivists have tended to neglect the difference between agent-practices and agent-theories. Neoclassicals have focused on agent-practices. Indeed, they concluded from the Machlup–Lester debate that one could, one should, one must, neglect agent-theories. Radical subjectivists have focused on agent-theories. They have studied subjective meanings and neglected objective meanings. To them, often, the objective meanings seem false and the subjective meanings seem real. The language games framework requires us to identify both agent-theories and agent-practices. It also requires that we establish an appropriate coherence between the two.

The Machlup–Lester debate illustrates the role of competition in shaping the language games of exchange. In a competitive market, businesses that did not adjust their discounts to changes in demand would suffer losses and lost opportunities for profits. Their reduced profit margins would make it harder for them to get credit. Eventually, should they continue to apply rigid markups unresponsive to fluctuations in demand, they would be flushed out of the market. The remaining firms would adjust their markups to accommodate fluctuations in demand. The remaining firms, in other words, would be those whose practice of price setting is described by the marginalist logic.

Our discussion of the Machlup–Lester debate shows one way the marginal principle may enter the analysis. The logic of marginalism might seem to have been banished by the rule-following perspective of the language games framework. It comes back in, however, through the scientist's description of the practices of the agents. In the case at hand marginalist logic passes two tests.

First, it satisfies Schutz's postulate of "adequacy." This postulate requires that the social scientist's model of action "must be constructed in such a way that a human act performed ... would be understandable for the actor himself as well as for his fellow-men in terms of common-sense interpretation of everyday life" (Schutz 1953, p. 44). This test must always be passed. The economist can apply marginalist language only if the imagined actions of his model would be subjectively plausible for the agents, even though they would not use the marginalist language.

Second, the marginalist result Machlup described was a stable outcome of the market process. Each surviving firm was *constrained* to obey the marginalist logic. It is not necessary that the constraint be supplied by market competition. But if there is nothing broadly similar to market competition constraining actors, then the predictions of the model are less reliable. In other words, the system constraint must be tight.

A famous sociological study also illustrates how the maximization principle can enter the language games framework. Westie (1965) conducted a survey of households regarding their racial attitudes. He found that many white subjects would express allegiance to the general principle of equality but object to a black neighbor. When confronted with the contradiction, most of the subjects who recognized the contradiction would abandon their discriminatory attitude rather than the general principle of equality. The decision to stick with a general principle does not reflect an unexplained preference for ethical principles. When once the contradiction is pointed out, the subjects had to make some sort of change. One might suppose the general principle to be so distant from the concrete choices of daily life as to be easily jettisoned. But the general principle plays a role in many inter-linked language games. These language games guide the individual through many activities for which, absent the principle, he or she would have no substitute. The computational costs of trying to reformulate so many habits and routines exceed the costs of expressing a willingness to have black neighbors. One might challenge the need to change the principle at all. Why not continue to live with the contradiction? But of course one cannot. I may choose to express allegiance to the principle of equality while resisting its concrete consequences. But to do so is to abandon the principle in favor of empty expressions of fealty to it. This option still abandons the principle and thus carries all the costs of such abandonment.

Westie's subjects did not want equal opportunity in housing. At the same time, they used the principle of equality to organize their thoughts and actions. It was easier for Westie's subjects to abide equal opportunity in housing than to get along without the principle of equality. In other words, abandoning the discriminatory attitudes was the cost-minimizing option.

The Westie case passes the two tests indicated above. First, the actions of Westie's subjects are subjectively plausible. We can understand why they are willing to mortify their bigotry in favor of the principle of equality. Second, there is a social process that maintains the high importance of the principle of equality. Repudiating the principle would expose one to criticism. Social relations would be harder to maintain. And so on. The system constraint favors fealty to equality.

I have proposed two tests introducing the maximization principle, namely adequacy and a tight system constraint. Schumpeter (1934) expressed the spirit of these tests. He said, "The assumption that conduct is prompt and rational is in all cases a fiction." He also noted, however, that the fiction would be "sufficiently near to reality if things have time to hammer logic into men." He correctly says that the medieval peasant "sells his calf just as cunningly and egoistically as the stock exchange member his portfolio of shares." Schumpeter seems to think a more or less stable evolutionary environment has shaped both sellers. The maximization principle can only be applied, he argued, where "precedents without number have formed conduct ... and have eliminated unadapted behavior" (1934, p. 80).

Within a given language game, choices must be made. Language games themselves may also be the objects between which one chooses.

There is choice within language games and choice among language games. The distinction between these two levels of choice is analogous to Buchanan's (1990) distinction between choice within rules and choice among rules. In some cases, a decision may be described as choice within a language game or choice from among language games according to the analytical purpose at hand. Consider the choice of career. In a theory of wage equalization, this choice might be modeled as choice within a language game. In another context it might be modeled as a choice between, say, the saintly rules of priesthood and the stealthy rules of thievery.

As the last example suggests, language games are arranged in a kind of nesting structure. Some language games are parts of other language games. The rules governing behavior in an elevator are a subset of the rules governing behavior in public. The nesting structure of language games is very complex. Some of the complexities of the structure of language games are explored in Appendix 3 (p. 210).

I believe the language-games framework is useful. But some economic problems are best left to the old tools. To explain why the price of butter rises when the supply of margarine falls, one probably should not bother about choice among language games. As Langlois and I (1994) have said, the language-games framework gives us a "way to represent individual choice and action. How widely to apply our model of choice is a matter of experience and judgment" (1994).

The economy as a network of language games

We may view the economy as a network of language games. The various language games will be more or less coordinated with one another depending on circumstances. The notion of economics as a coordination problem is a characteristically Hayekian one (Hayek 1937, O'Driscoll 1977) taken up by Lachmann, Loasby, and others. Hayek, though, discussed the coordination of plans and actions, not language games. There are at least two notions of coordination that may be useful in the language-games framework. The first corresponds to choice of language games and the second corresponds to choice within a language game.

First, there is *coordination among language games* when no actor has an incentive to change the repertoire of language games available to him. Second, there is *coordination within language games* when no actor has an incentive to change his choice of strategy for each language game he plays. Coordination among language games and coordination within language games are two equilibrium concepts. They will be useful for some purposes, but not for others. They do not displace other notions of equilibrium. The theory of the evolution of money illustrates each of these two equilibrium concepts.[3]

John Law (1705) seems to have been the first scholar to explain the existence of money by evolution rather than agreement (Menger 1871). Menger's exposition is a standard example of an invisible-hand explanation. The Law–Menger model reveals some underlying causal processes. It is not a fully realistic or historical account. Many modern models of a similar nature have been proposed (Howitt and Clower 2000, Jones 1976, Luo 1999). Menger's story can be represented as a path-dependent process fed by a network externality (Selgin n.d.). When several goods compete to be used as exchange media, traders will tend to prefer those goods that are frequently used by others for the same purpose. The greater the number of people who have chosen a given good, the greater is the chance the next comer will also choose it. Eventually, the system locks in to a small set, perhaps just one good. The winning good prevails in part because chance events caused it to get an early lead. Other goods will be excluded because of the "steering effect" of early choices.

The story begins with barter. In this initial equilibrium there is co-ordination among language games and coordination within language games. The evolutionary process starts when one trader innovates by engaging in indirect exchange. Once that has happened, many individuals have an incentive to expand their repertoires of language games to include the new language game, indirect exchange. The innovation induces discoordination among language games. When all traders practice indirect exchange, coordination among language games is restored.

Coordination among language games does not guarantee coordination within language games. Even if all traders in the economy practice indirect exchange, there may be no generally accepted medium of exchange. There may be no money. In this situation, many traders will have an incentive to change the choices they make from within the language game of indirect exchange. They will have an incentive to move away from less widely demanded goods to more widely demanded goods. In other words, they have an incentive to move to the goods that are more money-like. This process is not complete until some goods emerge as generally accepted exchange media. At this point coordination within language games is restored.

As I told the story above, the first decision to practice indirect exchange was an exogenous cause, kicking off a process of adjustment.

One might wish to view indirect exchange as, instead, an induced innovation. In that case, one would note that under barter all traders had an incentive to adopt the practice of indirect exchange. Neither account excludes the other. An analyst may wish to describe indirect exchange as an exogenous cause. In this case, the analysts will say that under barter there was coordination among language games. Another analyst may wish to describe indirect exchange as an induced innovation. In this case, the analyst will say that under barter there was discoordination among language games.

If the economy is a network of language games, then we may ask what makes them more coordinated and what less so. We may ask what effects different policy choices have on the array of language games used to guide action. And, we may consider how the language games available to guide action influence the preferences people reveal through their market decisions.

Two examples illustrate how the network of language games changes over time. Langlois and I have argued that general principles help organize and coordinate the language games an individual has in his repertoire. This fact helps to explain the rise of abolitionist sentiment in the United States during the 1850s. Drawing heavily on Fogel (1989), we argued that the abolitionist principle acquired a central organizing role in the Christian "witness" of the Yankee. "Abolitionism provided an intellectual 'bright spot' or focal point around which other aspects of Yankee religious faith and practice could be organized" (1989, p. 95). This bright spot served a mostly rhetorical function until the Republicans built a new political coalition in the 1850s. By the 1850s, immigration had slowed from the high levels it had reached earlier in the century. The nativist movement occasioned by immigration had similarly abated. The collapse of the nativist movement gave the Republicans a chance to stitch together a coalition of ex-nativist Yankees, Catholic workers, and others. The Republican strategy worked in part because the abolitionism they preached "served as a rhetorical least common denominator for a number of groups" (1989, p. 96). The rhetoric of abolitionism bound many persons to the Republican movement. The success of that movement gave abolitionist sentiments increasing power in the lives of those who espoused the doctrine. In this way many individuals were led to act on an ideology that did not serve their material interests. "Thus, what had started out as a ideological focal point for a homogeneous ethnic group came to serve a similar function for a larger coalition, for which, however, underlying material interests were both diverse and, in the end, not directly related to the existence of slavery" (1989, p. 96).

Adam Smith's account of "How the Commerce of the Towns Contributed to the Improvement of the Country" (1937, pp. 84–96) provides an example of how the invisible hand can cause some language games to prevail and others to pass away. The old manorial lords, Smith argued, had only a few ways to spend their incomes. They had little choice but to spend the annual produce of their estates on "a multitude of retainers and dependants" (Smith 1937, p. 385). With so many dependants, they had plenty of power and hardly felt the constraining hand of jurisprudence. But as commerce grew up they found new ways to spend. The purchase of "trinkets and baubles, fitter to be the play-things of children than the serious pursuits of men," (1937, p. 391) left them unable to support as many retainers as before. But with the number of dependants thus reduced, their power too was reduced. Thus, Smith argued, through their profligacy "they became as insignificant as any substantial burgher or tradesman in a city. A regular government was established in the country as well as in the city, nobody having sufficient power to disturb its operations in the one, any more than in the other" (1937, p. 391).

Corporate culture may also be viewed as a network of language games. Kristian Kreiner's (1989) study of a Danish construction company illustrates. An hourly wage masquerades as a piece rate. The company Kreiner studied hires gangs of six to ten men to perform specific tasks such as placing a basement. The company representative is the site engineer. He bargains with a "ganger" (1989, p. 68). The ganger represents the gang and typically put it together in the first place (1989, p. 80). The gang agrees to do the job for a given total price. In Denmark it is an "organizational principle" that the gang be hired under a piece-rate system. The piece-rate system in the construction trade was established as a part of an agreement between Denmark's official workers' association and Denmark's official employers' association. It has the force of legislation. Also, the corporate culture at the firm studied celebrates the piece-rate system as a reflection of the "achievement principle" (1989, p. 69).[4] The higher one's position within the firm, the more one's salary comes from commissions. Thus, any other payment scheme might have appeared dubious to the firm's management, regardless of the official sanction on the piece-rate system.

The realities of the work site, however, allow the site engineer to control the hourly wages of each member of the gang. The site engineer can influence how much help the gang gets, when a job is considered finished, and so on. The site engineer consciously used these tools to equalize hourly wages (1989, pp. 69–72). Norms of fairness and solidarity operate to produce this result (pp. 72–73). The site engineer knows how to set a piece rate that will bring the gang close to the desired wage. "There exists a correct answer," he explained to Kreiner, "and that is the one which gives a fair [hourly] wage. And that you normally reach. And everybody knows damned well what a fair wage is" (1989, p. 73).

In this case we have two rhetorics sustaining one practice. The construction company has to look like it uses a piece-rate system. Moreover, the rhetoric of achievement is probably essential to the firm. Without it, management and employees alike might be less alert to opportunities for profit. But at the gang level, we can guess, an ideology of achievement must compete with the steady wages gang members can get elsewhere. If the site engineer were to stick to the achievement principle and let hourly wages fluctuate, he might find himself unable to hire workers except at unacceptably high piece rates. Even without the sanction of the official system, competition in the firm's output market might have enforced the achievement principle. Competition in one of the firm's input markets enforces a norm of fairness. These two inconsistent norms clash for only one person, the site engineer. He must negotiate the two rhetorics required to sustain one practice. The site engineer "frequently jumped between the two frames of reference and did it comfortably – occasionally observing that 'nothing is perfect'" (1989, p. 75).

Kreiner infers that "we must abandon the notion of organizational culture as collective representations of reality, as shared universes of meaning and emotion" (1989, p. 79). Perhaps we can better conceive of corporate culture as a network of language games. The more public aspects of the culture will impose certain constraints on members of the organization. But within those constraints, they may sometimes act in ways inconsistent with the official culture. But if the organization is coherent, these inconsistencies need not subvert the overall order or the ends of the organization. In the organizational context, too, we may speak of coordination within and among language games.

Coordination does not require common rules

Coordination within and among language games does not require that we all follow the same rules. This point is relatively simple and easy to demonstrate. It has been neglected, however, by the literature on expectations, multiple equilibria, and self-fulfilling prophesies. It has also been somewhat neglected in Denzau and North's analysis of "shared mental models." Both points are taken up below. The logical possibility of coordination without universal rules does not imply that no such norms can exist, should exist, or do exist. This point is taken up at the end of the section.

The mathematician Karl Menger made the point of this section in his *Morality, Decision, and Social Organization* (1934). Menger used set theory to argue against Kant's categorical imperative. The essential point is captured with the example of a dinner party. (My example of the dinner party is a free adaptation of material in the original.) You are having a dinner party. You have several tables, each of which can seat five guests. A successful dinner party does not require that all guests be polite or even that every pair of guests be compatible.

Your potential guests are of four types. Some people are polite, others rude. Some people are thick-skinned. They don't mind rude people. Others are thin-skinned. They can't abide rude people. Thus, the four types are: (1) polite, thick-skinned people; (2) polite, thin-skinned people; (3) rude, thick-skinned people; and (4) rude, thin-skinned people.

Not every guest list will produce a successful party. You cannot seat a thin-skinned person at a table of rude people. But it is possible to have a successful party with representatives of all four types. They must be represented, however, in the right proportions. A polite thick-skinned person is universally compatible. It will never create trouble to add him to a group. Any table of all polite people is compatible. Not every table of all rude people is compatible. A rude person will offend any thin-skinned person whether or not that thin-skinned person is himself rude. Thus, a table with only rude people will be compatible only if they are also all thick-skinned. For each rude, thin-skinned person you invite, you must invite four polite, thick-skinned persons to sit with him. Knowing that guests must be seated in groups of five, you can determine, for any given list of potential guests, whether a dinner party with those guests could be successful and if so, which seating arrangements will make it so.

A successful party does not require that your guests follow any universal norm. Similarly, coordination of language games does not necessarily presuppose the existence of any universally shared rules. If we accept Karl Menger's analysis and the conclusion I have just drawn from it, then an important group of questions presents itself. When are common rules necessary for coordination among language games? How can individuals cooperate if they do not share a common set of rules? And so on. Menger discussed the possibility of allowing society to be composed of many different moral communities. Menger's pluralistic vision is vividly expressed in the following passage:

> If various groups work under a common system at cross-purposes, then even some of the most important features of the underlying ideas may fail to materialize so that their effects may never be clearly seen or the basic plan fully judged. A system of several self-imposed regulations of various groups makes the effects of their diverse ideas manifest. Only on this basis have moral plans, removed from primary passions and from the happinstances of many struggles, the opportunity to prove themselves. Only in this way do ideas and their effects become comparable with one another. Only the organization proposed in the thought-experiments [of co-existing voluntary communities] opens the possibility of a contest of plans. (Menger 1934, p. 91)

Menger's ideas also have a more narrowly economic application. International trade is often trade between persons who operate under very different language games. We might call such exchanges "trade across cultural systems." A middleman may be required to effect trade across cultural systems. The middleman knows the cultural system of each group and puts them in indirect communication. Experience has shown that trade across cultural systems is perfectly possible. When we consider internal political, legal, and economic questions, however, we often insist on the need for a common set of rules that should govern all parties. We feel the need for common legal rules, common moral rules, a common "lifestyle," a common mentality, and even a common language. But it is not clear that any such commonality is required for social cooperation. There can be multiple legal systems governing the same geographic area. In some "multi-ethnic" nations, such legal pluralism might encourage social harmony. There can be and are in many nations, competing moral and religious communities who constrain themselves to obey very different sets of rules. Consider, for example, the cultural variety of New York City. Domestic pluralism need not threaten "social cohesion."

Menger's model suggests a development of Denzau and North's analysis of shared mental models. Denzau and North argue that social cooperation depends on the evolution of shared mental models. I believe they are correct. There are at least two different ways, however, in which mental models (i.e. agent-theories) may be shared in society. It is not clear that Denzau and North distinguish these two ways. First, all members of society may share a model. This form is direct sharing of mental models. Second, a series of models may indirectly link members of society who share no common model. This form is indirect sharing of mental models. The cultural middlemen mentioned earlier can link long chains of cultural systems together into a potentially harmonious system of social cooperation. This cooperation does not require the direct sharing of any mental model, only the indirect sharing of an appropriate sequence of mental models. Denzau and North did not emphasize indirect sharing nor did they distinguish it from direct sharing. The indirect sharing of mental models permits trade across cultural systems. It permits more pluralism than could otherwise exist.

Many writers on expectations and multiple equilibria implicitly assume that all agents directly share the same mental model. In such models, therefore, expectations must be identical to be coordinated. In fact, different people have different mental models. Coordination does not require identity. A very simple model illustrates.

Imagine two agents repeatedly playing the following coordination game. (Figure 5.1)

Imagine, however, that each player is wrong about the payoff structure. Each one errs as shown in Figure 5.2.

In this situation, each player has a different mental model of the game and both mental models are wrong. But there will be coordination of

	A	B
a	20,20	0,0
b	0,0	10,10

Figure 5.1   A simple coordination game
Player One chooses strategy **A** or **B**. Player Two chooses strategy **a** or **b**. Player One gets the payoff on the left; Player Two gets the payoff on the right. Each player prefers **Aa** to **Bb**.

	A	B
a	10	0
b	0	20

Figure 5.2   Payoff structure
The grid represents each player's perception of the payoffs facing the other player. Each player knows his own payoffs. But each falsely imagines the other to prefer **Bb** to **Aa**.

action and expectation if the two players hit upon any Nash equilibrium, for instance **Aa** in each round or **Bb** in each round. There would be co-ordination of action and expectations if they hit upon the Nash equilibrium that selects **Aa** on odd-numbered rounds and **Bb** on even-numbered rounds. This solution would be a kind of sharing scheme based on the players' false mental models of the game. The players are oriented to different visions of the future and yet neither party is ever disappointed. Neither party has an incentive to change his strategy.

As a matter of logic, coordination does not require direct sharing of language games or mental models beyond that required for cultural middle men. Four considerations help show why we nevertheless do have or should have some widely shared rules and mental models. First, there seems to be a universal mental structure common to all of humanity (Barkow *et al.* 1992). We all recognize a smile or a threatening posture. We can imagine a different possibility. Creatures with perfectly incommensurable mental structures could cooperate through the indirect sharing of mental models. But this logical possibility does not fit our actual situation. Any two humans have common mental models because of their common biological history.

Second, any heterogeneous society seems to require a minimal set of shared laws and norms. If the society is indeed one society and not a collection of perfectly distinct nations, then there will be the possibility of spontaneous encounters between members of distinct groups. This possibility requires some set of rules to govern such interactions. Some of these rules will have the force of law, others will be norms enforced by social sanctions. In either case, the rules have universal validity within the society.

Third, all men are created equal. Justice demands a presumption in favor of the principle of equality before the law. Unfortunately, no practical necessity backs this principle of justice. As Adam Smith pointed out, a republic of free persons may keep slaves without threatening social cohesion. Women have suffered under special legal restrictions in many times and places. Equality before the law is not always respected, nor should it be. Children are not equal to adults before the law. But we should keep a strong presumption in favor of legal equality. The true doctrine of the universal brotherhood of all mankind greatly strengthens the moral force of this presumption.

Finally, distinct groups may experience conflict. Without a set of rules to adjudicate disputes, a set of meta-rules if you like, war threatens.

In the "Postscript to the English Edition," written in 1974, Menger (1934) provided a related list of four obstacles to the complete realization of his pluralistic vision. First, history has led to powerful interests opposed to change. Second, the "tight geographical and economic interconnections ... and its standardization" tend to favor "monisitic regulations." Third, "some ideas ... require the cooperation of exceedingly large numbers" of people who must act with some degree of unity. Finally, Menger notes poignantly, "is the existence of individuals who decide to limit or suppress decisions of others – in a few extreme cases, to exterminate some other groups" (1934, p. 104).

Natural selection of language games

Exchange, as we have seen, is a language game. Thus, buying and selling on a given market are governed by the rules of a set of language games. Each party to each trade is performing according to the rules of some language game of trade, a trading game as we might call it. Which game is at work depends on who the trader is. Those traders who operate according to the rules of a trading game that – for whatever reason – happens to induce actions that are, in some sense, "appropriate" or "correct" or "better," will profit. Others will lose. Which sense of "appropriate," "correct," or "better" is the right one will depend on the particular market. In a modern asset market, the "correct" actions are the ones that best correspond to the future history of the asset's price. The filter of profit and loss tends to weed out the losers. Traders with the "fittest" trading games tend to survive. This phenomenon of selection among language games according to their fitness is analogous to processes of natural selection in biology. I call it, therefore, "natural selection of language games." Without using the term, I have already discussed the natural selection of language games when discussing Machlup's defense of marginalism and the Westie (1965) study.

What makes a language game of trade "fit" is not its truth. What makes it fit is only its ability to induce successful actions on a particular market given a particular institutional regime. A trading game will tend to survive market competition if it does a better job at inducing profitable trades than its competitors. The market ranks trading games on an ordinal scale. Thus, "fit" does not mean "optimal." It means "better than average; good enough." The fittest trading games meet an external criterion of good design. They solve a kind of engineering problem in signal extraction. What signals tell me to buy? To sell? To raise my price? To lower it? The winners in this design contest are the "fittest" trading games. The contest, of course, is ongoing. There is no once-and-for-all winner.

If competition is stiff enough, then the particulars of the language games guiding trade do not matter. If we wish to know only what the overall behavior of the market will be, that is, how it will respond to changes in market fundamentals, then we need not bother about the theoretical and rhetorical aspects of the operative language games. Our assumption of stiff competition implies that the market will respond "rationally" to news about the fundamentals. In sufficiently competitive asset markets, whatever ideas might be guiding actions, whatever the theory of the operative trading games, the actions induced will tend to be the "right" ones. (As I shall argue presently, the literature on "sun spots" gives us no exception.) Should there be a change of regime, rivalrous competition among language games will be renewed. This will create a shakeout, and the surviving, now-fittest, trading games will again tend to induce the "right" actions. These new language games may be similar to the old ones or wildly different. They may be heterogeneous or all about the same. The market process selects useful language games, not true theories.

The claim that sufficiently stiff competition tends to induce the right actions may seem to be contradicted by models of sunspots. In a sunspot model, an asset's price is kept equal to its present value and rational expectations prevail. But "rational bubbles" may arise on the basis of some stochastic process that is unrelated to the stochastic process generating the asset's cash flow. Thus we can have "rational" deviations from an asset's fundamental values. While I consider this possibility rather more theoretical than empirical, it does not contradict the claim that competition induces "correct" actions. If the market follows sunspots, then the "right" thing for any one trader is to follow those same sunspots. The trader should follow these sunspots even if he knows they are not intrinsically related to the asset's cash flow. Selection pressures will ensure that each trader who survives will follow the sunspots, whatever his conscious ideas about the matter might be.

The particulars of the language games guiding trade, I have argued, do not matter "if competition is stiff enough." When competition is "stiff enough" individual traders do not have much influence on the market. The anonymous forces of supply and demand impel each trader to keep his actions closely in line with market conditions. When competition is stiff in this sense, the "system constraint" (Langlois 1986a) is tight. The logic of the situation facing each actor leaves only one plausible "exit" or course of action.

A tight system constraint lets us ignore the particulars of the language games guiding action. From any change in market fundamentals, we may infer the resulting changes in prices and quantities without first calculating how each individual trader will respond. But the system constraint is not always tight. The looser it is, the more scope there is for multiple exits, path-dependency, and indeterminacy.

A tight system constraint can produce "rational" outcomes even when the individual agents are not "rational." Gode and Sunder (1993), provide an example. They put algorithms called "zero-intelligence traders" in a large computer program meant to simulate exchange among stupid agents. They found that certain constraints on the exchange process led to economic efficiency in spite of the lack of individual rationality. More recently, Howitt and Clower (2000) have used computer programs to simulate "The emergence of economic organization." Their imaginary agents have only bounded rationality. Market structure emerges unintendedly from an initial autarky. In most runs monetary exchange emerges and the system exploits almost all of the possible gains from trade. The aggregate results often closely approximate the implications of rational-choice theory. "Although firms are following simple rules, they may be led (by the visible hand of the functioning system) to act as if they were maximizing profits" (2000, p. 66). Their concluding paragraph is worth quoting in full.

One implication of our analysis is that market forces are in some ways less and in other ways more powerful than one would infer from general equilibrium theory. They are less powerful in the sense that the process of creating and maintaining markets consumes resources that usually are invisible to equilibrium theory, and also in the sense that they do not always bring the economy near an equilibrium with actual GDP close to potential. But they are more powerful in that they often allow such a situation to be approximated even though no one in the economy is capable of performing the elaborate maximization problems postulated by equilibrium theory. (Howitt and Clower 2000, p. 81)

The computer simulations of Gode and Sunder (1993) and of Howitt and Clower (2000) are consistent with Alchian's (1950) claim that natural selection operates in the market. Hayek has cited Alchian's essay as important to his own evolutionary ideas.

6
Expectations

Introduction

Expectations depend on institutions. As I indicated in Chapter 1, expectations will be more prescient in some institutional environments than in others. Stable environments tend to produce prescient expectations. Instability reduces the reliability of economic expectations. This point is the central result of the theory of Big Players. It is also a statement about learning in the market process. Expectations depend on institutions because institutions influence, in Hayek's words, "the process by which individual knowledge is changed" (1937, p. 45).

A theory of expectations is, in part, a theory of learning and of change. When cognitive expectations change, learning has occurred. When acognitive expectations change, new habits have been formed. Thus, a theory of expectations requires a theory of change and of learning. The agent of change in economic theory is the entrepreneur. Thus, a theory of expectations begins with a theory of entrepreneurship.

Entrepreneurship

My account of entrepreneurship builds on Butos and Koppl (1999) and Minniti and Koppl (1999). It thus follows Kirzner (1973). But, like the two papers just cited, I will develop Kirzner's account in ways that Kirzner has not.

For Kirzner, entrepreneurship is a "praxeological category." It is an aspect of action and implicit in the very concept of action. It is a category of the pure *a priori* "logic of choice" as developed by Ludwig von Mises. His version of the logic of choice, like the neoclassical version, takes each action as an isolated unit. The analysis recognizes no necessary links between one action and the next. It does not recognize the structure of action into a lifeplan. Nor does it recognize the logical relations among actions such as those I have outlined in Appendix 3 (p. 210). The praxeological context also omits the rhetorical dimension of entrepreneurship. "The entrepreneur," McCloskey and Klamer note, "is above all a persuader" (1995, p. 194). Recasting Kirzner's theory in the language-games framework allows us to recognize, with McCloskey and Klamer, that entrepreneurs are not mute. They are often teachers and translators; they are always rhetors.

Kirzner follows Mises closely. Recall from Chapter 2 that Mises viewed theory as *a priori*. It can say nothing about the content of action, only its form. Entrepreneurship changes the content of action. Thus, in Mises' system, theory can say essentially nothing about entrepreneurship except that it is present in every action. Kirzner's theory identifies an essential feature of action and of the market. But his larger theoretical framework prevents him from drawing out as many theoretical implications as seem, in fact, to follow from his basic insight.

With Kirzner's view of action, entrepreneurship must be an uncaused cause. It comes from outside the maximization framework and cannot be further explained. Kirzner does recognize that entrepreneurial "alertness" is "switched on" by the existence of available opportunities. But he can press the argument no further. The language-games framework, building on Hayek and Schutz, can draw inferences from Kirzner's basic idea. His praxeological perspective closes off these inferences.

The theory given here is not in conflict with Kirzner's theory. It simply adds a cognitive element not present in Kirzner's writings. This cognitive element is "theoretical." But in Kirzner's highly Misesian system, accounts of this cognitive element are not "theoretical." What I am calling "theoretical" he would label "applied."

Before returning to the exposition and extension of Kirzner's theory, some extra comments may be appropriate for readers with a special interest in the theory of entrepreneurship. At the highest theoretical level, I view entrepreneurship as a praxeological category. The language-games framework is a pure praxeology, though distinct from Mises' pure praxeology. The language-games framework is preferable wherever it is more useful than that of Mises. I doubt the two praxeological theories are in direct conflict on any but, perhaps, a few minor points. Thus, I agree with Kirzner that entrepreneurship is an aspect of any action and that the entrepreneur is a functional type, not a sociological type. The emerging discipline of "entrepreneurship" studies specific forms of Kirznerian entrepreneurship such as new-venture entrepreneurship. This emerging discipline may be based on a Kirznerian theory, but it goes beyond Kirzner to study the special forms of entrepreneurship in commercial society.

For Kirzner, the term "entrepreneurship" identifies the element in human action that corresponds to the passage of time, that makes things happens, that creates change. Entrepreneurship is not present in the "neoclassical" model of action. In that model, human action is the allocation of known and scarce resources among known and competing ends. The agent allocates his resources to maximize his utility. This process of allocation is "Robbinsian" maximizing. Kirzner uses the term "Robbinsian" because Lionel Robbins (1932) gave the definitive statement of the neoclassical view of choice.

In Kirzner's system, "there is present in all human action an element which, although crucial to economizing, maximizing, or efficiency criteria, cannot itself be analyzed in [those] terms" (Kirzner 1973, p. 31). This " entrepreneurial element" in human action distinguishes "action" from "maximizing." The entrepreneurial element in human action is the cause of changes at the individual level. Similarly, the "entrepreneurial role" in the market produces change there (1973, pp. 31-32). It "occupies precisely the same logical relationship to the more narrow 'economizing' elements in the market that, in individual action, is occupied by the entrepreneurial elements in relation to the efficiency aspects of decision-making" (Kirzner 1973, p. 32). The market process cannot emerge, Kirzner argues, unless entrepreneurship operates.

Kirzner develops his theory of entrepreneurship with the concepts of alertness and discovery. Kirzner has defined "alertness" as "the 'knowledge' of where to find market data" (1973, p. 67). He puts the word "knowledge" in inverted commas to warn the reader that the entrepreneur possesses this "knowledge" only through his capacity to act on it. He cannot write it down and may not know that he possesses it. His knowledge "is a rarefied, abstract type of knowledge – the knowledge of where to obtain information (or other resources) and how to deploy it" (1979, p. 8).

Alertness leads to the "discovery" of opportunities. The entrepreneur did not previously know of the opportunity he acts upon; nor does anyone else. If he or someone else had known of it, it would already have been seized. The exploitation of the opportunity would not, then, constitute a change in any meaningful sense. Thus, the entrepreneur's alertness leads to something previously unimagined. It leads to the discovery of a new way of doing things. Thus, it may lead to unanticipated improvements in the human condition. The opposite result is also possible. A criminal, for instance, exhibits entrepreneurial alertness when he thinks of new ways to foil anti-theft devices. The general tendency of entrepreneurship to produce good or evil depends on the overall institutional order as the theory of Big Players illustrates.

The role of entrepreneurship in the evolution of language games can be illustrated with an important example of the evolution of money. Before the evolution of money, all trade is barter exchange. The problem of finding a double-coincidence of wants frustrates many attempts to exchange. One or more frustrated trader may seize upon the idea of indirect exchange. The trader who thinks of indirect exchange is an innovator, an entrepreneur. He finds a new strategy in the game of market exchange, namely, indirect exchange. He thereby devises the rules of a new language game, namely, indirect exchange. The network externality at work will drive the path-dependent process to converge on the good that becomes a generally accepted exchange medium.

As this process unfolds, the language game changes. In the earliest stages, each trader who practices indirect exchange has an incentive to know with whom he will trade the intermediate good for the good that he ultimately desires. The indirect exchanger needs a concrete plan. As the practice of indirect exchange spreads, the trader may be more vague about what final exchanges will complete the process. As the number of exchange media shrinks, a trader can be more confident that someone unknown to him will take his exchange medium for the goods he ultimately desires. Eventually, some highly marketable good is accepted in exchange *because it is money.* (The process might produce more than one money.) In a fully monetized economy, traders are guided by the rules of money exchange even though they may not quite understand that they are engaged in indirect exchange. The rules surrounding money's use define the language game of monetary exchange. That language game guides them adequately for practical purposes.

Entrepreneurship enters this process through the original innovation of indirect exchange. Further acts of entrepreneurial alertness induce others to imitate the innovator. The imitators discover the new possibility by observing others. Still more acts of entrepreneurship cause traders to recognize that some goods are better exchange media than others, and so on. Entrepreneurial revisions to the language games of exchange do not stop until the process has fully run its course.

Kiznerian entrepreneurs are "alert" to opportunities for gain. They are alert to new things to do and to new ways of doing things. The entrepreneur "discovers" new opportunities. The quality of alertness suggests an active awareness and engagement with the external environment. A

Kirznerian entrepreneur is not a passive receptor of information. He is engaged in the ordering and selection of information germane to his particular situation and objectives. The entrepreneur interprets his environment. Going beyond Kirzner's "praxeological" framework and studying the structure of interpretation helps us to see how the entrepreneur's pre-existing interpretations shape his future discoveries. Knowledge and history shape entrepreneurial discovery.

In Chapter 3 we saw that common-sense knowledge is a system of typifications. It is a system of stereotypes and recipes that guides us through our daily activities. The entrepreneur's knowledge, too, is such a structure. The entrepreneur (like any actor) organizes his collection of typifications through a "system of relevancies" fixed by his "biographically determined situation" (Schutz 1951 p. 76). His "prevailing system of interests" determines which elements of his "stock of knowledge" are relevant to him. It determines which elements are relevant to his interests and purposes. This system of relevancies guides the entrepreneur and influences the sorts of discoveries he can make. Schutz's analysis of relevance applies to all action. I will apply it only to entrepreneurship. But, because entrepreneurship is an aspect of action, this restriction is a matter of vocabulary, not substance.

Schutz distinguishes "four regions of decreasing relevance" (1946, p. 124). First, there is the *field of action*, what Schutz calls the "zone of primary relevance" (1946, p. 124). The field of action is the part of the world the entrepreneur thinks he can control at least in some degree. "It is that sector of the world within which our projects can be materialized and brought forth" (1946, p. 124). It is in the field of action that we place the highest demands on our knowledge. "In order to master a situation we have to possess the know-how – the technique and the skill – and also the [relatively] precise understanding of why, when, and where to use them" (1946, p. 124). The field of action is where we attempt to realize our plans.

For a farmer, the field of action includes the state of repair of his equipment, his inventories of feed, fertilizer, and seed, his credit with the local bank, and so on. These things are highly relevant to his interests. His (subjective) knowledge of them will be very salient in his mental map of the world. They are all things he views as subject to his influence. In some degree he can control them. The condition of his equipment, we may imagine, is almost perfectly in his control. Only very unlikely contingencies could prevent him from keeping his machines in good repair. The state of his credit may be less subject to his control. For the current season, it depends mostly on his credit history, a thing now beyond human control. But he can visit his banker and attempt to assuage any doubts that may have arisen.

Second there is the *milieu of action*. Schutz refers to the "other fields not open to our domination but mediately connected with the zone of primary relevance [i.e. the field of action] because, for instance, they furnish ready-made tools to be used for attaining the projected goal or they establish the conditions upon which our planning itself or its execution depends" (1946, pp. 124–125). The context of action is our knowledge of things that influence the results of our actions, but are not in our control.

For our farmer, the weather is a part of the milieu of action. His actions depend vitally upon the weather. But he considers the weather beyond his control. He cannot decide if it will rain, only whether to irrigate. The methods of delivering feed are also a part of the farmer's context of action. He cannot schedule the trucks that bring it or direct their maintenance. He has only a very vague idea about how scheduling is arranged or what might be appropriate maintenance for the delivery trucks. But it serves his interest to know that his feed is delivered by truck. His plans depend on the reliability of those trucks. He wants to know how rain, snow, and labor actions influence feed deliveries.

Third, there is the *relatively irrelevant zone of knowledge*. Schutz explains that "there are other zones which, *for the time being*, have no ... connection with the interest at hand. We shall call them relatively irrelevant, indicating thereby that we may continue to take them for granted as long as no changes occur within them which might influence the relevant sectors by novel and unexpected chances or risks" (1946, p. 125, emphasis in original).

At one time all knowledge of computers fell into the relatively irrelevant zone of our farmer's knowledge. Computers were large expensive objects operated by university scientists. The interests of our farmer required only the most vague ideas about computers. But the arrival of inexpensive personal computers, of course, changed the relevance of computers in the structure of his knowledge. Most farmers now own a computer and use it as a daily tool.

Finally, there is the *absolutely irrelevant zone of knowledge*. This is the zone the entrepreneur imagines to be "absolutely irrelevant because no possible change occurring within [it] would – or so we believe – influence our objective at hand" (1946, p. 125). Our farmer's beliefs about extra-terrestrials or life during the Renaissance are in this category. His knowledge in this zone may be extremely vague. He may vaguely feel that talk about UFOs is "bunk." As a farmer, he has no need to clarify this knowledge. He does not need to have the slightest idea why such talk is to be rejected. Indeed, he may have a very different opinion. He may hold elaborate beliefs about who is visiting the planet and what they want. Those beliefs do not change his plans and actions as a farmer. For his farming interests, they are absolutely irrelevant. Henry Ford's knowledge of history was absolutely irrelevant to his business activities.

The field of action and the milieu of action are the *inner zones of relevance*. Knowledge in these zones directly governs action. The relatively irrelevant zone of knowledge and the absolutely irrelevant zone of knowledge are the *outer zones of relevancy*. Knowledge in the outer zones cannot govern action until it is moved to the inner zones of relevancy.

As Schutz points out, the four zones of relevancy are not four separate airtight compartments. They "are intermingled, showing the most manifold interpenetrations and enclaves" (1946, p. 126). The "interpenetrations" of these zones of relevance create "twilight zones of sliding transitions" (1946, p. 126). A given piece of knowledge may be hovering between two zones of relevance. In his choosing and acting, the ambiguous bit of knowledge may not require clarification in order to apply the agent's tried and true recipes for negotiating his daily life. But if the ambiguous bit of knowledge is once recognized as such, the agent must decide which zone it belongs to.

Any act of entrepreneurship is a change in the content of the entrepreneur's knowledge in some area. It also entails the movement of knowledge from one zone of relevance to another. Consider Kirzner's example of simple arbitrage. A man discovers apples selling for one price on one side of the street and another price on the other side of the street. Before the discovery, the price of apples bore no relation to his business activities. The alert discovery of an exploitable price difference moved his knowledge of the price of apples from the relatively irrelevant zone of his knowledge to the milieu and field of action. He may imagine that his buying and selling do not influence the price of apples on either side of the street. In that case, his input prices are part of the milieu of action; his output prices are a part of the field of action. If he thinks his selling lowers the price of apples in his output market, then the price of all apples in that market are in his field of action even though only his own prices are within his direct control. The perfectly competitive firm views only its own prices and quantities as within its field of action. Those of competitors are a part of the milieu of action; they are beyond his control. An oligopolist imagines his actions to influence his competitors. Their decisions are thus a part of his field of action.

Schumpeter listed five types of entrepreneurial innovation. In each case the entrepreneur's knowledge of some area is moved from one zone of relevance to another. The five cases are "(1) The introduction of a new good ... (2) The introduction of a new method of production ... (3) The opening of a new market ... (4) The conquest of a new source of supply [and] ... (5) The carrying out of the new organisation of any industry" (Schumpeter 1934, p. 66). When opening a new market, for example, the entrepreneur moves the knowledge of the conditions of that market from the outer zones of relevancy to the inner zones of relevancy.

The entrepreneur may profit from the opposite movement. If he discovers that an item in his field of action is not really subject to his control at all, he will no longer waste resources trying to influence what he cannot influence. The farmer who stops trying to appease the gods may produce a richer harvest.

Any act of entrepreneurship has its meaning for the entrepreneur within the entrepreneur's system of relevancy even as it transforms that system. In the example considered above, Kirzner's pure arbitrageur discovers apples selling for one price on one side of the street and another price on the other side. This discovery has meaning only within the entrepreneur's existing system of relevancy. The entrepreneur knows already what apples are and recognizes the apples on each side of the street to be "the same." He knows what buying and selling are. He knows how to make a purchase, carry inventory, and make a sale. Without this pre-existing body of knowledge, he cannot make his discovery. His interests must be engaged as well. The desire of money profits must be present before he turns himself away from other activities and toward apple dealing. Without that desire, he would not have been alert to the prices of apples and to the possibilities implicit in price differences. As a pure consumer, he might have noted that "it is better to buy apples on this side of the street." But only the desire for wealth transforms that knowledge into the perception of a profit opportunity. For a mendicant monk, the same knowledge is not the perception of a profit opportunity.

The act of discovery transforms the entrepreneur's knowledge. The entrepreneur views apples differently after his act of discovery. They occupy a different place in his system of relevancies. And the properties of apples that interest him change as do the characteristics of two sides of the street. The initial act of discovery is itself a change in the entrepreneur's system of types and in his system of relevancies. The actions following from the initial discovery induce further change in his knowledge. He learns who buys and sells apples on each side of the street, what sort of apples are more easily sold, and so on.

Entrepreneurship is change in the actor's knowledge. Thus, entrepreneurship is learning. Of course, what is learned may be false. Entrepreneurs may fail. The market system is not a system of profit and profit; it is a system of profit and loss. (Unfortunately, there is some truth to the quip that in the United States, profits are privatized and losses are socialized.) Nevertheless, entrepreneurship is learning. A theory of entrepreneurship, therefore, requires a theory of learning. Schutz's theory of relevancy provides some elements for such a theory. Further elements are provided by Hayek's cognitive theory.[1]

Hayek's discussion of the "map" and the "model" applies to acts of entrepreneurship. The "map" is the agent's structure of knowledge, including his system of relevancies. The "model" is the agent's interpretation of his present situation, an interpretation based on his knowledge. As we have seen in Chapter 4, Hayek's notion of the actor's cognitive "map" requires that the map reflect the individual's personal history as well as his social and biological history. Each entrepreneur's map is unique in some degree. Thus, any observation will have a different interpretation, a different meaning, for any two entrepreneurs.

Hayek's discussion of "attention" in *The Sensory Order* fits nicely with Kirzner's notion of "alertness" and Schutz's notion of "relevancy." Hayek notes that "the experiences to which our attention is directed are more fully discriminated and given in greater detail" than others. "We notice more in them and are more fully prepared to respond adequately to their occurrence." This describes precisely the peculiar position "alertness" occupies between calculation and luck. Hayek understands as well that this "alertness," as Kirzner calls it, must be switched on. It is, says Hayek "characteristic of attention that it has these effects" of greater discrimination and detail "only with regard to events which are in some sense expected or anticipated." Attention, Hayek infers, "is thus always directed, or confined to a particular class of events for which we are on the look-out and which, in consequence, we perceive with greater distinctness when one of them occurs" (Hayek 1952a, p. 139).

Hayek's theory of mind draws our attention to the ways we are shaped by our environments. This evolutionary shaping prepares us better for some contingencies than others. In some contexts we are lighter on our feet than in others. Kirzner's discussion of alertness and Schutz's discussion of relevancy come to much the same end. As we have seen, Hayek used the term "map" in discussing the structure of subjective knowledge. Schutz, too, uses a cartographic metaphor. He compared zones of relevancy to contour lines:

If we had to draw a map depicting such a distribution [of relevancies] figuratively it would not resemble a political map showing the various countries with their well-established frontiers but rather a topographical map representing the shape of a mountain range in the customary way by contour lines connecting points of equal altitude. Peaks and valleys, foothills and slopes, are spread over the map in infinitely diversified configurations. The system of relevancies is much more similar to such a system of isohypses than to a system of coordinates originating in a center 0 and permitting measurement by an equidistant network. (1946, p. 126).

Schutz's description is reminiscent of the idea of "fitness landscape" from complexity theory. And as I have said on another occasion, entrepreneurs operate on a rugged and shifting fitness landscape. "Entrepreneurship is governed by the sort of non-directed search complexity theorists have studied. The entrepreneur does his share of 'hill climbing.' But he also jumps, periodically, in new and untried directions." On a shifting fitness landscape, "entrepreneurial leaps are necessary to keep the actions of different persons reasonably adjusted to one another" (Koppl 2000b, p. 103).

The entrepreneur's pre-existing knowledge and relevancies shape what he learns. So does the institutional environment within which he operates; it influences what the entrepreneur learns and his level of alertness. These influences are illustrated by several examples.

Adam Smith (1937) lists several reasons for the "encrease of opulence" occasioned by the division of labor. One reason is that workers who specialize in a given task will invent machines and techniques that improve the execution of that task. Entrepreneurial discovery depends on local knowledge.

Benny Gilad (1981) reports on the effects of introducing money-like tokens to patients in mental institutions. Before the introduction of tokens, the patients were completely lacking in alertness. It would be quite normal for a patient to gaze limply at an out-of-focus television waiting for a nurse or attendant to adjust the tuning. Later a system of tokens was introduced. A patient would be give so many tokens for making his bed, so many for mopping the floor in a given area, and so on. The tokens could be used to buy a better lunch or some other small reward. After learning to use such tokens, many patients showed a marked increase in alertness. Without special prompting, they would perform many tasks that earned tokens. They also performed alert actions that did not earn them tokens. After the tokens, the typical patient would get up and adjust the television for himself. These results show that incentives influence not only the direction of entre-preneurship, but also the amount of it.

Maria Minniti (1999) has constructed a model in which entrepre-neurship breeds entrepreneurship. (See also Minniti and Bygrave 1999, 2000.) She restricts her attention to what Minniti and Koppl (1999) call "new-venture entrepreneurship," which is "any case of Kirznerian entrepreneurship that results in the formation of a new venture" (1999, p. 575). The key mechanism for this self-reinforcing process is a kind of emulation. Some people live in communities with much new-venture formation. They are more inclined to imagine that a new venture may be successful. They are also likely to know more about how one forms a new venture. Their perceptions and knowledge will more naturally incline them to acts of new-venture entrepreneurship. Minniti uses non-linear stochastic dynamics to model the process. Her model predicts clustering of new-venture entrepreneurship. Empirical studies by Minniti and others are consistent with her theory. Minniti's work shows that the existing level of entrepreneurship influences each individual's disposition toward entrepreneurship.

Some evidence suggests that, among rich nations, those with the highest rates of new-venture entrepreneurship are also those with the highest rates of immigration. These countries include the United States, Canada, and Israel (see Zacharakis *et al.* 1999). Immigration may be an important influence on entrepreneurship in an area. The immigrant's system of relevancies differs from that of the native. He thus sees different entrepreneurial possibilities. Apparently, he also sees more of them.

These examples illustrate my claim that pre-existing knowledge and relevancies as well as the institutional regime influence the direction of entrepreneurial learning and the volume of entrepreneurship.

Cognitive expectations

Keynesian conventions and the relativity of plan futurity

In Chapter 1, I defined "cognitive expectations" as our thoughts about the future. Cognitive expectations are a part of the agent-theory of language games. The "horizon principle," explained below, shows that the very concept of cognitive expectations implies the subjective predictability of the future.

Cognitive expectations are structured by the agent's system of relevan-cies. When an agent's cognitive expectations change, then his system of relevancies changes. Thus, any change in cognitive expectations is an example of entrepreneurial learning. Conversely, any entrepreneurial act entails learning and a corresponding change in cognitive expectations.

The term "cognitive expectation" covers ideas in all four zones of relevancy. But the observing social scientist will usually be interested only in the inner zones of relevance. The inner zones of relevance cover the field of action and the milieu of action; they cover events we do not control and events we do control. For events we do not control, we assume that what has held true in the past will hold true in the future as well (Schutz 1951, p. 75). This sort of assumption is a Keynesian convention. "In practice," Keynes argued, "we have tacitly agreed, as a rule, to fall back on what is, in truth, a *convention*. The essence of this convention -- though it does not, of course, work out quite so simply -- lies in assuming that the existing state of affairs will continue indefinitely, except in so far as we have specific reasons to expect a change" (1936, p. 152, emphasis in original).

Our expectations about events we do control are quite differently structured. This is our knowledge of the field of action. This knowledge exists in the form of plans we might carry out. The field of action is filled, therefore, with hypothetical propositions. "If I do this, that follows." The point of our plans is precisely to change events, to move them from the path they would otherwise take. Keynesian conventions enter only by shaping the assumed background conditions of the plan, that is, the milieu of action. Even in that role, however, they are not rigid or arbitrary.

Each convention in the milieu of action contains within it a certain degree of imagined possible variation. We know the world changes. And we know that some things are more subject to change than others. We know the sun will come up tomorrow. We do not know if it will be covered by clouds. The conventions that govern the milieu of action, therefore, are festooned in the actor's mind with all sorts of predicates and qualifiers. They are judged for their variability, for their reliability, and for the reliability of the judgment of reliability. They are labeled with markers telling us when to learn more about them and how to do so. They are, in other words, complex structures of meaning that serve our practical interests.

As Keynes correctly argued, ignorance of the future discourages action aimed at the future. Thus, we plan only where the inner zones of relevancy give us enough subjective predictability to expect the desired result with the required degree of confidence. We plan for the foreseeable future. We do not plan for the unforeseeable future. The very concept of cognitive expectations contains within it the notion of the predictability of the future. This notion of predictability is a pragmatic and subjective one, not a philosophical one. Our pragmatic judgment may be mistaken.

I have noted a similarity between Keynes' and Schutz's discussions of conventions. But I think there is an important difference. As I have just argued, in the Schutzian perspective, we plan for the foreseeable future only. Keynes seems to have imagined that we plan for the unforeseeable future.

Keynes distinguishes short-term and long-term expectations. Short-term expectations govern daily output decisions. They are subject to a feedback loop that usually operates so well that we may dispense with direct reference to expectations. Long-term expectations govern capacity decisions. No feedback loop keeps them in check. Rational forecasting is impossible in this sphere. But our "animal spirits" impel us to action anyway. To act in a state of ignorance requires some sort of convention. Keynes thought any such convention would necessarily be arbitrary. Because it is objectively baseless, it is also fragile. "But it is not surprising that a convention, in an absolute view of things arbitrary, should have its weak points. It is its precariousness which creates no small part of our contemporary problem of securing sufficient investment" (Keynes 1936, p. 153). Our animal spirits constantly lead us into disappointment.

Keynes' distinction between short-term and long-term expectations puts a dichotomy where a continuum belongs. Tomorrow is predictable. The next day is less predictable. The day after that is still less predictable. And so on. Our investment decisions can aim at a more distant future or a less distant future. We cannot see one thousand years ahead; we do not plan one thousand years ahead. We can see more than one day ahead; we plan more than one day ahead. We may freely choose our planning horizon. The more distant the future to which our actions are aimed, the more open-ended our plans will be. The less subject they will be, therefore, to disappointment by surprises.

It is useful to give a name to the idea that our planning horizons are subjectively determined and our plans grow more open-ended as the goal is more temporally distant. I will call this idea the *relativity of plan futurity*. The structure of plan futurity is relative to the agent's subjective knowledge. A simpler, but less descriptive name is the *horizon principle*.

It is because of the relativity of plan futurity that the concept of cognitive expectations implies subjective predictability of the future. Many Austrian and Post Keynesian economists have followed Keynes in neglecting the relativity of plan futurity. Thus, Paul Davidson (1989) insists that the supposed "nonergodicity" of the future puts an end to rational economic planning under capitalism. Other Post Keynesians make similar arguments. If the horizon principle is good, then these Post Keynesian arguments are miscast.

Invisible-hand processes ensure that agents will typically be about right in their understanding of how predictable the future is. Stuart Kauffman (1993, pp. 401–402; 1994, pp. 128–129) has carefully explored the logic of such invisible-hand processes. Kauffmann's argument addresses a somewhat different issue. But it is easily adapted to demonstrate the horizon principle.

Imagine we have short planning horizons. If our planning horizons are short enough, there will be very little uncertainty in our plans. Each of us could plan for a more distant future without suffering much increase of uncertainty. In this case, each of us has an incentive to expand his planning horizon. If my competitors hold no inventories, for example, they must make to order. A little advance planning lets me hold inventories. My speedier delivery gives me a competitive advantage. Eventually, planning horizons will grow.

In the opposite case of very long planning horizons, the future for which we are currently planning is so far off that it is almost completely obscured by uncertainty. Resources devoted to such distant ends are wasted; the likelihood of realizing the desired end is very low. In this case, each of us has an incentive to shrink his planning horizon. Planning horizons will shrink. At the equilibrium planning horizon, there is considerable uncertainty about the most distant future for which we plan, but not enough to discourage action.

Profit-seeking firms must approximate the equilibrium planning horizon. Firms that fall short will be passing up profitable opportunities. Their earnings will be below normal. Firms that overshoot will waste resources in the vain pursuit of distant ends. Their earnings, too, will be below normal. The filter of profit and loss tends to enforce the equilibrium planning horizon among profit-seeking enterprises.

Now hold the planning horizon constant and consider the degree of plan specificity. Plans that are too specific and lacking in contingencies provisions will be frequently disappointed. Plans that are too open-ended will waste resources on needless contingency provisions. They will also fail to exploit opportunities for gain by relatively specific sequences of planned actions. There is an equilibrium degree of plan specificity for every plan horizon. Households have an incentive to reach this equilibrium. Firms must approximate it well enough to avoid economic losses. Firms too far from this equilibrium will suffer losses. The filter of profit and loss tends to enforce the equilibrium degree of plan specificity for any given planning horizon.

My argument simplifies. In reality, each decision maker will have his own planning horizon. Indeed, he will have many different planning horizons because he will have many different plans. Similarly, each plan will have its own degree of specificity. But market processes such as I have described tend to bring about an equilibrium constellation of planning horizons and an equilibrium constellation of degrees of plan specificity.

An invisible-hand process tends to enforce the horizon principle. In the equilibrium position, there will be considerable complexity in the plans of agents. The future will be perfectly knowable in many respects. But many important matters will be clouded in uncertainty. There will be complexity, but not chaos.[2]

Our knowledge of future events[3]

Post Keynesians such as Burczak (2001) argue that market economies are subject to serious bouts of unemployment because of uncertainty and surprise. Discretionary government policies are required to compensate for this tendency and thereby maintain full employment. They use a statistical analogy to make their point. The business investor is like a statistician who wishes to forecast a non-ergodic time series. He cannot simply extrapolate time averages gathered from past results. The business investor loses his way in a non-ergodic world.[4]

This statistical simile mistakes the nature of our knowledge of future events. As theater patrons, we are in a position much like that described in Post Keynesian theory. We may try to forecast a sequence of events that is out of our control. Whatever we do, however, the third act contains surprises. As actors in the world, we are in a radically different position. We act only where we have influence, or think we do. In such cases, our knowledge of future events is in the form of a kind of architecture of the situation. The future is not a sequence of specific events, but a field of action. Indeed, if the future were not uncertain for the passive observer, it could not be the object of action for the active participant. We act in the world precisely to change the course of events. Uncertainty does not prohibit action; it makes action possible. (See Schutz 1959 for a deeper analysis of these issues.)

Anonymity and reflexivity

Anonymity

Agent-theories include representations of other agents. As we have seen in Chapter 3, these representations or "typifications" can be more or less "anonymous."

A "concrete" typification includes many details of psychological programming. It represents the person typified in relative detail. An "anonymous" typification is largely devoid of psychological programming. The perfectly anonymous typification is "anyone" without regard to time or place.

My agent-theory of the post office is filled with anonymous pictures of people called "postal workers" who somehow sort and deliver. A person's agent-theory of his workplace may include a very concrete picture of his boss.

In the band-level society of man's beginnings, a society was composed of a few known persons. This was the face-to-face society. In these groups each person had a concrete picture of everyone else in the group. The emergence of civilization greatly enlarged the numbers cooperating in the social process of production. Civilization meant cooperation with strangers. But one cannot form a concrete typification of strangers. By the time one had acquired enough knowledge to fill in the details, the stranger would be a stranger no more. Thus, social cooperation with strangers leads necessarily to the use of anonymous typifications. Their use allows strangers to cooperate.

Anonymous typifications can be very reliable. When we ride elevators, we rely on anonymous typifications. We take it for granted, "until further notice," that our fellow passengers will follow the rules of elevator etiquette. They are anonymous others to us. We need to know very little about them in order to confidently apply the anonymous typification "typical elevator passenger." When I mail a letter I rely on the anonymous typification of "postal worker." I confidently expect that faceless people I do not know will do things I do not really understand and that, as a result, my letter will arrive in the proper place more or less promptly.

Anonymous types are not always reliable, however. If I learn that the old boss has been fired and replaced with someone "from outside," I may have no grounds for imputing any habits or meanings to him. He will be a highly anonymous type for me. But this anonymity notwithstanding, I cannot form reliable expectations about him. I may be possessed, indeed, by considerable anxiety precisely because of my lack of familiarity with him.

Anonymity is a necessary, but not sufficient condition for cooperation with strangers. The crucial issue is one of "reflexivity," to which I now turn. I will argue that my expectations of others are reliable in cases of "closed reflexivity," but not in cases of "open reflexivity."

Reflexivity

Economic expectations refer to the reciprocal expectations of others. I drive on the right partly because I expect you to drive on the right. This expectation, in turn, is based partly on the expectation that you expect me to drive on the right. I think that you think that I think. This mutual interlocking of expectations creates self-reference. Following Arthur (1994b), I will call this interlocking "reflexivity." (Arthur credits George Soros with coining the term.) Appendix 4 (p. 212) has further notes on reflexivity. See also Knudsen (1993) for an excellent and unusually acute treatment of the problem.

In a reflexive situation, I can rely on my expectations if my model of you is *complete*. My agent-theory must contain all the information I need to orient my action to you. "Completeness" is defined only with respect to those matters touching our mutual interactions. (These interactions may be direct or indirect.) My model of you does not need to be complete in some absolute sense. It needs to be complete only with respect to those of your thoughts and actions that touch my plans. Completeness is a relative thing in another sense as well. No model is so complete as to utterly close off all open-ended possibilities. But some models are less open-ended than others. Some models are relatively complete; others are relatively open.

My model of you contains within it a representation of your model of me. That representation is my model of your model of me. If my model of you is to be complete in the sense just indicated, my model of your model of me must be complete in the same sense. Otherwise I cannot be sure how you will react to uncertainty about me.

I cannot be confident that I know how you will act unless I can be confident that you know how I will act. And I must be confident that you know that I know, and so on.

When each agent's model of every other agent is complete, then the situation is one of *closed reflexivity*. The reflexivity is "closed" because the mutual completeness of the agents' models closes off paradox. There are no open-ended possibilities through which the paradoxes of reflexivity might enter. When some agents' models are not complete, then the situation is one of *open reflexivity*. The incompleteness of some agents' models opens the door to paradox.

When two partners are face to face, each partner can continuously update his model of the other. In an ongoing personal relationship as well, the updating will be continual. This updating may keep each party's model relatively complete. Each meeting enriches and corrects each party's model of the other. In intimate relationships, even unfriendly ones, each party has a relatively intimate model of the other party or parties. Everyone relies on concrete typifications. In less personal relationships, the parties will necessarily rely on typifications that are more anonymous. Reflexivity may be closed even when some or all parties are relying on anonymous typifications.

Closed reflexivity with anonymous types

Each of us knows that his fellow social actors are guided by anonymous typifications of other actors. This knowledge gives each of us an incentive to fit his own actions into the stereotyped patterns expected by others. Others must understand you if your actions are to succeed or have, at least, an objective probability of success. To be understood by strangers, however, you must fit into their pre-existing structures of knowledge.

Each of us must rely on anonymous typifications to understand the social world. Each of us must fit his actions to the anonymous typifications of others. Thus, there is a kind of double reinforcement of anonymous typifications in society. Because we can and do rely on them, we can formulate reliable expectations about the social world, including those aspects we think of as "economic." Anonymity coordinates expectations.

Some "radical subjectivists" have neglected the coordinative function of anonymity. G.L.S. Shackle and J.M. Keynes were leading theorists of this description. They emphasized the possibility of "surprise" and novelty. Keynes argued that in the stock market, conventions close reflexivity. But partly because he did not recognize the role of anonymity in coordinating expectations, he imagined these conventions to be arbitrary and fragile. Burczak (2001) is a more recent example of this sort of thinking. Surprise and novelty are very real phenomena. But many radical subjectivists have exaggerated their power to disappoint our expectations. Considering the role of anonymous typifications in society leads us to see novelty as less threatening of order. Each actor aiming at that future must constrain himself to act in the typical ways expected by others. When they do constrain themselves in this way, they create relatively closed reflexivity where highly open reflexivity would otherwise prevail.

Acognitive expectations

"Acognitive expectations" are dispositions or propensities to act in certain ways. Acognitive expectations are implicit in the agent-practices of the language games operative in society. They are agent-practices, described in a particular way. The description tells us what the agent would have to be expecting if the practice were the deliberate choice of a rational individual. It is thus an objective meaning. In some cases, acognitive expectations will be the objective meaning of a series of acts of one individual. An example is the American crossing the street in London. But in other cases, acognitive expectations describe the "actions" of a representative agent. In such cases, acognitive expectations describe aspects of relatively complex social interactions, not the actions of any one person. An example is asset pricing under rational expectations.

In Chapter 5, I argued that language games are subject to a process of natural selection. Thus, acognitive expectations are subject to natural selection. Theories of natural selection in the social sciences can be plausibly traced back at least as far as Adam Smith and the Scottish Enlightenment (Hayek 1988, p. 146). Armen Alchian (1950) wrote a classic essay on the subject. The essay was a direct source and inspiration for much of Hayek's work on the evolution of social institutions. More recent examples of economic arguments relying on natural selection include Gode and Sunder (1993) and Howitt and Clower (2000).

The idea that the language games operative in some market are subject to natural selection works best when the constitutional rules governing the market are relatively stable and competition is more or less atomistic (Butos and Koppl 1993, Koppl and Yeager 1996). Competition is "atomistic" in the relevant sense when each competitor feels "that he is 'competing' with heaven-knows-how-many ... the feeling that the others would not care about what he does." It is the "absence of real rivalry or rival-consciousness" (Machlup 1952, p. 85). Stability is harder to define, but it may be sufficient to say that more stability means smaller and less frequent changes in the rules.

Under the "filtering conditions" of stability and atomicity, profits will go to traders whose chosen language games happen, for whatever reason, to lead them to prescient actions; they will be "weeded in." Those whose chosen language games happen to lead to losses will be weeded out. The losing language games may be theoretically superior to the winners. The winning language games may be social-science fiction. What matters is not the reasonability of the ideas animating the habits and routines of traders, but their profitability. Since the constitutional rules governing the market are stable, many of the incumbent traders will be successful again in the future. The conditions that made their routines work in the past have not changed much. Thus, these routines will generally produce appropriate actions again in the current period. In sufficiently "thick" markets, efficient markets models may fit the data reasonably well.

Natural selection has three parts: variation, selection, and retention. Selection operates over objects that vary from time to time. In biology, the objects were traditionally organisms. More recently, genes are the main objects of selection. Variation occurs in each generation. Variation implies that the array of objects present at any time is heterogeneous. In biology, the individuals of any species differ from one another. The heterogeneity of objects implies that some are more fit than others for the current environment. Thus, some objects will have more "success" than others. They are more likely to be "selected" by the system; others will be more likely to be rejected or weeded out. In biology, greater fitness traditionally meant (the probability of) differential reproductive success. Today, fitness is given by Hamilton's concept of "inclusive fitness." Retention is memory. In order to survive, the selected variations must persist somehow. In biology, retention is achieved mostly through genes.

In economics, I propose, the objects are language games. Variation occurs through "entrepreneurship." Selection will typically occur through the realization of profit and loss. Of course, as in biology, chance plays a role. We are very interested in when the filter of profit and loss is tight and when it is not. In Chapter 7, I will argue that Big Players make chance count for more and skill count for less.

Almost by definition, a tight system constraint implies that cognitive expectations don't much matter. In one sense, of course, they always matter. Each language game a trader uses entails some cognitive expectations. Those cognitive expectations are a necessary part of the action for the trader. The ideas embodied in the language games operative in the market do matter. But in another sense, when competition is stiff, they do not. The rhetoric and theory of an actor's trading game may correspond somehow to the truth. Or it may be social-science fiction. In either event, it will lead the agent to take appropriate action. Otherwise, the agent will be weeded out of the market process.

In many contexts, including that of the Big Players' theory, I will view acognitive expectations as the outcome of an evolutionary process. The economic environment selects them. In such cases, the same selection processes will influence cognitive expectations. But as I have just argued, this does not imply correct cognitive expectations.

Hayekian expectations

The notion of acognitive expectations is enriched by placing it within the context of Hayek's theory of mind. Doing so expands the notion and causes it to overlap the notion of cognitive expectations. But the perspective remains external, not internal. That is, the description of expectations is not phenomenological. In Schutzian terms, the meanings are relatively objective. The description runs in terms of the rules and behaviors of the actor even when reference is made to the actor's internal states of mind. The overlap between cognitive and acognitive expectations reflects the continuity between subjective and objective meanings.

Sometimes, acognitive expectations will describe complex social processes. For example, we may say that in a given financial market the traders have "rational expectations." This statement would not imply that any one trader knows the best available estimates of present value. It says, rather, that the complex interactions of many traders result in price movements that would prevent an imaginary actor armed with such estimates from earning above-normal profits.[5] In this case the word "expectations" describes an interaction among many people, not the meaning of any one person's actions. But in such a case, expectations do refer to the dispositions of economic actors. Thus, while the notion of acognitive expectations is enriched by Hayek's theory of mind, it also carries us beyond the context of individual action to that of interaction.

In Hayek's theory of mind, any individual's knowledge and actions are inextricably linked to the patterned stimuli of its external environment. In this sense, it is not possible for an individual to set himself cognitively apart from external reality. What the individual knows is shaped by the particulars of the environment within which he operates.

In the broadest sense, our expectations are endogenous to the world. The most deeply seated of them are endogenous to our "environment of evolutionary adaptedness" (Symons 1992, p. 143). It is an extension of this idea to say that we should view economic expectations the same way. Just as or deepest expectations are shaped to the environment of evolutionary adaptedness, so too are economic expectations shaped to *their* evolutionary environment. But that environment may not exercise much control of our expectations if, for example, it changes rapidly. So we should say that economic expectations have a *degree* of endogeneity determined by the time scale and the economic environment.

Our "knowledge of the external world" Hayek claims, "consists in the action patterns" that "stimuli tend to evoke, or, with special reference to the human mind, that which we call knowledge is primarily a system of rules of action assisted and modified by rules indicating equivalences or differences of various combinations of stimuli" (1969, p. 41). Hayek warns us against thinking of the "formation of abstractions" as "actions of the mind." We should think of the formation of concepts "as something which happens to the mind, or that alters that structure of relationships which we call the mind, and which consists of the system of abstract rules which govern its operation" (1969, p. 43).

Hayek's remarks about the formation of abstractions reflect his opinion that we should liken the mind to "a system of abstract rules of action" (1969, p. 43). And "every appearance of a new rule (or abstraction) constitutes a change in that system, something which," Hayek holds, "its own operations cannot produce but which is brought about by extraneous factors" (1969, p. 43). Experience induces change in the taxonomic rules that constitute the mind. The changes promote a better fit with the agent's environment.

The structure and mechanisms of the cognitive apparatus are "designed" by evolution to improve the agent's fit with the environment. The design is imperfect because it was not a true design, contrived by a planning mind. It was the product of selective mechanisms acting to improve the differential reproductive success of genes.

By nature's "design," a complicated feedback loop connects the mind and the world. This relationship enables the individual to adapt to changes in the world through an ongoing evolution of knowledge: adaptive modification of the individual's knowledge produces adaptive modifications of his actions. Indeed, what an individual "knows" is not so much how things are as what to do (Hayek 1967b). When action is inconsistent with the environment, the individual changes his habits. This implies a change in his expectations and his theories of reality.

In the Hayekian view of cognition, there is no guarantee that the individual's knowledge and actions will correspond adequately to external reality. The mind's classificatory process constructs its representation of the external world "in a partial and imperfect manner" (1952a, p. 145). The agent's "model" provides "only a very distorted reproduction of the relationships existing in that world" and thus the "classification of these events ... will often prove to be false, that is, give rise to expectations which will not be borne out by events" (1952a, p. 145). This gives rise to "reclassification" by which the mind rearranges nervous impulses (sensory inputs) into new configurations that allow better predictions to be made about reality. In short, those ideas that are "fit" tend to survive while those that are "unfit" tend to be weeded out. The criterion of fitness is confirmation of expectation.

The competitive process among expectations occurs, in Hayek's writings, at three levels. There is competition between ideas within the individual, between the ideas of separate individuals within society, and between the ideas of societies. At all three levels the logic of selection is the same. The better ideas lead to actions that better promote survival and success. Success causes the spread of the ideas that produced it.

In Hayek's framework, expectations correspond to the habits, practices, norms, and traditions of the society or, in other words, to the social rules governing action. For Hayek, these rules are products of social and biological evolution. In this evolutionary view there is no reason to see in the uncertainty of the future a special cause for discoordination of actions. Expectations have some tendency toward coherence and coordination. The evolutionary selection processes at work among thoughts and actions tend to select "fit" expectations and to weed out "unfit" ones. The evolutionary environment determines how much this tendency to coordination is blocked by other factors.

Correlating cognitive and acognitive expectations

The language-games framework gives us a way to discuss and correlate cognitive and acognitive expectations. As I suggested in Chapter 1, these two types of expectations are separate, but related.

Consider our story (from Chapter 1) of the Italian labor leader who opposed the government's low inflation target because low inflation would erode the real value of wages. Low inflation may hurt the union and its members. Thus, this leader's disposition to oppose monetary restraint may have reflected the correct "expectation" that low inflation is bad for his workers. (For the point at hand, it does not matter whether inflation is good only for union leaders, but not for the workers.) His good instincts about the desirability of inflation were translated into a true acognitive expectation. "Inflation is good for the union." His good instincts about the desirability of inflation were translated into a false cognitive expectation. "Inflation raises the real value of a given wage." It would be hard to explain the leader's error if we did not see that it emerged from an understandable preference for inflation.

Cognitive and acognitive expectations are distinct. But they do not inhabit separate worlds. We cannot have just any combination of the two at work. There must be an appropriate degree of congruence between them. The notion of action as performance under a language game may help us to decide which combinations of cognitive and acognitive expectations are plausible.

Acognitive expectations refer to objective meanings; cognitive expectations refer to subjective meanings. There is continuity between subjective and objective meanings. There is an overlap between cognitive and acognitive expectations. Nevertheless, they play somewhat different roles in economic explanation. Reference to acognitive expectations may be appropriate to cases in which the analyst wishes to emphasize the role of the economic environment in shaping events. Reference to cognitive expectations may be appropriate when the analyst wishes to emphasize the cognitive processes of individuals.

7
Big Players[1]

The general theory of Big Players

Big Players are privileged actors who disrupt markets. A Big Player has three defining characteristics. He is big in the sense that his actions influence the market under study. He is insensitive to the discipline of profit and loss. He is arbitrary in the sense that his actions are based on discretion rather than any set of rules. Big Players have power and use it.

Big Players disrupt markets by reducing the reliability of expectations. This disruption occurs in two ways. First, Big Players make each market participant less able to predict the future. Second, Big Players make the market process less likely to weed out traders who are bad at forecasting, and more likely to weed out traders who are good at forecasting. The first way is discussed in Koppl and Yeager (1996). The second way is discussed in Butos and Koppl (1993) and Koppl and Langlois (1994). I will treat each in turn.

Big Players and cognitive expectations

The actions of Big Players are hard to predict, but they influence the market. Big Players divert a portion of entrepreneurial attention away from more narrowly economic data onto aspects of the economic environment – actions of policymakers – that are inherently subject to unpredictable change. (For models of the allocation of attention see Baumol 1990, Gifford 1998, Radner 1975, Radner and Rothschild 1975.) Traders must pay attention to the actions and possible actions of the Big Player. Doing so means diverting attention from other factors, the fundamentals. (One would say the "other fundamentals" if one wished to call the Big Player a fundamental factor.) But the object onto which the diverted attention is moved is intrinsically hard to predict. Thus there is a net loss of prescience in each actor's interpretation of the future.

Economic expectations are based, implicitly or explicitly, on assumptions about what people will do. A judgment about what bad weather will do to wheat prices is based on reasonable assumptions about the actions of many persons, each of whom is subject to the discipline of profit and loss. There is little chance that idiosyncratic behavior of wheat farmers or wholesalers will prove our judgment mistaken. In contrast, a judgment about how the central bank will respond to, say, weakness in the manufacturing sector rests on assumptions about what a few known individuals will do. However reasonable these assumptions may be, there is always the chance that the persons in question will act out of character and disappoint our expectations. Fed watching is an inexact science.

The vulnerability of expectations to disappointment in particular cases is illustrated by Machlup's three propositions discussed in Chapter 1. Consider again his third proposition. "If, because of heavy withdrawals of foreign deposits, the banks are in danger of insolvency, the Central Bank Authorities will extend the necessary credit" (1936, p. 64). As a description of general trends, this seems a sound rule of thumb. But particular cases may go either way. "It will make a great difference," in Machlup's example, "whether Mr. Keynes or Professor von Hayek is governor or expert adviser of the central bank" (1936, p. 68).

Discretionary policymaking focuses entrepreneurial attention on the politics of the market. For the reasons just outlined, these are typically less knowable than more narrowly economic influences. When discretionary policymaking thus reduces the knowability of markets and the reliability of expectations, it devalues skill and makes luck count for more. Economic actors have less reliable and more transient knowledge about their environment when discretionary policymaking is an important dimension of that environment.

The presence of a Big Player forces other market participants to use an ideal type of low anonymity in their models of the market. The Big Player creates a situation of open reflexivity. The concept of open reflexivity was explained in Chapter 6. As I indicated there, open reflexivity frustrates coordination.

The argument of this subsection is similar to Machlup's argument in his "Why Bother with Methodology?" (1936), where he applies ideas of Schutz (1967). Machlup's argument concerns epistemological problems of economic theorists. Mine derives from applying his analysis to epistemic problems of economic actors.

Axel Leijonhufvud seems to have had something like this is mind when he discussed the corrosive effects of a high and variable rate of inflation. He points out that when money growth rates are determined by the discretion of the monetary authorities, "being good at real productive activities – being competitive in the ordinary sense – no longer has the same priority. Playing the inflation right is vital" (1986, p. 35). But it is hard to play the inflation right. The winners in this game owe more to luck than do the winners in the game of ordinary market competition.

Steve Horwitz (2000, 2002) has expressed similar ideas in his recent discussion of inflation. He argues that people try to avoid the bad effects of inflation. Such actions are socially wasteful coping costs. He also argues that inflation increases the volume of political rent seeking as well as the opportunities for politicians to give out special favors. As Horwitz points out, this increase in the volume of political exchange corrupts both market and political values in dangerous and costly ways.

Big Players and acognitive expectations

In Chapter 6, I identified two important conditions of market competition, namely, atomism and stability. When these conditions are violated, the filter of profit and loss is less likely to weed out unfit habits of action. It is less likely to weed out acognitive expectations that are not prescient. Big Players violate the condition of atomism. Thus, Big Players tend to corrupt acognitive expectations.

Big Players influence the markets in which they act. Their actions help determine which traders enjoy profits and which suffer losses. But the Big Player actions that help to determine profit and loss are more or less unrelated to anything objective, regular, and predictable. In the presence of Big Players, plain bad luck is more likely to bring losses to traders with otherwise meritorious trading habits. Sheer good luck may more easily bring profits to traders with otherwise poor interpretations of the market. The filter of profit and loss is less efficient under Big Player influence. The individuals who remain as participants in the market are likely to have, on average, more irregular trading habits, less real understanding of the market, and inferior methods of forecasting.

Big Players reduce the informational efficiency of markets by reducing the knowability of the future and by increasing the element of chance in determining who trades in the market.

Who are Big Players?

Bigness does not a Big Player make, but it helps. To be a Big Player in some market, it is not enough that you be able to influence the market, that you be largely immune from competitive pressures, nor even both. You must also be in the habit of using your discretion. Big Players have power and use it. Finance ministers and central bankers are paradigmatic Big Players, but only when they engage in discretionary policymaking. Private actors, too, may be Big Players. Each seller in oligopoly is one, which is what makes modeling oligopoly so difficult. In Oskar Morgenstern's discussion of Holmes and Moriarty (1935), both characters are Big Players.

It is difficult for private actors to be Big Players. Private actors who are big are not usually insensitive to profit and loss. If they become insensitive to profit and loss, they will probably suffer losses large enough to either remove them from the market or induce reform. Nomura Securities, U.S. seems to have been a private Big Player for a time (Ahmed *et al.* 1997). It is now defunct. It seems probable that only two types of actors may be Big Players beyond the short run, namely, governments and government-protected monopolists. Only they have enough immunity from the possible bad consequences of their decisions to act arbitrarily, yet stay in the market. Of course, my argument depends on a theory of markets that may be mistaken. In Post Keynesian theory, competition creates oligopolists nearly immune from potential competition. If such a theory were assumed, the theory of Big Players would apply to private actors even in relatively long runs. In any event, the prototypical Big Player is an activist finance minister or central bank. When finance ministers and central banks stick to rules, they are not acting as Big Players.

Modeling Big Players[2]

I have argued that the politics of the market are less knowable than more narrowly economic factors. This may seem unreasonable. Surely the authorities exercising this "discretion" have an objective function or a reaction function? Cannot such a function be mapped with just as much (and just as little) confidence as the equations describing underlying conditions of demand and supply? The assumption that a discretionary authority has an objective function or a reaction function is, at best, one that cannot be put to good use.

If the central bank, say, is exercising its discretion, then it is not committing itself to any course of action except that which seems best to it at the time of each decision. Each decision is based on the information available at the time the decision is made. Moreover, the weights given to each bit of information and the interpretation of it are those that seem best at the time the decision is made. Thus, the variables appearing in the bank's reaction function may change from decision to decision and the weights given to each variable change from decision to decision. The functional form of the reaction function may also change from decision to decision. Were such changes in the function ruled out, the bank would be following a rule and not using its discretion. The central bank, in my example, may be said to have a reaction function or a utility function. But because the function changes with each observation of it, the econometric identification problem is necessarily insuperable. The assumption that such a function exists cannot be used to guide expectations.

We may put the matter in another way. If a decision-making body (a person, a family, a committee) is using its discretion, then it will learn over time. But "real" learning implies more than the accretion of information. It implies a change in knowledge, a change in the way news is "framed," "filtered," or interpreted. A change in knowledge implies some novelty. If a decision-making body is using its discretion, there will be an element of novelty in its every action. We are always a little surprised by what real people do. Just as we would not expect to succeed in modeling our loved ones with mathematical reaction functions, we should not expect to succeed in modeling central bank presidents with mathematical reaction functions.

About the behavior of Big Players, to paraphrase J. M. Keynes, there is no scientific basis on which to form any calculable reaction function whatever. We simply do not know (Keynes 1937 p. 114).

The argument that Big Players cannot be modeled may be made as a kind of logical proof. It is not a practical impossibility, but a logical impossibility that Big Players be completely modeled.[3] Any model of a Big Player is necessarily simpler than the model-builder by at least one order of magnitude. If Big Players and economists are of about the same order of complexity, then no social scientist is capable of writing out a complete model of a Big Player.

A complete model of the Big Player would describe the environment in which he acts, and would predict his behavior in each of the different states of the environment. A Big Player acts in the context of some environment. This environment is the market under study and the set of other influences on the Big Player such as his bureaucratic position within his agency, the political status of this agency within the government, the weather, and the recent performance of his favorite sports team. The environment may also include elements of the larger political and social system within which the market is embedded. Let L denote the number of different states of the environment the model can distinguish. For the purposes at hand, it doesn't matter if the list of L states is in any sense true or complete. The number L describes a property of the model, namely, the number of states of the environment it can distinguish. This number may or may not reflect something about the true environment.

The Big Player will not behave in the same way in all states of the environment. He has, say, R different behaviors he might exhibit. Again, the number R reflects something about our model, namely, the number of Big Player behaviors it can distinguish. That number may or may not reflect something about the true behavioral repertoire of the Big Player. The Big Player might have three behaviors, namely, "expand the money supply," "contract the money supply," and "no change." The responses might be more complex. For instance, the Big Player might express concern over "irrational exuberance" while acting to keep interest rates constant. In any event, the model can describe R different behaviors of the Big Player. R is not greater than L. Each state of the environment corresponds to exactly one of the R behaviors of the Big Player. If one state were to correspond to two or more of the Big Player's R behaviors, the model would be incomplete.

If the Big Player learns over time, he may react differently to two environments which are the same except for their times of emergence. This role of time must be reflected somehow in the model. The model may include a time index. In this case, one of the dimensions of the model's description of the environment would be time. This device may not be adequate. It may not be so much time as experience that causes similar environments to induce dissimilar behaviors. The Big Player might be represented as having an internal state whose value is somehow related to the history of the Big Player in his environment. In any event, some way to capture this temporal dimension must be built into the model if it is to be a complete model of the Big Player.

In a complete model of the Big Player we can vary the environment (in imagination) and read off the implied variation in the behavior of the Big Player. We say the environmental change "caused" the behavioral change. A complete model gives necessary and sufficient conditions for each behavior.

To explain the Big Player's behavior, the model must say for each of the Big Player's R behaviors what elements of the set of possible environmental states do and what do not correspond to that behavior. Thus, for each of the R behaviors of the Big Player and each of the L states of the environment the model must describe the behavior, describe the environment and indicate (somehow) whether or not the two correspond. The model must be capable of generating RL separate statements. This number is greater than R. Thus, the model must be capable of a larger variety of behaviors than the Big Player whose behavior it explains. It follows that the model-builder, too, must be capable of a larger variety of behaviors than the Big Player whose behavior he would explain.

This simple calculus, it may be objected, depends on the assumption that R and L are finite numbers. But there is an infinite number of behaviors the Big Player might choose. The number may be infinite in reality, but it is finite in the model. Our theory may contain statements such as "The Big Player chooses a probability, p, between zero and one half." This statement seems to imply that any agent's behavior may take on a continuum of values. But typically our theory will distinguish only a few cases. We may want to know only if p is "sufficiently large" for some condition to hold. Consider the simple supply and demand model of freshman economics classes. Each demander is seemingly free to buy any of a continuum of units. But our description distinguishes only quantities greater than, less than, and equal to those of the initial equilibrium. Far from a continuum of actions, we have only three. This is typical. Any model distinguishes only a finite number of possibilities. This point may be illuminated by a thought experiment.

Imagine we have a complete formal language for some model of a Big Player. (Carnap 1958 contains some complete formal models for physics and biology.) Such a language would be composed of a finite number of symbols and a finite number of rules for combining the symbols. The rules determine what are well-formed formulae. The number of well-formed formulae is necessarily countable. If we imagine *any* finite limit to the length of a formula, then the language can distinguish only a finite number of cases. Given any amount of time required to write a symbol, however brief, one can calculate a finite formula length so great that it would require more time to write the formula than has yet passed in the history of the universe. Thus, whether or not one can calculate a least upper bound to formula length, some upper bound does exist. It seems reasonable to conclude that only finite numbers of states and behaviors can be distinguished by any theory.

A Big Player would be less complex than the typical small player if he would restrict himself to a relatively simple repertoire of behaviors. However complex the Big Player might be in other dimensions, those of his behaviors that matter to the small players would be relatively simple and easy to predict. But then he would be following a rule. By definition, a Big Player uses discretion. He does not commit himself in advance to any pre-programmed response to pre-determined environmental variables. He takes into account all available information at the moment of choice and weighs it and processes it in the manner that seems best at the time. He learns and changes. To predict the movements of a Big Player requires a complete model of him. As we have just seen, that model would have to be more complex than the Big Player. Small players cannot create complete model of Big Players. Big Players introduce an unpredictable element to the markets they affect.

A Big Player is a cipher. We cannot predict his actions or model him completely. This limit to knowledge applies to both finance researchers and market participants. If one were to attempt to construct a "rigorous" model of a market troubled by a Big Player, this double limit would have to be considered. The model would necessarily represent the Big Player as less complex than he really is. To be "rigorous," it would have to represent other market participants as themselves modeling the Big Players. But their models would have to be represented as less complex than the model's representation of the Big Player, and by at least one order of magnitude. (Otherwise, we should impute to market participants an ability to model that we lack ourselves.) Thus, a "rigorous" model of a market under Big Players' influence would have to represent its agents as acting on the basis of models at least two orders of magnitude less complex than that which they would need in order to calculate an optimal strategy. It is doubtful that the artificial time series generated by such a model would resemble the empirical series it is intended to mimic. We seem to have encountered a limit to knowledge in finance and economics. The apparent limit is a matter of logic. A part of the model must be less complex than the whole. It would be nonsense in the strict sense to deny it. This difference between part and whole seems to imply a fundamental limit to our knowledge, a limit we cannot overcome.

If Big Players impose on us the limits I have argued for, we cannot always get beyond what Hayek called "explanation of the principle" (1952b, p. 42). An explanation of the principle is one in which only general features of some phenomenon are accounted for. When the phenomena studied are sufficiently complex, this is all that can be hoped for. When studying social phenomena, "the number of separate variables which ... will determine the result" may be "far too large for any human mind to master them and manipulate them effectively" (1952b, 42). In such cases, "our knowledge of the principle by which these phenomena are produced" will not "enable us to predict the precise result of any concrete situation" (1952b, p. 42). When we can have only an explanation of the principle, our theoretical knowledge "will merely enable us to preclude certain results but not enable us to narrow the range of possibilities sufficiently so that only one remains" (1952b, p. 42).

The distinction between explanation of the principle and explanation of the particular had gone more or less unnoticed in the physical sciences before the emergence of theories of chaos and complexity. This may be because in the physical sciences "usually there [was] no great difficulty about elaborating any explanation of the principle so as to make it approximate to almost any desired degree to the circumstances of a particular situation" (Hayek 1952a, p. 183). One simply added the necessary complexities to one's model. As we have seen above, this device is logically impossible in at least some cases of scientific problems in economics.

Big Players in asset markets

In asset markets, the presence of Big Players can induce "herding" or "bandwagon effects" and therefore "irrational bubbles." The strength of such bubbles will depend on many particulars, including how active the Big Players are. The greater their activity and influence, the stronger the bandwagon effects. I develop this argument by using Ronald Heiner's (1983) model of choice among routines.

Heiner's reliability condition

If you are buying and selling assets on financial markets, you must respond to signals. Some say "buy" and some say "sell." All of these signals are more or less unreliable. Your job is to decide which to respond to and which to ignore. Heiner's "reliability condition" (1983) suggests a criterion. You respond to those signals for which the expected value of responding is positive. In Heiner's notation,

$$r / w > (l / g) * [(1 - \pi) / \pi] \tag{7.1}$$

where
r = the probability of getting a true signal to act (buy or sell as the case may be),
w = the probability of getting a false signal to act
l = the loss from acting when you should not
g = the gain from acting when you should, and
π = the relative frequency or *ex ante* probability of there being a favorable occasion to act.
(Heiner restates the condition that expected gain be positive: $r*g*\pi - w*l*(1 - \pi) > 0$.)

Discretion encourages herding

Discretionary interventions of a Big Player, threatening to override the fundamentals, weaken the reliability of the old signals about wise buy and sell decisions. In Heiner's notation, r/w falls below $(l/g)*[(1 - \pi)/\pi]$ for many signals.

My argument so far has not shown that herd behavior results. It has shown only that discretionary intervention dilutes the influence of fundamentals on trading. But why should more trading occur on the basis of herd behavior?

Following Scharfstein and Stein (1990), we must look a little more closely at what the people actually making buy and sell decisions stand to gain and lose. Many of the real decision makers are managers trading with other people's money. Accordingly, an important part of the gains and losses from good and bad trades is the effect on one's reputation as a hired hand. Reputation typically hinges on relative performance. If most banks are failing, including yours, you are not considered a bad banker, just the unlucky victim of an industry crisis. On the other hand, if you defy prevailing wisdom and lose, your reputation is shot and you must look for a new line of work. This is the sharing-the-blame effect (Scharfstein and Stein 1990, p. 466). When you go along with the common wisdom and things work out, your wisdom is proved. When you go along with the common wisdom and things go bad, you can share the blame with everyone else. Your relative performance is still pretty good. The really dangerous thing is to defy common wisdom.

The share-the-blame effect can lead to herding (Scharfstein and Stein 1990). I think Keynes exaggerated, however, when he said, "Worldly wisdom teaches that it is better for reputation to fail conventionally than to succeed unconventionally" (1936, p. 158). Incentives influence the choice between idiosyncrasy and herding. If the penalty for a bad idiosyncratic decision is high compared with the penalty for the same bad decision made along with everyone else, then one has an incentive to ignore buy and sell signals except those that indicate what other traders are doing. If signals about the fundamentals are "reliable" in Heiner's sense, however, then they provide a powerful counter-weight to this incentive, namely, the large gains to be expected from making good idiosyncratic decisions with some regularity. When most of the signals about fundamentals have been rendered unreliable by a Big Player's discretionary interventions, this counter-weight no longer exists. The prospective gain from idiosyncratic decisions then becomes too small to discourage herd behavior. Herd behavior is encouraged by discretionary interventions because of the role of reputation in the market for the labor of money managers.

The process is self-reinforcing. If herding begins, movement in an asset's price conveys information about how other traders are acting, information that will lead traders to amplify the movement. If the price of a stock should start to rise, then some traders will buy it on this sign of bullishness by other traders. The further price rise now strengthens the common wisdom that the stock is on its way up. And so on. The less reliable are the signals about fundamentals, the longer such self-reinforcing movements can go unchecked. The stronger the actual or conjectured influence of Big Players, the more frequent and persistent such bubbles are likely to be.

Other consequences of Big Players in asset markets

Broussard and Koppl (1999) identify further consequences of Big Players in asset markets.[4] By reducing the reliability of expectations, Big Players diminish the informativeness of markets. Markets become less efficient mechanisms for the generation and transmission of information. Broussard and Koppl argue that Big Players reduce the informational efficiency of markets by increasing unconditional volatility and increasing the persistence of conditional volatility. (It increases the "volatility dynamics" one may model as a GARCH process.)

In the presence of Big Players, market participants are more likely to act on information containing little intrinsic merit, especially if that information concerns possible actions of the Big Player. Bogus reports and rumors will be acted upon with greater frequency. More traders will begin exchanging more money than the amount indicated by fundamentals. The greater the quantity and variety of bogus reports influencing the market, the more frequently will chance accumulations of seemingly favorable news drive up prices. By the same logic, the more frequently will chance accumulations of seemingly unfavorable news drive prices down. Thus we should expect the variance of changes in asset prices to rise in the presence of Big Players.

A simple model illustrates the principle. Imagine we had a model of returns in which $y_t = e_t$ with $e \sim N(0, \sigma^2)$. In such a model var(y) = var(e). If traders begin to pay attention to rumor and surmise about Big Player behavior, the model becomes $y_t = e_t + u_t$. The second error term (u_t) represents the effect of trading based on rumors about the Big Player. Under the new regime of Big Player influence var(y) = var(e) + var(u) + 2cov(e,u). If the two error terms are not too strongly correlated in the negative direction, the variance of y grows. Although this model is too simple to capture all known regularities in asset return series or the full effects of Big Player influence, it may help show why Big Players are likely to increase the variability of asset returns.

Big Players are also likely to increase the apparent persistence of conditional volatility. By reducing the value of economic information, Big Players increase attention paid to an asset's recent price behavior. Traders will attach more meaning to transient increases in asset-price volatility. One day's unusually large price change may be imagined to be the result of the Big Player's actions, or a movement to which the Big Player is likely to respond. Some will see a trend, others will expect reversal. Whichever view happens to gain more adherents, the exaggerated attention paid to the price movement encourages another large movement the next day or the day after, perhaps in the same direction, perhaps in the opposite direction. In this way, Big Players are likely to increase the measured persistence of conditional volatility. Diebold and Nerlove (1989) also discuss how GARCH effects may result from differences in the interpretability of information.

I said Big Players will increase the "apparent" and "measured" persistence of conditional volatility. The analysis of Chapter 9 shows that herding and contra-herding may create "X-skewing," a statistical pattern that resembles GARCH, but is not GARCH. A simulation discussed in Chapter 9 shows that standard tests will mistake X-skewing for GARCH.

Big Player influence, then, should cause both an increase in the unconditional variance of asset prices and returns as well as an increase in the apparent persistence of that variance. Testing the implications of Big Player theory is possible if a clear case of regime shifting from less to more Big Player influence exists. Chapter 8 studies such a case.

Modeling asset prices in the presence of Big Players

My discussion of herding was based on Scharfstein and Stein's (1990) sharing the blame effect and on Heiner's earlier contribution. Moreover, one can draw a rough parallel between the variables used in Heiner's general analysis of decision making and Scharfstein and Stein's analysis of herding.[5] One might, then, expect us to derive an explicit model based on the equations of Heiner and Scharfstein and Stein. I could then test my prediction that Big Players induce herding by estimating the parameters of my model. For reasons discussed in this section, I will not do that. I will instead use a non-parametric procedure to test my prediction.

As I argued earlier in this chapter, we cannot put to good use the idea that a Big Player has a reaction function or objective function. If it is sensible to say that such a function exists, then its continual changes prevent econometric identification. But a fully specified model would have to incorporate the behavior of the Big Players whose actions, after all, do influence the behavior of the asset's price. Thus, any model of the time series data generated in an asset market with Big Players must either specify the asset's behavior incompletely or misspecify its behavior by positing some unchanging reaction function for the Big Player.

Even if we had, somehow, a "true" reaction function for the Big Player (an impossibility given the assumption of discretionary decisionmaking) we would still need to model the dynamics of the interaction between the Big Player and the rest of the market.

The Big Player knows that the rest of the market participants are trying to guess what he will do. He takes this knowledge into account when making choices. The rest of the market traders know this about the Big Player and factor this knowledge into their choices. All of this is known, of course, to the Big Player. He thinks that they think that he thinks, and so on. Such situations present problems of convergence. (See also Morgenstern 1935 and the discussion of it in Appendix 4, p. 212.)

If I were to specify a time series model and attempt to estimate the parameters of the model, I would have to make some rather specific assumptions about the structure of the time series data under study. Beyond the prediction of "memory" to be discussed below, we have little basis for preferring one choice of model to another. The hypothesis that Big Players induce herding does not tell us if marginal distributions will be Gaussian or non-Gaussian. Nor does it give us a functional form for the asymptotic behavior of the autocorrelation function. It tells us only, as I shall explain on p. 154, that "persistent dependence" should increase with Big Player influence.

If I were to estimate a parametric model of the time series data I study, I would multiply the number of ancillary hypotheses being tested together with the prediction of increased herding. This would multiply the number of excuses I might make should my prediction go awry. This multiplication of excuses would immunize the prediction from falsification. Standard philosophy of science has accepted Karl Popper's admonition to expose our ideas to potentially falsifying tests and that these tests should be as strong as possible. (For a good overview of twentieth-century philosophy of science, see Caldwell 1984.) Making excuses is not good science. If I were to estimate a parametric model of asset-price time series data, I would produce plenty of good excuses and little in the way of rigorous testing.

The theory outlined in this chapter leads to a kind of middle-ground position on financial markets. There is a core of truth in efficient markets theory, but herding exists. Moreover, the degree of herding is a function of the market regime. It can be influenced, for good or bad, by policy.

Standard economic theory predicts that an asset's price, $P(t)$, will tend toward the discounted sum of its price at the end of next period, $P(t + 1)$, and the value of any services it renders during the period, $z(t + 1)$. If agents have rational expectations, this tendency is fully realized and an asset's price will equal the discounted expected value of $P(t + 1) + z(t + 1)$. Under the assumption of rational expectations, the value of an asset at time t can be represented by the equation:

$$P(t) = (1+r)^{-1} E[P(t+1) + z(t+1)|\Phi(t)] \qquad (7.2)$$

where $\Phi(t)$ is the information available at time t. Forward substitution shows that the asset's price will equal its "fundamental value," $F(t)$, plus a residual "rational bubble," $B(t)$:

$$P(t) = F(t) + B(t) \qquad (7.3)$$

where

$$F(t) = \sum_{\tau=1}^{\infty} (1+r)^{-\tau} E[z(t+\tau)|\Phi(t)] \qquad (7.4)$$

and

$$B(t) = (1 + r)^{-1} E[B(t + 1)|\Phi(t)] \qquad (7.5)$$

This present value model has been challenged by models in which agents who do not formulate rational expectations influence asset prices (e.g. DeLong *et al.* 1990). Following Black (1986), economists often call these "irrational" agents "noise traders." (See Shleifer and Summers 1990 for a review of noise trader models.) In the work of Shiller (1989) and others, noise traders are subject to fads and fashions or, as Topol (1991) puts it, "mimetic contagion." Following Scharfstein and Stein (1990) I will use the term "herding." Papers on noise trading and herding often cite J. M. Keynes as inspiration or precursor. (But see Piron 1991.) The assets to which noise trader and present value models are often applied include stocks, bonds, and foreign currency.

Empirical studies have not yielded results clear enough to make the choice between present value and noise trader models unambiguous. (See Cochrane 1991, LeRoy 1989, Meese 1990, and West 1988 for reviews of relevant literature.) Econometric studies necessarily test specific versions of a theory. If the theory fails an empirical test, the trouble may lie with a particular assumption of the model tested, not the general theory. Early volatility studies, for instance, did not "falsify" the present value model, just the version assuming a constant discount rate (Cochrane 1991, pp. 465–67). Similarly, in models of exchange rates that contain more than one "fundamental" factor, exchange rates may be "even more volatile than their component fundamental factors" (Meese 1990, p. 123). West concludes his survey by noting that "there is little formal positive evidence to sway someone unsympathetic to fads models" (1988, p. 654). Just as the positive evidence for fads or present value models in the stock market is weak, the positive evidence for competing models of short-to-medium-run movements in exchange rates is weak (Meese 1990). The weakness of econometric tests designed to distinguish present value and noise models was noted by Black, who defended his ideas about noise even though he could not "think of any conventional empirical tests that would distinguish between [his] views and the views of others" (1986, p. 530).

In this book I propose an approach to explaining asset prices that contains testable implications while largely skirting the difficulties of modeling the time series data generated by asset markets. In my approach to understanding asset prices, the degree of herding and, therefore, the relative merits of fads and fundamentals as explanatory variables depend on exogenous market conditions. At least some of these exogenous market conditions can be identified and, therefore, the implications of the model can be tested.

In my approach to asset markets, prices tend to equal present values. Noise traders prevent this tendency from being fully realized. Noise trading will have a greater tendency to keep prices away from their present values in some circumstances than in others. In particular, the discretionary actions of "Big Players" such as interventionist finance ministers encourage herding and thus weaken the tendency of asset prices to equal their rationally expected present values. Discretionary actions of governments and other Big Players reduce market efficiency.

Big Players are not always bad. Mramor and I (Koppl and Mramor 2000) analyze a recent episode in Slovenian monetary history. In 1994 the Bank of Slovenia, the central bank, was forced to defend the value of its currency by issuing a large volume of bonds. We show that this action was interpreted as a basic change in central bank policy. The bank had followed a hands-off policy up to then. Beginning in 1994, the Bank of Slovenia became a Big Player. We applied R/S analysis to stock-market data. Our results indicate an increase in herding on the Ljubljana Stock Exchange. In this case, the Big Player intervention was necessary to defend the currency. The Big Player promoted price stability. The Big Player had an unfortunate effect on the stock market. But the overall effect seems to have been quite beneficial to the people of Slovenia.

Big Players are not always governments. Ahmed, Rosser, White, and I (Ahmed *et al.* 1997) have studied the behavior of closed-end countries funds in the late 1980s. We find strong evidence of herding and bubbles in this market. We conjecture that Nomura Securities, U.S. may have acted as a Big Player in this market. In the long run, only government actors or governmentally protected actors can be Big Players. But private Big Players may emerge in the short run. Nomura securities may be an example.

Herding and contra-herding as error duration

Parke's "error duration" model (1999) gives us a simple model of the herding and contra-herding produced by Big Players in asset markets.[6] In Parke's error duration model, "the basic mechanism ... is a sequence of shocks of stochastic magnitude and stochastic duration. The variable observed in a given period is the sum of those shocks that survive to that point" (1999, p. 632). The model will produce long memory if the probability of an error enduring k periods, p_k, declines slowly as k grows. The values p_k are called "survival probabilities." When autocorrelations exist, their rate of decline is determined by partial sums of the survival probabilities. I will model bubbles as error duration processes. Big Players increase the survival probabilities of the errors and decrease their rate of decline. With Big Players, noise stays in the system longer. Thus, Big Players increase volatility, and herding. Big Players may also induce or increase long memory. Contra-herding is consistent with this error duration model.

The price of an asset can be described by

$$P_t = F_t + B_t + \varepsilon_t, \tag{7.6}$$

where P_t is the asset's price, F_t is its fundamental value, B_t is a bubble, and ε_t is an i.i.d. error term. The bubble can be modeled as an error duration process.

Let $\{\epsilon_t\ t = 1,2,\ ...\}$ be a series of i.i.d. shocks having mean zero and common variance σ^2. Each error is a price movement induced by news that does not convey new information about the asset's fundamental value. These errors are distinct from the ε_t.

There are two distinct sets of traders in the market, namely fundamentalists and noise traders. (This common assumption is used, for instance, by Day and Huang 1990.) The fundamentalists correctly estimate F_t up to an i.i.d error, ε_t. Noise traders behave like fundamentalists except that they respond to false signals ignored by fundamentalists. Past price changes are one example of such false signals. Through its effect on noise traders, each false signal induces a price change of ϵ_t. Some of them may be movements in excess of the level properly implied by the news to which fundamentalists respond. Each error ϵ_s lasts n_s periods beyond s, where n_s is a random variable. The error disappears when noise traders revise their initial interpretation of the false signal. Following Parke, let $g_{s,t}$ denote "an indicator function for the event that error ϵ_s survives to period t" (1999, p. 632). The indicator, $g_{s,t}$, switches from one to zero after period $s + n_s$ and stays at zero thereafter. The indicator is one as long as the error endures. Assume ϵ_s and $g_{s,t}$ are independent for $t \geq s$. The probability of an error enduring at least k periods is p_k. Thus, $p_k = P(g_{s,s+k} = 1)$. Clearly, $p_0 = 1$ and the series $\{p_0,\ p_1,\ p_2,\ ...\}$ is monotone non-increasing. The realization of the process is just the sum of the errors. Thus,

$$B_t = \sum_{s=-\infty}^{t} g_{s,t}\epsilon_s \tag{7.7}$$

As Parke notes, the survival probabilities "are the fundamental parameters" of the model (1999, p. 632). He shows (pp. 632–633) that if autocovariances exist, they are given by

$$\gamma_k = \sigma^2 \sum_{j=k}^{\infty} p_j \tag{7.8}$$

If λ exists, the variance is $\sigma^2(1 + \lambda)$, where

$$\lambda = \sum_{i=1}^{\infty} p_i \tag{7.9}$$

In this case, the first-order autocorrelation is $\rho_1 = \lambda/(1 + \lambda)$. The process has a long memory if $\lim_{n\to\infty} \sum_{k=1}^{n} kp_k$ is infinite (1999, p. 633). Assume the survival probabilities have the form $p_k = k^{-2+2d}$ with $d \le 1/2$. In that case λ and the γ_ks exist. The process has a long memory for $0 < d \le 1/2$, and a short memory if $d \le 0$. (If $1/2 \le d \le 1$, λ and the λ_ks do not exist. (If $d > 1$, $p_k > 1$.)

In this model, a sufficiently small (i.e. large, negative) value for d will make any bubbles difficult to detect; p_k will be close to zero even for small k. As d grows, bubbles are increasingly large and persistent. If $0 < d \le 1/2$, the bubble process is stationary with a long memory.

Many of the effects of Big Players can be represented by an increase in d. A larger d means larger survival probabilities. The increase of d results from the greater ignorance of traders regarding the meaning of any piece of news. Noise traders will thus take longer, on average, to revise their interpretations of false signals. The history of the credit ruble, recounted in Chapter 8, provides a good example. In 1890, false rumors circulated that the ruble would soon be put onto the gold standard. These rumors drove up the ruble's international value. The rumors persisted and were believed in spite of disconfirming evidence. This persistence is probably attributable to the heavy Big Player influence of Ivan Vyshnegradsky, the contemporary finance minister. Under his Big Player influence, once the error entered the system, it was slow to exit.

The increase in d raises the autocorrelations of the bubble process. If the increase is from a value below 0 to one above 0, then the Big Player will produce long memory. If long memory is already present, he will cause it to increase. It is perfectly possible, however, that the Big Player will cause d to increase from one value below 0 to another value that is still below 0. Big Players cause or increase herding, but they need not cause long memory. I will return to this point in Chapter 8 when I argue in favor of the "classic Hurst" estimating technique.

The increase in d will cause an increase in λ and thus in $\sigma^2(1 + \lambda)$, the variance of the bubble process. Thus Big Players cause an increase in volatility. Big Players may also cause an increase in σ^2, the variance of the ϵ_t. Assume ϵ_t is the sum of several independent random variables each corresponding to a process unrelated to the asset's fundamental value. Big Players may increase the number of unrelated processes noise traders respond to. In that case, the variance of the ϵ_t will grow.[7]

This representation of the effects of Big Players is consistent with contra-herding. One of the false signals followed by noise traders may be last period's movement, u_{t-1}, in the non-bubble part of the asset price. Some noise traders will see a trend. Others may expect a "correction."

If the sheep prevail, $\epsilon_t = u_{t-1}$. If the contrarians prevail, $\epsilon_t = -u_{t-1}$. In either event, $|\epsilon_t| = |u_{t-1}|$. (More generally, u_{t-1} error will be added to or subtracted from ϵ_t according whether sheep or contrarians prevail.) The winning interpretation will then endure for n_t periods beyond t. This form of herding and contra-herding would produce the "X-skewing" described in Chapter 8. As noted there, X-skewing is not GARCH, but it produces apparent GARCH effects.

Part IV
Applications

8
Big Players in Czarist Russia[1]

The policies of Bunge and Vyshnegradsky

The contrasting policies of two Russian finance ministers, Nikolai Bunge and Ivan Vyshnegradsky, provide a case study in the Big Players effect. Bunge served from 1881 through 1886, Vyshnegradsky from 1887 through 1891.[2] Bunge was a strict rule-follower and thus not a Big Player. Vyshnegradsky was an interventionist and very much a Big Player in the international market for the ruble. Under Bunge's regime, as we shall see, the ruble exchange rate fluctuated more narrowly than under Vyshnegradsky. The statistical results of this chapter and Chapter 9 suggest that Big Player effects were stronger under Vyshnegradsky.

The theory of Big Players predicts that the greater Big Player influence of Vyshnegradsky will have had several effects. First, Vyshnegradsky's activism should have induced an increase in the variance of ruble returns. Second, Vyshnegradsky should also have induced an increase in volatility dynamics. Finally, Vyshnegradsky should have induced more herding in the international market for rubles. The statistical results of this chapter are consistent with these predictions.

During the decade under study, Russia had an irredeemable paper currency, the "credit ruble." The country had gone off its traditional silver standard during the Crimean War of 1853–6, and not until 1897 did it return to a metallic standard, this time gold. Meanwhile, the ruble floated on foreign exchange markets under greater or lesser degrees of influence from the Finance Ministry.

Unlike most other Russian finance ministers, Nikolai Bunge was a principled non-interventionist. In the words of the economist Migulin, Bunge "followed the system of nonintervention in bourse affairs, attempts at which (made under N. Kh. Bunge's predecessors) had led to a negative result and which, therefore, N. Kh. Bunge considered harmful rather than useful" (Migulin 1899–1904, I, pp. 491, 597.) In an article published the year before he became finance minister, Bunge had described the disadvantages of intervention at length (1880, pp. 97ff.). He distinguished between two types of official intervention. First, the government agency might continuously buy and sell foreign exchange, acting differently from private banks and exchange offices only in taking smaller profit margins. Doing so would drive private institutions out of business and leave a monopoly. That situation seemed likely to cause "larger fluctuations in the exchange rate ... than with the combined activity of the exchange offices and private credit institutions." Alternatively, the agency might try to regulate the exchange rate by buying metallic currencies when they were in ample supply and selling them at other times to meet net demands for them. Such intervention, Bunge said, "not only does not withstand criticism but is condemned by experience."

As finance minister, Bunge repeatedly emphasized that his administration had not been intervening on the market. In his report accompanying the budget proposal for 1883, for example, he argued that "Every attempt to raise the rate of the credit ruble at once could have only momentary success and would unavoidably end in failure, having served only to give profit to bourse gaming" (quoted in Migulin 1899–1904, I, pp. 481–82). In his 1886 budget proposal, similarly, Bunge reported that "The Finance Ministry abstained, as previously, from any influence on the price of the credit ruble and for this purpose did not even sell gold received in payment of customs duties but transferred it to the operating cash of the State Bank in exchange for credit notes accumulated in the latter" (quoted in Gurjev 1896, part 2, supplement 1, pp. 182–83). One indication that Bunge was telling the truth is the absence, in all the newspapers and books we consulted, of any mention of intervention during Bunge's administration.

Taking office in January 1887, "I. A. Vyshnegradsky was more energetic," according to Migulin, "and up to the end of his activity he did not renounce intervention on the bourses, but, acquiring gold, in a significant degree on account of credit notes belonging to the Treasury and the State Bank, he naturally was interested in bourse gaming on the difference in the prices of the credit ruble" (1899–1904, II, part 2, p. 133). He thus reinstated an old Russian tradition. (Intervention or proposals for it date as early as 1771.)

Under Vyshnegradsky, rumors and fears of imminent action moved the ruble as much as direct intervention. The financial press was keenly aware of both Vyshnegradsky's presence and his capacity to act surreptitiously.

In 1888 Russia had an abundant harvest but most of the rest of the world a bad one. The ruble rose. Its rise was particularly sharp in June and again in September. Towards mid-September the German newspaper *Aktionär* judged from all available reports that the chief motor in the rise of the ruble, more important even than foreign demand for rubles to pay for Russian grain, was the Russian finance minister himself. He must have welcomed the cheapening of the gold currencies he needed to pay interest abroad. His methods of strengthening the ruble suggested an ingeniously thought-out plan. He was taking full advantage of the international political détente and was supposedly trying to make paper rubles scarcer both at home and abroad. He was tightening credit and raising interest rates at home, evidently hoping to check the repatriation and even promote the export of Russian securities. Abroad, his agents were apparently buying up ruble notes every month. An article on "Russische Noten" in the *Aktionär* of 16 September 1888 reported that Bourse operators were becoming wary, however, as they recognized that the partly artificial character of the rise might bring on a reaction. This interpretation is, on its very face, more a conjecture or an inference than an account of well-established fact; but right or wrong, it does illustrate the ideas that were circulating and influencing market behavior at the time.

I. F. Tsion, who had been Vyshnegradsky's financial representative in Paris for a while but later became his bitter personal enemy, accused Vyshnegradsky in some detail of destabilizing intervention. At a German spa in the summer of 1888, Tsion met the banker Bleichröder, who told him that his firm was serving as Vyshnegradsky's intermediary in buying rubles to raise their price. Skeptical at first, Tsion warned Bleichröder that private banks were probably misusing the finance minister's name to promote their speculations (Tsion 1892, pp. 17–18).

Early in October 1888, just about the time when the ruble had in fact reached its peak for the year, *Aktionär* surmised (wrongly) that its rise had been interrupted only momentarily. It suggested that conjectures about official intervention were influencing speculation:

> People see, in this, purchases being continually carried out by the very first side and believe that these purchases are connected with the secret operations of the Russian finance minister. Meanwhile, speculation also takes a hand with greater verve than hitherto in the trading in Russian notes; and, indeed, some large speculators are documenting their good opinion for the Russian currency through continuing additional firm purchases and, namely, through big

option purchases, while the bulk of the little speculation, in this sector as on the whole market, engages itself bearishly. (October 7, 1888, 642)

Not all accounts agree on which way the finance minister was intervening in 1888. It would not have been out of line with his character to switch back and forth capriciously between reinforcing and restraining the rise of the ruble.

One scandal of 1890 illustrates the sort of disturbances caused by Vyshnegradsky's interventions – and conjectures about them. Before seeking the Czar's approval of a plan to push down the ruble rate, Vyshnegradsky discussed it with A. A. Abaza, a former finance minister and President of the Department of State Economy at the time. He entrusted Abaza with close participation in conducting the intervention. During the summer of 1890, when the ruble rate was still rising strongly, Abaza arranged with Aleksandr Rafalovich, an Odessa banker, to carry out bear speculation in rubles on his personal account. Inferring that Abaza must have had inside information, Rafalovich himself undertook the same speculations as his customer. Yet the ruble kept on rising. After each man had lost nearly 800,000 rubles, Rafalovich asked Abaza whether he had not been mistaken. Abaza answered, in effect: That is none of your business; continue executing my orders. Still believing Abaza mistaken, Rafalovich switched to a bull position on the ruble. He began acting himself as counterparty to Abaza'a transactions: instead of executing Abaza's orders abroad, Rafalovich bought all the rubles Abaza sold. At first, as the ruble continued rising, Abaza'a cumulative losses grew, while Rafalovich's shrank. But after the ruble trend switched in mid-September to a rapid decline, Abaza recouped his earlier losses and won a handsome profit, while Rafalovich's new losses, added to his earlier losses, made his banking firm insolvent. (As we argued earlier, it is generally harder to know what a named person will do than to predict the anonymous forces of supply and demand. The politics of the market are typically less knowable than its economic data.)

Rafalovich paid Abaza his winnings but had to obtain two loans from the State Bank to pacify his firm's other creditors. Vyshnegradsky and his successor as finance minister, Sergej Witte, reluctantly agreed to these shaky loans to keep the scandal from becoming public. Witte eventually informed the Czar. Abaza begged the Czar's forgiveness and promised never to do such things again; but the Czar, also recalling an earlier scandal about his gambling, did not trust him. Abaza had to resign his government post.[3]

A further wrinkle to the story of the Abaza scandal and the ruble's 1890 rise and fall makes another contribution to our picture of Vyshnegradsky the Big Player inducing uncertainty and destabilizing speculation. One reason the ruble kept on rising until mid-September developed from an interview in August between Vyshnegradsky and the editor of the *Berliner Börsen-Courier*. Vyshnegradsky made remarks suggesting that he intended soon to peg the ruble upward onto gold at its supposed old parity, about 22 per cent above its highest rate actually reached in mid-September. If the editor had misunderstood his meaning, Vyshnegradsky let the misinterpretation go uncorrected.

The *Börsen-Courier* repeated in many issues its conviction that Vyshnegradsky would soon put the ruble onto the gold standard at par. It repeatedly replied to the skeptics and cited new bits of supposed evidence, including alleged remarks of the Czar. It implied that the continuing rise of the ruble rate was itself a sign of policy intentions. Other newspapers gave the gold-standard rumors further circulation. The *Frankfurter Zeitung* and *Aktionär* were skeptical. For this reason, their own dismay at other people's gullibility carries weight as a clue to prevalent opinion.

A number of Russian and foreign economists later also testified to the strong influence of the gold-standard rumors in 1890. Not until two weeks after the ruble-rate trend had in fact sharply reversed itself did the *Börsen-Courier* begin to crawl back, with amusing artfulness, from its earlier confident assertions.[4] The relapse of the ruble itself tended to discredit the gold-standard rumors. By October 24, at the latest, *Aktionär's* Berlin correspondent could report a great change of front on the ruble market. The same groups of speculators who had asserted to high heaven their exact knowledge that the Russian currency restoration would take place at once – or in January at the latest – and who had therefore expected an exchange rate corresponding to the ruble's supposed par value had gone over bag and baggage to the opposite camp. Nobody still expected immediate introduction of the gold standard, said *Aktionär's* correspondent, hinting that his own articles had helped bring this return to good sense (October 26, 1890, p. 688).

It may seem inconsistent of Vyshnegradsky to have incited bullish speculation on the ruble by actively promoting or at least passively tolerating momentous rumors about his intentions while at the same time selling rubles to buy gold and foreign exchange. One conjecture reported in *Aktionär* was that he welcomed the rise of the ruble rate as an excuse for raising import duties; another was that he welcome the opportunity to buy gold and foreign exchange on the cheap by hanging rubles on the necks of speculators (September 7, 1890, p. 609, October 12, 1890 p. 668). In any case such apparent inconsistencies were not out of line with Vyshnegradsky's character. S. M. Propper, a Russian financial journalist, reports that Vyshnegradsky rubbed his hands in glee on this occasion at having gotten the better of the Berlin speculators. More generally, Propper described Vyshnegradsky as a friend of large-scale bourse operation. The struggle with speculators in Berlin was one of his favorite activities. He was always inventing new schemes, which were not always worthy of a finance minister (Propper 1929, p. 145).

Showing the kind of mood that Vyshnegradsky had created, *Aktionär* warned speculators on July 24, 1892 that Vyshnegradsky might be "once again preparing one of those surprises ... in which he has always shown himself such a master" (p. 427).

The episodes we have been surveying, and others, point to some generalizations that contemporary observers did in fact make. Migulin said that

> the fluctuations of the rates in the course of 1888, 1890, and 1891 [all Vyshnegradsky years] were such as to be comparable only with the fluctuations of 1877–1878 [when Russia was at war with Turkey]; moreover, they were stronger under Vyshnegradsky than during the war ... in regards to the steadying of the currency, a step backward rather than forward was taken during Vyshnegradsky's ministry in comparison with N. Kh. Bunge's ministry, since such sharp fluctuations of the rate did not occur under Bunge. (1899–1904, II, p. 504)

Fajans (1909) also judged that "Vyshnegradsky himself had a certain guilt for the size of the rate fluctuations." His fanaticism in promoting exports for the sake of an active balance of trade "drew him into the whirlpool of bourse-gaming and accordingly gave him occasion to promote a factor that impaired the stability of the rate in a high degree: ruble speculation ... the ruble gradually became a favorite object of bourse gaming, in which the Russian bank houses also and ... the Russian Finance Ministry during Vyshnegradsky's term of office zealously took part" (1909, pp. 17–19).

Under Vyshnegradsky's system, according to Tsion:

> the chief factor in the determination of the rate of the ruble became the bourse gaming, the agiotage of our Financial Administration. Thanks to this, in recent years we have witnessed a leaping of our rate completely unprecedented in Europe.

Only countries suffering from chronic revolutions and the systematic plundering of public treasuries, such as for example the South American republics, sometimes present the example of such frenzied fluctuations of the rate as the credit ruble of Autocratic Russia was subjected to during the administration of Mr. Vyshnegradsky ...

These leaps, inconceivable for the public, were caused only by bourse gaming and agiotage and proceeded not from Berlin speculators wishing to disrupt Russian trade and the Russian national economy, – but from Russia's Finance Minister, from I. A. Vyshnegradsky! (Tsion 1892, pp. 16–17)

In short, the most conspicuous fluctuations of the ruble rate did not occur in a market fully free from official manipulation. On the contrary, intervention seems at times to have incited speculation and promoted instability, just as the Big Player theory predicts. The contrast between intervention under Vyshnegradsky and non-intervention under Bunge is one piece of evidence. So is the contrast between the fluctuations of the ruble and of the Austro-Hungarian paper gulden over the same years. One among several apparent reasons why the gulden fluctuated much more mildly was its freedom from official intervention. The occasions when the gulden's fluctuations were significantly wider than usual – though still not as wide as the ruble's – were times when intervention was expected in the form of pegging onto silver or gold at an exchange rate different from the rate currently prevailing (Yeager 1969).

The ruble in 1890, as we have seen, provided a striking example of the destabilizing influence of expectations of the adoption of a metallic parity different from the currently prevailing exchange rate. Several European currencies fluctuating after the First World War – fluctuating not freely, however, but under the influence of expectations that they would sooner or later be restored to their prewar parities – provide further examples.

The behavior of the ruble under Bunge and Vyshnegradsky as chronicled above counts as evidence in favor of the general theory of Big Players. This evidence comes from books and newspapers, not from calculations with numbers. Let us now turn to some statistical evidence.[5]

The ruble and GARCH

Big Players and GARCH models

Explaining the time series behavior of asset prices and returns is a central issue in economics and finance. Investigators hope that observed empirical regularities have theoretical explanations. In its present state, however, standard theory cannot account for all the regularities that seem to exist. Standard economic theory contains predictions about the first moments of price and return distributions, but offers little with regards to explaining the behavior of second moments. Moreover, the Big Players theory makes predictions absent from standard theory, such as the increase of herding under Big Players. This section studies evidence regarding the influence of Vyshnegradsky on volatility dynamics. The following section studies evidence that he encouraged herding in the market for the ruble.

Engle's (1982) ARCH model shows that variances of asset price changes tend to run in clumps. (Engle 1982 studied inflation data. But he and others have applied his techniques to financial data. Several important articles are collected in Engle 1995.) The high-variance days are not evenly distributed across time. Instead, we see bursts of volatility separated by periods of relative calm. Bollerslev's (1986) GARCH model and its modifications are most commonly used to model volatility characteristics across numerous financial markets and assets.[6] Most of the GARCH literature, however, *describes* the characteristics of the behavior of the second moment, but does not *explain* why those characteristics exist. As Diebold and Lopez (1995) note, GARCH models "do not arise directly from economic theory."

One attempt to link GARCH processes to theoretical considerations relates to the literature on mixture of distributions. The basis of the argument is that stochastic news arrival makes asset prices move. Since the quantum of information arrival is random within any specified time frame, changes in asset prices follow a mixture of distributions process. The mixing variable in these cases is information.

Although information proxies are difficult to quantify, the most widely used proxy is volume as the mixing variable. Tauchen and Pitts (1983) use volume as the mixing variable and provide evidence that changes in asset prices follow a mixture of distributions stochastic process. Lamoreaux and Lastrapes (1993) show that if volume is the proxy for information, the existence of GARCH effects can be explained by the rate of information arrival. Hence, they provide support for the mixture of distributions hypothesis' ability to *explain* persistence in asset volatility.

However, the mixture of distributions explanation is only one argument and cannot be tested in many markets or time frames due to the lack of sufficient information proxies. Diebold and Lopez (1995) conclude that "a consensus economic model producing persistence in conditional volatility does not exist," and that "measurement is simply ahead of theory." Even if one theory could sufficiently explain the persistence volatility phenomenon, no hypotheses exist that explain *changes* in GARCH effects. The economic theory of Big Players offers one possible explanation

This chapter provides evidence that the presence of Big Players in asset markets increases the unconditional variance of asset returns as well as the persistence in their conditional variances. Although the Big Player argument may not constitute a complete, closed-form model of the second moment, it suggests a fruitful area for the theoretical explanation of volatility dynamics.

In Chapter 7, I argued that Big Players should cause both an increase in the unconditional variance of asset prices and returns as well as an increase in the persistence of that variance. Testing the implications of Big Player theory is possible if a clear case of regime shifting from less to more Big Player influence exists.

Statistical results

Broussard and Koppl (1999) analyzed Yeager's ruble data. These data are day-to-day values of the ruble exchange rate. The rates are in marks per 100 rubles. The mark was a gold-based currency at the time. Yeager took his data from reports on the Berlin market appearing in *Aktionar* and *Frankfurter Zeitung*. The data set contains all 2808 daily price changes from January 3, 1883 to March 31, 1892. The first 1225 of these price changes occurred during the Bunge period whose last day was January 12, 1887. The remaining 1583 occurred during the Vyshnegradsky period.

Figure 8.1 plots the daily exchange rate levels. As one can see, the ruble exchange rate during Bunge's period appears more stable than that found during Vyshnegradsky's regime. However, since we are dealing with the level of an asset, tests to indicate whether a unit root exists in the data must be performed. Table 8.1 reports both Augmented Dickey–Fuller and Phillips–Perron tests for the presence of non-stationary data. The results indicate that a unit root exists in the level of the exchange rate, but that first differencing yields (weak) stationarity. Therefore, the rest of the statistical analyses will be performed on the first difference of log exchange rate data.

Table 8.2 presents some general statistics on this data. The data do not appear to be skewed, but exhibit kurtosis. The data have fat tails. The LB(6), or Leung–Box autocorrelation test at 6 lags indicates dependence in the first moment, while the Lagrange Multiplier test indicates the presence of ARCH effects. The results presented in

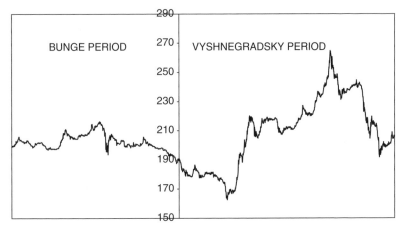

Figure 8.1 Daily exchange rate levels
The graph shows daily price levels for the ruble. The vertical line separating the two periods indicates the regime shift from Bunge to Vishnegradsky.

Table 8.1 ADF and Phillips–Perron tests

	Panel A	ADF unit root tests	
	Full period	*Bunge period*	*Vyshnegradsky period*
Level	−1.357	−1.777	−0.743
	(0.873)	(0.716)	(0.969)
First difference	−39.097	−26.377	−29.303
	(<0.0001)	(<0.0001)	(<0.0001)

	Panel B	Phillips–Perron unit root tests	
	Full period	*Bunge period*	*Vyshnegradsky period*
Level	−1.832	−1.998	−0.748
	(0.866)	(0.602)	(0.969)
First difference	−55.097	−41.309	−39.690
	(<0.0001)	(<0.0001)	(<0.0001)

Note: ADF represents the Augmented Dickey–Fuller (ADF) test (Dickey and Fuller 1979, 1981). The model estimated is $\Delta Y_t^* = a_0 + a_1 t + a_2 y_{t-1} + \Sigma c_s \Delta Y_{t-s} + u_t$. The null hypothesis is that $a_2 = 0$ vs. the alternative that $a_2 < 0$. The Phillips–Perron test (Phillips and Perron 1988) is similar, but makes corrections for serial dependence in the error term as opposed to estimating lagged dependent variables in the estimated equation. The Phillips–Perron test estimates $y_t = b_0 + b_1(t - T/2) + b_2 y_{t-1} + u_t$ and tests the null whether $b_2 = 1$ vs. the alternative $b_2 < 1$.

Table 8.2 General statistical information for ruble data

	All data	Bunge period	Vyshnegradsky period
N	2808	1225	1583
Mean	0.000014	–0.00003	0.000052
Maximum	0.03107	0.021707	0.03107
Minimum	–0.03347	–0.03347	–0.02591
Variance	0.00002	0.000011	0.000027
Skewness	–0.26287	–1.06925	–0.08402
Kurtosis	6.961972	21.18195	3.531403
Normality test	0.095***	0.838***	0.961***
LB(6) autocorrelation test	27.10***	85.85***	19.35***
LM(6) ARCH test	376.84***	225.82***	173.07***

Note: The normality test is size-dependent. If the sample size is less than 2000, the Shapiro–Wilk statistic is used. If the sample size is greater than 2000, the Kolmogorov D statistic is calculated. The LB(6) autocorrelation test is that of Ljung and Box (1978) to test for white noise of the raw data series with lag set to 6. The LM(6) proposed by Engle (1982) tests whether the squared series are correlated to lag 6.
*** significant at the 1% confidence level.

Tables 8.1 and 8.2 are further evidence that asset price changes from very different times and places all have similar distributional characteristics (Goetzmann 1993, Harrison 1996). It is nice to see these effects, because it gives an indication that if the theoretical arguments concerning Big Players provide explanatory power, even on an obscure series such as this, the theory may have implications for more recent and intensely studied series.

Figure 8.2 presents the price-change (calculated as differences in logarithms) data. Looking at the graph may cause one to suspect that the unconditional variance has increased. Overall, there seems to be more vertical movement in the latter part of the graph than in the earlier part. We test this assumption using a straightforward variance ratio test. Table 8.3 presents the results of this unconditional variance test. The test rejects the hypothesis of a constant variance at very high confidence levels. Specifically, the result indicates that the volatility found during Vyshnegradsky's regime is approximately 2.7 times higher than that exhibited during Bunge's reign as finance minister. Thus variance seems higher under Vyshnegradsky, the Big Player than under Bunge, the noninterventionist.

This result indicates that high volatility may have clouded resource allocation decisions during Vyshnegradsky's regime. In any event, it provides evidence that Big Players increase the volatility of changes in asset prices.

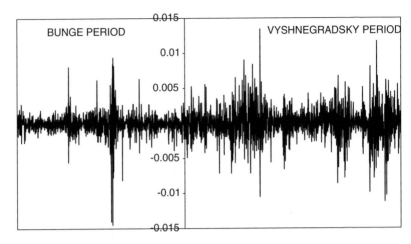

Figure 8.2   Price-change data
The graph shows daily price changes for the ruble. The vertical like separating
the two periods indicates the regime shift from Bunge to Vishnegradsky.

Table 8.3   *F* test for equal unconditional variances between Bunge and
Vyshnegradsky periods

Period	Variance	F-test[a]
Bunge	0.000011	
Vyshnegradsky	0.000027	
		2.33***

Notes: [a] *F* test examines the null hypothesis that $\sigma^2_{Bunge} = \sigma^2_{Vyshnegradsky}$ vs. the alternative
that $\sigma^2_{Bunge} < \sigma^2_{Vyshnegradsky}$.
*** Significant at the 0.0001 *p*-level.

Similarly, Figure 8.2 suggests that the correlation of conditional
volatility has also increased, because there seems to be more clumping
or clustering in volatility. The tests reported below support this view.
To test our hypothesis that Big Players increase the correlation of conditional variance, we fit a both a traditional and a modified
GARCH(1,1) model to the data. The modification consists in the addition of a dummy interaction term.

A traditional GARCH (1,1) model is given by

$$y_t = e_t, \tag{8.1}$$

$$e|\Omega \sim N(0,h_t) \tag{8.2}$$

$$h_t = \omega + \alpha_1 e_{t-1}^2 + \beta_1 h_{t-1} \tag{8.3}$$

$$\omega > 0; \alpha_i \geq 0, \ \beta_i \geq 0, \ \text{and} \ \alpha_1 + \beta_1 < 1 \tag{8.4}$$

Broussard and Koppl adapted this model to account for the effects of a change in regime by adding dummy-interaction terms as follows

$$h_t = \omega + \alpha_1 e_{t-1}^2 + \beta_1 h_{t-1} + \alpha_1^d \ d_{t-1} e_{t-1}^2 + \beta_1^d \ d_{t-1} h_{t-1} \tag{8.5}$$

where $d_{t-1} = 1$ for the Vyshnegradsky period and 0 for the Bunge period.

The results reported in Tables 8.4 and 8.5 are consistent with their hypothesis. Panel A of Table 8.4 estimates a GARCH(1,1) model for the Bunge data period. The parameters on the lagged innovations and the lagged conditional variance are statistically significant. The half-life of a shock to the system lasts approximately 6.5 days during Bunge's regime. Panel B, on the other hand, indicates that volatility persistence increased during Vyshnegradsky's period. The half-life of a shock to the system is increased to 57.4 days. Therefore, persistence in conditional volatility appears to have increased during the interventionist's reign.

Table 8.5 presents similar evidence, only this time, the modified GARCH(1,1) model is employed to test whether a structural shift in the data occurred. During the Vyshnegradsky period, the persistence component of conditional variance increased from 0.66 to 0.75, as

Table 8.4   Parameter estimates from a traditional GARCH(1,1) model with no dummy interaction variables
The particular model estimated was:
$h_t = \omega + \alpha \ e_{t-1}^2 + \beta h_{t-1}$

		Panel A *Bunge period*			
	ω	α	β	$\alpha + \beta$	HL
Estimate	9.52e-7	0.229	0.670	0.899	6.5
Std error	1.35e-7	0.0243	0.0343		
Probability	<0.0001	<0.0001	<0.0001		

		Panel B *Vyshnegradsky period*			
	ω	α	β	$\alpha + \beta$	HL
Estimate	9.31e-7	0.229	0.759	0.988	57.4
Std error	1.84e-7	0.022	0.021		
Probability	<0.0001	<0.0001	<0.0001		

Table 8.5   Parameter estimates from GARCH(1,1) model with dummy interaction variables on the conditional squared error term and conditional variance term
The model estimated was:
$$h_t = \omega + \alpha_1 e_{t-1}^2 + \beta_1 h_{t-1} + \alpha_1 d\, d_{t-1} e_{t-1}^2 + \beta_1^d d_{t-1} h_{t-1}$$

	Parameter est.	Standard error	T-stat	Prob.
ω	0	0	8.9	0
α	0.235	0.23	10.2	0
β	0.663	0.28	23.3	0
α^d	−0.004	0.03	−0.14	0.888
β^d	0.09	0.026	3.50	0.0005

evidenced by the estimate of the value of the dummy variable. During Vyshnegradsky's reign, Big Player influence affected not only the overall variance of ruble price changes, but also how that variance changed through time. The economic significance of our result is that Vyshnegradsky's interventionist policies affected traders who attached more meaning to large recent, or transient, price movements.

There is evidence that the increase in Big Player influence resulting from Vyshnegradsky's replacement of Bunge produced the expected result. The unconditional variance of volatility seems to have gone up as does the persistence of conditional volatility. Current theories of asset prices do not restrict the behavior of conditional volatility. But the fact of GARCH effects has been well documented. Broussard and Koppl have shown that the theory of Big Players has testable implications for the behavior of conditional volatility.

R/S analysis

Persistent dependence as a consequence of herding

The evidence suggests that Bunge was not a Big Player but that his successor, Vyshnegradsky, was. According to my theory then, there should have been more herding or follow-the-leader or "mimetic contagion" (Topol 1991) under Vyshnegradsky than under Bunge. To test this conjecture statistically, Koppl and Yeager (1996) used R/S analysis to measure the "persistence," or "memory", in exchange rates under the two regimes.

Herd behavior should generate "persistent dependence" in time-series data generated by financial markets. This statistical concept is explained below. Together with the use of R/S analysis as a test, it was developed by the hydrologist H. E. Hurst (Hurst *et al.* 1965), by Benoit

Mandelbrot (1971, 1972), and by Mandelbrot and Wallis (1968, 1969a, 1969b). (Mirowski 1990 contains interesting historical notes.) Persistent dependence in time-series data creates "aperiodic cycles," irregular ups and downs in the data that cannot be attributed to "short-period" autocorrelation.

Persistent dependence or memory in a stationary time series is simply the failure of the autocorrelations to die off quickly, i.e. at least exponentially. The influence of each innovation "persists" indefinitely. Such a time series is not ergodic. When a time series has a long memory, it will swing up and down about its long-term expected value in irregular waves or "aperiodic cycles." If a positive (negative) innovation in any one period tends to produce positive (negative) innovations in later periods, there is "positive persistence." In this case the waves will be longer, on average, than the pseudo-cycles of a white-noise process. Graphs of the time series will undulate too much to have been generated by white noise. If a positive (negative) innovation in any one period tends to produce negative (positive) innovations in later periods, there is "negative persistence." In this case the aperiodic cycles will be shorter on average than the pseudo-cycles of a white-noise process. In this case the graph of the time series will be too spiky to have been generated by white noise. (See the graphs in Mandelbrot 1972.) The aperiodic cycles created by persistent dependence are just these too-undulant or too-spiky pseudo-cycles in the graph of the time series.

Hurst (1965) performed an experiment with playing cards that nicely illustrates the nature of positive persistence – the case of interest to us. He relabeled the 52 cards with the numbers +1, −1, +3, −3, +5, −5, +7, and −7 in proportions designed to approximate a normal distribution. He then shuffled the deck and picked a card at random by cutting the deck. After writing down the number of the card turned over, +5 for example, he shuffled the deck again and dealt out two hands of 26 cards each. He then biased one of hands by replacing some of its cards according to the number written down earlier. In our example the number was +5, so Hurst would have created the biased hand by removing the five lowest cards and replacing them with the five highest cards of the other hand. The final step in preparing the biased hand was adding a joker. Hurst would repeatedly shuffle the biased hand, cut it, and record the number of the card turned over. This shuffling and cutting would go on until the joker came up, at which point a new biased hand would be created and the process repeated. The sequence of values generated through this experiment was characterized by persistent dependence and aperiodic cycles.

Hurst's experiment provides a nice metaphor for the bubbles created by herding in asset markets. Something causes an asset's price to rise. Herding transforms this price hike into an upward trend. Though the asset's price is going up and down, movements up tend to be larger and more frequent. The trend has no internal tendency to weaken and will thus continue indefinitely. Finally, some chance event such as a rumor about the plans of the finance minister will, like the drawing of the joker, remove the bias and a new trend in the same or the opposite direction will kick in. Over sufficiently long stretches the biases tend to cancel out and the asset tracks its fundamental value. But deviations from trend tend to form and to persist. Note that the length of time a bubble may be expected to continue does not depend on how old the bubble is, so it is hard to know when to jump off the bandwagon. Since the autocorrelations die off slowly, the trend is your friend even on rather long views. Thus, if the market's tendency toward herding is strong enough, even traders who prefer to analyze the fundamentals have good reason to ride the bandwagon.

The joker in this story need not always be the Big Player. While some action of his may cause a change in trend, other events too can play this role. The rise of the ruble in the fall of 1890 seems to have been driven entirely by the rumor that Vyshnegradsky was going to peg the ruble to gold at the old parity. Apparently his buying and selling had nothing to do with it. Of course his actions did matter in another sense. He created the rumor in the first place, or at least did not squelch it. The Big Player need not play even this indirect role in creating a wave of optimism or pessimism. The Big Player creates an atmosphere in which it is sensible to follow trends and dangerous to buck them. This will create herding and aperiodic cycles. Some changes in trend will be directly attributable to actions (or inactions) of the Big Player, others will not.

This story about how asset markets work in the presence of Big Players bears some similarity to Keynes' description of the stock market. In this story, as with Keynes, waves of optimism and pessimism "which are unreasoning and yet in a sense legitimate" (1936, p. 154) create fluctuations of price unrelated to changes in the fundamentals. In the Big Players' theory too, such movements are possible only because of the market participants' necessary ignorance of the future. But there is an important difference. In Keynes's view, "These tendencies are a scarcely avoidable outcome of our having successfully organised 'liquid' investment markets" (1936, p. 159). In my view bubbles have more to do with the role of Big Players than liquidity. While it seems unlikely that herding should ever disappear completely, we should expect more of it when Big Players exert their influence and less of it when they are absent.

Persistent dependence in past studies of asset markets

Persistent dependence has been found in foreign exchange markets (Booth *et al.* 1981, 1982), the New York Stock Exchange (Greene and Fielitz 1977, Peters 1989), the commodity futures market (Helms *et al.* 1984), gold and silver spot markets (Booth and Kaen 1979), Treasury-bond returns (Peters 1989), and sports scores (Hurst *et al.* 1965). The phenomenon of memory in asset-market time series tends to contradict martingale models. Thus, it is important to develop and test models of this phenomenon.

As far as I know the only explanation of persistent dependence in asset prices is that of Kaen and Rosenman (1986) who were building on Heiner (1983). This chapter has some close similarities to the analysis of Kaen and Rosenman. But my objectives are not the same. Kaen and Rosenman were trying to explain persistence as such, not the effects of Big Players. As befits their purpose, they do not offer any testable hypotheses about when the degree of persistence should be greater and when less. Nor do they develop the connection between herding and persistence. (But they do mention it briefly.) Thus, while my use of R/S analysis owes much to their example and might be viewed as something of an extension or development of their ideas, the theoretical and empirical content of our argument is distinct from theirs.

R/S analysis as a test for persistent dependence

Today's most popular techniques of times–series analysis assume that the series under study has a "short memory." They assume, that is, that the autocorrelation between X_t and X_{t+k}, $\rho(k)$, declines rapidly as k goes to infinity. The decline in the correlation is rapid when

$$|\rho(k)| \le Cr^{-k} \tag{8.6}$$

where C is positive and r is between zero and 1 (Brockwell and Davis 1991, p. 520). When this condition fails, the series is characterized by "memory," "persistence," "persistent dependence," or, as Mandelbrot and Wallis put it, the Joseph Effect. ("Behold, there come seven years of great plenty ... And there shall arise after them seven years of famine", Genesis 41:29.) The presence of persistence is consistent with both short-term autocorrelation and its absence. I do not assume any particular functional form for $\rho(k)$.

R/S analysis tests for persistence assuming the series is "stationary" in the sense that the expected value of any function of $\{X_t\}$ is the same for $\{X_{t-k}\}$. Recall that the tests reported in Table 8.1 are consistent with the hypothesis of weak stationarity. Let us consider such a series $\{X_t\}$ for which we have a sample of size T. The cumulative sum of the series, $X^*(t)$, is just the sum of the values up to t:

$$X^*(t) = \sum_{u=1}^{t} X_u \tag{8.7}$$

where $t \geq 1$. For $t = 0$ we define $X^*(t) = 0$. For any interval of length s beginning at t, the range of the interval is

$$R(t,s) = \max_{0 \leq u \leq s} \{X^*(t + u) - X^*(t) - (u/s)[X^*(t + s) - X^*(t)]\}$$

$$= \min_{0 \leq u \leq s} \{X^*(t + u) - X^*(t) - (u/s)[X^*(t + s) - X^*(t)]\} \tag{8.8}$$

To rescale the range, divide through by the sample standard deviation, $S(t,s)$, of the original series $\{X_t\}$, where

$$S^2(t,s) = s^{-1} \sum_{u=1}^{s} \{X_{t+u} - s^{-1}[X^*(t + s) - X^*(t)]\}^2$$

$$= [s^{-1} \sum_{u=1}^{s} X^2_{t+u}] - [s^{-1} \sum_{u=1}^{s} X_{t+u}]^2 \tag{8.9}$$

and $S(t,s) = \sqrt{S^2(t,s)}$.

The rescaled range, R/S, is just the ratio $R(t,s)/S(t,s)$. The expected value of the rescaled range is independent of t because the series $\{X_t\}$ is stationary. It is not, however, independent of s. The rescaled range can only grow with the length of the sample. (This will be more obvious when we turn to the graphical representation of R/S analysis.) Its asymptotic rate of growth, moreover, is a measure of the degree of persistent dependence. Mandelbrot and Wallis (1969a, 1969b) report that R/S is asymptotically proportional to a fractional power of interval length. That is,

$$R(t,s)/S(t,s) \sim Cs^h \tag{8.10}$$

where $C > 0$ and $0 < h < 1$. The Hurst coefficient, h, is a measure of persistence. If $h = 0.5$, there is no persistence. If $h > 0.5$ there is positive persistence and if $h < 0.5$, there is negative persistence.

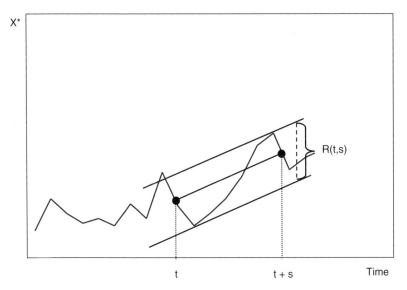

Figure 8.3   R/S analysis

Figure 8.3 illustrates R/S analysis. X^* is plotted on the vertical axis and time is plotted on the horizontal analysis. The line showing the cumulative values of X_t goes up and down because $\{X_t\}$ is stationary with some values positive and some negative. The range, $R(t,s)$, of an interval is the vertical distance between two straight lines tangent to the cumulative series and parallel to the straight line connecting $X^*(t)$ and $X^*(t + s)$. The range just measures how much the cumulative series deviates from trend over an interval. The rescaled range adjusts this figure to correct for the size of the variance of the original series over the interval.

The Hurst coefficient, h, measures the rate at which the rescaled range of the cumulative series grows with interval length. If the original series is white noise, this growth rate is 0.5. Even if there is autocorrelation, the asymptotic rate of growth is still 0 5 as long as the correlellogram dies off "quickly." If there is positive persistence, then deviations from trend tend to persist. In this case, the rate at which the rescaled range grows with interval length will exceed the rate given by chance: $h > 0.5$. Similarly, if there is negative persistence, then deviations from trend tend to be reversed more promptly than chance alone would have implied. In this case the rescaled range of the cumulative series will grow more slowly than the rate given by chance: $h < 0.5$.

If an asset's price is subject to bubbles because of herding occasioned by Big Players, then there should be positive persistence in the time series of its price. The measured value of the Hurst coefficient should exceed 0.5. The greater the influence of Big Players, the larger the Hurst coefficient will be, *ceteris paribus*. Big Players are not the only reason for herding and thus persistence to exist. But their presence should increase the degree of persistence. The results of the next section tend to support this conclusion.

Statistical results

Koppl and Yeager used the classical Hurst. The classical Hurst has been criticized by Lo (1991). I prefer it to Lo's technique, however, for the reasons given in Ahmed *et al.* (1997, pp. 30–31). I review them in the next two paragraphs.

Lo argues that the classical Hurst may mistake short-term dependence for long-term dependence. His result, however, depends on the existence of second and fourth moments. Mandelbrot (1997) continues to argue against the existence of second moments in financial time series even though his stable Paretian hypothesis is not widely accepted. Loretan and Phillips (1994) show that fourth moments may be asymptotically infinite in stock market data. Hiemstra (1993) shows that Lo's critique does not hold up under these conditions.

Finally, we are looking for evidence of herding, not necessarily long-term memory. What is significant for us is the increase in persistence, be it long-term or short-term. Thus, we have no need to be concerned if our technique may sometimes mistake short-term dependence for long-term dependence. The implication for herding is unchanged.

To estimate separately the value of the Hurst coefficient, h, under Bunge and Vyshnegradsky, Yeager and I divided our data set into two pieces, an initial segment corresponding to Bunge's tenure and a final segment for the Vyshnegradsky years. We estimated the Hurst coefficient separately for each period. Our data consisted of daily price changes of the ruble against the German mark. Our prices are quoted in German marks per 100 rubles in Russian banknotes. (The mark was a gold-standard currency at the time.) The rates were compiled from *Aktionär* and *Frankfurter Zeitung*, contemporary German newspapers. We calculated the "percentage" change of each trading day's rate from the previous rate as the difference of the natural logarithms. For the Bunge years we have approximately 1200 data points and for the Vyshnegradsky years we have approximately 1500 data points. In both cases there are no gaps in the data. We used an estimating technique explained in Wallis and Matalas (1970).

As we have seen, Wallis and Matalas report that

$$R(t,s)/S(t,s) \sim Cs^h \tag{8.11}$$

Taking the natural logarithm of each side of this equation gives us

$$\ln(R/S) = \ln(C) + h^*\ln(s) \tag{8.12}$$

The coefficients of this equation can be estimated by ordinary least squares regression if the value of R/S is calculated for at least two intervals of different length. The more intervals for which the value of R/S is known, the more precise the coefficient estimates are likely to be.[7] But trying to use too many intervals can impose high costs of calculation. Thus, there is a tradeoff in deciding how to pick intervals.

Wallis and Matalas recommend an "F Hurst" and a "G Hurst" technique for picking intervals. They found that, for the computer-generated series they used in their simulation study, other procedures "led to larger biases and variances than F Hurst and G Hurst" (Wallis and Matalas 1970, p. 1590).

F Hurst uses all possible intervals except those of length five and below. As Wallis and Matalas note, for big data sets such as we are using "an enormous amount of computation is involved" (1970, p. 1586). Koppl and Yeager used instead G Hurst, which selects a large, but not prohibitively large, set of intervals ranging in length from 10 to 1000 (or the length on one's data set if it is less than 1000).

The G Hurst technique has two variants. GH(10) calculates R/S for 39 interval lengths between 10 and 1000 inclusive. For each of these interval lengths, the technique selects up to 15 evenly spaced intervals of that length, calculates R/S for each such interval, and then averages them to arrive at one, average, R/S value for the interval length. The R/S values for each interval length are then regressed against their corresponding interval lengths using ordinary least squares regression. Since the number of R/S values averaged together shrinks as interval length grows, this averaging procedure has the desirable effect of reducing the influence on the coefficient estimates of the short intervals where low-order autocorrelation may be at work (Wallis and Matalas 1970, p. 1587).

GH(50) is like GH(10) except that it uses only interval lengths of 50 and above. Ignoring the short intervals reduces the chance that one's

Table 8.6   Estimated values of the Hurst coefficient
(Standard errors are in parentheses)

	Bunge years	*Vyshnegradsky years*
GH(10)	0.672	0.732
	(0.014)	(0.006)
GH(50)	0.595	0.715
	(0.025)	(0.011)

estimate will be biased by short-term autocorrelation, but it reduces the number of observations used in the linear regression of R/S on *s*. There is no telling how this tradeoff works in our case, so Koppl and Yeager calculated both GH(10) and GH(50) estimates of *h*. Their results are reported in Table 8.6

Table 8.6 shows that measured persistence is greater during the Vyshnegradsky years. The relatively low numbers for the Bunge period may be too high and the relatively high numbers for the Vyshnegradsky period may be too low. Wallis and Matalas report on the different estimation biases of G Hurst as do Booth *et al.* (1982). The most important result for interpreting our data was discovered by Wallis and Matalas. Their simulations suggest that when *h* is less than 0.7, estimated values tend to be too high; when *h* is more than 0.7, estimated values tend to be too low (Wallis and Matalas 1970, pp. 1593 and 1594).

Chow tests suggest that the measured differences between the two regimes studied did not arise from chance variations in our samples. For both the GH(10) and the GH(50) regressions Yeager and I ran two sets of tests. In one case, we tested the hypothesis that both slope and intercept were the same in the two regimes. For this hypothesis the *F* ratios were approximately 65 (for the GH(10) regression) and 51 (for the GH(50) regression). Both ratios are well above the 1 per cent critical values of about 5. The other pair of Chow tests tested the hypothesis that the only the slopes were the same in the two regimes. This may be a more appropriate test since changes in the intercept have no particular bearing on our results, whereas the slope is our measure of persistence. For this weaker hypothesis the F ratios were approximately 15 for both the GH(10) and GH(50) regressions. This value is well above the 1 per cent critical values of about 7. For both sets of tests, and both sets of estimates then, the Chow-test procedures imply that we may quite confidently reject the hypothesis of no change between the

Bunge and Vyshnegradsky regimes. In this sense, our results are statistically significant.

Koppl and Yeager's results may help account for the difficulty of "explaining" exchange rates in the short to medium run (cf. Meese 1990). Even though the fundamentals may override the influence of Big Players in the long run, animal spirits, herding, and rumors may drive markets in the short run. These things are difficult to "explain" econometrically. Furthermore, a Big Player's activity may have consequences even outside its own immediate arena. Even though, for example, a government allows its fiat currency to float freely against other currencies, if it pursues discretionary and changeable monetary policies for domestic purposes, traders' efforts to fathom its intentions may produce herding in the foreign-exchange market. These considerations tend to support rules over discretion in policymaking. (See Kydland and Prescott 1977, Yeager 1981 for discussion of rules versus discretion.)

9

The Angular Distribution of Asset Returns in Delay Space[1]

In Chapter 7 I reported on a GARCH study of Yeager's ruble data. At least two considerations limit the value of that study. First, the GARCH model assumes that the underlying error term is normally distributed. But, as Broussard and Koppl (1999) report, Yeager's ruble returns exhibit kurtosis. The distribution of returns has fat tails; it is not a normal distribution. Second, the model assumes the data are continuous, not discrete. But the ruble data are discrete. The price of hundred-ruble notes moved in jumps of 0.05 marks. It is possible to overcome these two difficulties with non-parametric tools designed to handle discrete data. This chapter reports on a test for herding and contra-herding that uses such tools. It builds on Crack and Ledoit's (1996) analysis of the "compass rose."

Crack and Ledoit (1996) plot daily stock returns against themselves with one day's lag. Doing so produces the "compass rose" pattern of Figures 9.1 and 9.2. The points of the graph are concentrated along several evenly spaced rays from the origin. The rays corresponding to the major directions of the compass accumulate the most points. This "strikingly geometrical" pattern "is indisputably present in every stock." The existence of a non-zero tick size produces discreteness in the data which, in turn, generates the compass rose.

The compass rose biases some standard statistical tools of financial analysis. The Monte Carlo study of Kramer and Runde (1997) proves that the BDS test will falsely indicate chaotic structure when applied to discrete data. The larger the (simulated) tick size, the greater this false propensity of the BDS test. Crack and Ledoit (1996) conjecture that discreteness biases the standard tests for autoregressive conditional hetero-skedasticity (ARCH). Apparently, financial researchers cannot rely on the statistical tools most commonly used to study volatility dynamics.

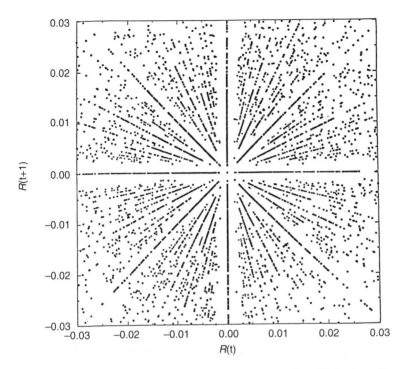

Figure 9.1 Daily returns for Weyerhauser stock on the NYSE, December 1963–December 1993
The horizontal axis shows a given day's return for Weyerhauser stock on the New York Stock Exchange (NYSE). The vertical axis shows the next day's return.

Surprisingly, Crack and Ledoit do not call for new tools of time series analysis specifically suited to the existence of ticks and of the compass rose pattern. They seem to have assumed objective tools of analysis cannot be created for use on the compass rose. Their explanation of the pattern uses "subjective language," they report, "because the above statement 'the compass rose appears clearly' is itself subjective" (1996, p. 754). This reasoning is not persuasive. If our current tools are biased, we should try to create new "objective" tools that are not biased by discreteness.

Chen (1997) takes a step in that direction by using the information in the compass rose to construct improved forecasts within an ARMA–GARCH framework. He reports improved forecasts in all cases. If Chen's result is sustained by future studies, it will contradict Crack and Ledoit's conjecture that the compass rose "cannot be used for predictive purposes," because "it is an artifact of market microstructure"

(1996, p. 751). Chen's forecasting algorithm corrects for discreteness, at least partly. His GARCH coefficient estimates, however, do not. Chen's ARMA–GARCH models, therefore, are subject to the same discreteness-induced biases likely to affect other ARCH techniques.

New objective techniques can be devised which are not biased by discreteness and are suitable for the compass rose. Plotting the number of points along a given ray of the compass rose against the angle of that ray creates a "theta histogram" which describes the angular distribution of the points in delay space. This distribution can be compared to a standard theta histogram created by a simple bootstrap procedure. A χ^2 test is then performed in order to estimate quantitatively the consistency of the actual data with the standard theta histogram. Other hypotheses can be tested using the Bernoulli distribution.

The tests reported below suggest that returns on stocks and other assets have a greater tendency to accumulate along the main diagonals of the compass rose than they would if they were statistically independent. An X pattern is embedded within the compass rose. In this sense, there are typically "too many" points along the main diagonals of the compass rose. This X pattern skews the compass rose away from the pattern that would exist if returns were statistically independent. We may call this pattern "X-skewing." A simple simulation shows that X-skewing of the compass rose can cause standard tests to indicate autocorrelation in conditional heteroskedasticity even when the underlying stochastic process is not consistent with standard ARCH models. X-skewing of the compass rose is a product of human actions that are subject to economic influences. The policy regime governing an asset market helps determine how much the compass rose is skewed. In particular, Big Players induce X-skewing.

The compass rose

Crack and Ledoit (1996) chronicle the (brief) history of the compass rose in finance. Huang and Stoll (1994) explain in a footnote that a graph of intra-day returns plotted against themselves with a five-minute lag shows "clusters of points that radiate from the zero" (Huang and Stoll 1994, p. 199, as quoted in Crack and Ledoit 1996, p. 753). They do not pursue the issue, however.

Brealy and Meyers (1991) plot daily Weyerhauser stock returns against themselves with one day's lag (13–2, p. 293). They said "it is obvious from a glance that there is very little pattern in these price movements" (1991, p. 291). Crack and Ledoit showed, however, that

Brealy and Meyers did "overlook a *significant* pattern," namely, the compass rose (1996, p. 752; emphasis in original). Brealy and Meyers would have seen the compass rose if they had used more data and a better graphical package. In the next edition of their textbook, Brealy and Meyers (1996) replace their earlier graph with Crack and Ledoit's Figure 2 (our Figure 9.1) and include a footnote explaining the compass rose. They still say, however, "it is obvious from a glance that there is very little pattern in these price movements" (1996, p. 326). The sentence continues "but we can test this more precisely by calculating the coefficient of correlation between each day's price change and the next" (1996, p. 326). Brealy and Meyers thus neglect the difference between correlation and statistical dependence. As shown below, they overlook a significant pattern, as do Crack and Ledoit. That pattern is X-skewing. Like the ARCH behavior to which it is related, X-skewing is a case of statistical dependence without linear correlation.

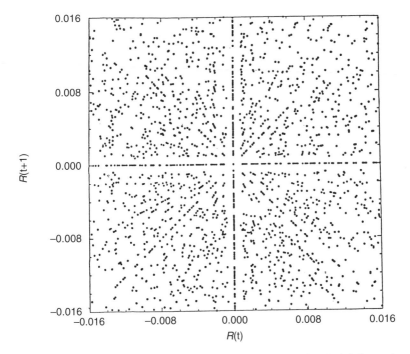

Figure 9.2 Crack and Ledoit's (1986) "compass rose" graph for IBM daily stock returns, January 1, 1980–October 8, 1992

Crack and Ledoit list three conditions for the compass rose pattern to emerge: daily price changes are small relative to the price level; daily price changes are in discrete jumps of a small number of ticks; and the price varies over a relatively wide range. The explanation of these three conditions is straightforward. Following their notation, let P_t and R_t be the price and return of some stock on day t.

If price changes are small relative to price level ($(P_t - P_{t-1}) \ll P_t$), and ignoring dividends and splits, the following approximation holds:

$$\frac{R_{t+1}}{R_t} = \frac{(P_{t+1} - P_t)/P_t}{(P_t - P_{t-1})/P_{t-1}} \approx \frac{(P_{t+1} - P_t)}{(P_t - P_{t-1})} = \frac{n_{t+1}h}{n_t h} = \frac{n_{t+1}}{n_t} \tag{9.1}$$

where h is the tick size and $n_t = (P_t - P_{t-1})/h$ is the day-t price change calculated in ticks. Equation (9.1) shows that the ordered pairs (R_t, R_{t+1}) will be close to the rays through the origin that pass through (n_t, n_{t+1}).

If prices usually change by a small number of ticks, then most points will accumulate along the major directions of the compass rose. The ticks that induce discreteness need not be official. As Crack and Ledoit (1996) explain, an official tick size is neither necessary nor sufficient for the compass rose. "The correct criterion for the existence of the compass rose is whether the effective tick size is of the same order of magnitude as typical price changes" (1996, p. 758).

Finally, Crack and Ledoit explain, if the price varied only slightly around the value P_t, a grid pattern would result, not the compass rose. "On any given ray (m, n) data points would cluster at discrete distances from the origin: $(mh/P_t, nh/P_t)$, $(2mh/P_t, 2nh/P_t)$, and so on" (1996, p. 754). Price variations produce "centrifugal smudging" which, in turn, produces the compass rose pattern.

Hypothesis testing with theta histograms

Crack and Ledoit describe the compass rose pattern as "subjective." It is possible, however, to transform the data of the compass rose and apply objective techniques to them. The transformation we propose is the result of a two-step procedure. First, express the points of the compass rose in polar coordinates. The point (R_t, R_{t+1}) becomes (r_t, θ_t) where

$$r_t = \sqrt{R_t^2 + R_{t+1}^2}$$

$$\theta_t = \begin{cases} \arctan(R_{t+1}/R_t) & \text{if } R_t \geq 0, \\ \arctan(R_{t+1}/R_t) + \pi & \text{if } R_t < 0, R_{t+1} \geq 0, \\ \arctan(R_{t+1}/R_t) - \pi & \text{if } R_t, R_{t+1} < 0, (9.2) \end{cases} \tag{9.2}$$

(arctan conventionally ranges from $-\pi/2$ to $\pi/2$).

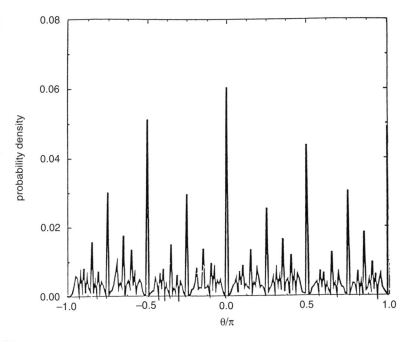

Figure 9.3 "Theta histogram" (angular distribution in delay space) of Weyerhauser stock returns

Second, associate each θ_t not with any of the corresponding r_t values but with the number of such values corresponding to a narrow interval around θ_t. Finally, normalize by π in order to plot histograms in the interval $[-1,1]$. Call the result a "theta histogram." A theta histogram represents the angular distribution of asset returns in delay space.

Figure 9.3 illustrates. The horizontal axis shows the value of θ/π. The θ/π values have been partitioned into 201 bins of width 0.01. (Details are in Koppl and Nardone 2001.) The vertical axis shows the relative frequency of points in each bin. For each θ/π value, it shows the number of points in that bin divided by the total number of points.

The theta histogram just described is an empirical theta histogram. Before we can engage in hypothesis testing, we need a benchmark with which to compare it. A simple bootstrap creates such a benchmark. To construct a bootstrapped theta histogram, one takes the observed relative frequency of each return in the data under study. Assume each period's return was draw from this distribution, and assume every period's return

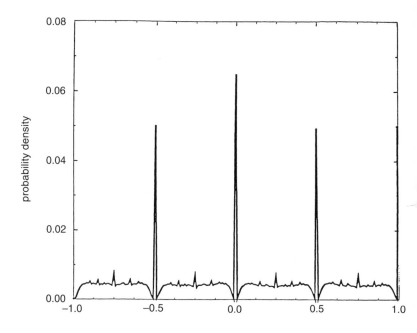

Figure 9.4   Bootstrapped theta histogram created using the data used to construct Figure 9.3

is independent of every other period. Repeated sampling (with replacement) from the empirical distribution of asset returns allows one to generate a bootstrapped theta histogram. Figure 9.4 illustrates.

Hypothesis tests can be conducted by comparing the empirical and bootstrapped theta histograms. The null hypothesis, H_0, is that the R_t are statistically independent. Under the null hypothesis, some values of R_{t+1}/R_t are more likely than others. If we had an infinite pool of identically, independently distributed returns, each ratio R_{t+1}/R_t would have a given relative frequency. Thus, each corresponding θ value would have its relative frequency. For a given distribution, statistical independence implies a certain relative frequency of "hits" for each ray of the compass rose; it implies a certain profile for the theta histogram. If the observed relative frequencies of a sample are close to the hypothetical values, we have no reason to reject the null hypothesis of statistical independence. If, on the other hand, the observed relative frequencies of some sample were sufficiently far from the hypothetical values, we should reject the null hypothesis.

An unrealistically simple hypothetical example provides an easy illustration. Assume we had a sample of 100 returns in which one half of the returns were 0.001 and the other half were 0.002. Under the null hypothesis of statistical independence, we would expect about half the points of the compass rose to fall along the 45-degree line, i.e. the ray bisecting the positive quadrant. For this ray, $\theta/\pi = 0.25$. The remaining points would be about evenly split between the rays at $\theta/\pi = 0.125$ and $\theta/\pi = 0.375$, i.e. those at 22.5 degrees and 67.5 degrees. The bootstrapped theta histogram of our sample would have three spikes. The relative frequency for the spike at $\theta/\pi = 0.25$ would be one-half. The relative frequency for the other two spikes would be one-fourth each.

Since our hypothetical sample contains 100 returns, it gives us 99 points of the compass rose. Assume we observed, say, 45 points at $\theta/\pi = 0.25$, 26 at $\theta/\pi = 0.125$, and 28 at $\theta/\pi = 0.375$. In this case, the empirical theta histogram would be similar to the bootstrapped theta histogram. We would have no cause to reject the null hypothesis. The tests we describe below would not reject H_0 for this sample. A different sample, however, might yield a different result. We would reject the null if the original returns had come in the following sequence: 0.001, 0.002, 0.001, 0.002, ... In this case statistical dependence is obviously present. The empirical theta histogram would have one spike of approximate length one half at $\theta/\pi = 0.125$ and another of the about same length at $\theta/\pi = 0.375$. (Details are in Koppl and Nardone 2001.) The compass rose would have no points along the 45-degree line instead of the 50 or so to be expected under the null hypothesis. The tests we describe below would reject H_0 for this sample.

In the example just given, statistical dependence caused us to reject H_0. The statistical dependence considered would also have shown up as (negative) linear correlation. But correlation and dependence are distinct. If a sufficiently large fraction of the points of the compass rose accumulate along the main diagonals, forming an X pattern, there is statistical dependence, but zero correlation. As shown below, X-skewing exists in the data. A more careful explanation of the test follows.

Let n be the number of observations. That is, n is the number of R_{t+1}/R_t ratios in our sample and $n + 1$ is the number of returns. (Now, n_t is no longer being used to denote the number of ticks by which price moved on day t.) Consider a narrow interval of a ray θ/π, namely, $\omega \pm \delta\omega$. Let p be the relative frequency of points in that interval under H_0. One reads p off of the bootstrapped theta histogram. Given the sample size n and the null hypothesis of independence, the expected number of points in ω is np. Let k denote the observed number of points in the interval. Define χ^2_{obs} as follows:

$$\chi^2_{obs} \equiv \sum_\omega \frac{(k - np)^2}{np} \tag{9.3}$$

where $\sum_\omega k = n$. Assuming H_0, in the limit of a large number υ of partitions, the complement cumulative distribution of χ^2_{obs} is $Q(\chi^2|\upsilon)$, an incomplete gamma function (Press *et al.* 1992). Selecting the customary confidence level of 0.05, we reject H_0 if

$$P(\chi^2 \geq \chi^2_{obs}) \equiv Q(\chi^2|\nu) = \frac{1}{\Gamma(\chi^2_{obs})} \int_\nu^\infty e^{-t} t^{(\chi^2_{obs} - 1)} dt < 0.05 \tag{9.4}$$

where $\Gamma(x)$ is the gamma function.

This χ^2 test probes the distribution as a whole. One may wish to know, however, if a particular ray or subset of rays of the compass rose has more (or fewer) points than would be expected under the null hypothesis of statistical independence. For example, to test for X-skewing we want to know, in effect, if the four rays making up the main diagonals of the compass rose have collected "too many" points. Let us consider the test as it would apply to one ray. The extension to groups of rays will be obvious. Consider, then, the interval $\omega \pm \delta\omega$. We can easily determine the relative frequency of theta histograms of size n for which the number of hits in that interval, k, is at least equal to the number, h, observed in our sample. Assuming H_0, we have a sequence of Bernoulli trials in which the probability of a hit is p. For every integer k such that $0 \leq k \leq n$, there are $C(k,n) \equiv n!/[k!(n - k)!]$ ways you could get k hits. The probability of exactly k hits is $C(k,n) p^k (1 - p)^{(n-k)}$. Thus, the probability of $k \geq h$ is

$$P(k \geq h) \equiv B(h) = \sum_{k=h}^n C(k,h) p^k (1 - p)^{(n-k)} \tag{9.5}$$

We reject H_0 if $P(k \geq h) < 0.05$.

Nardone and I used our tests on the Weyerhauser data studied by Crack and Ledoit (1996). We used CRSP data on daily returns from the period studied by Crack and Ledoit, namely, December 6, 1963 to December 31, 1993. This gives us 7559 returns and 7558 points of the compass rose. As explained earlier, our data are partitioned into 201 bins of width 0.01. Comparing Figure 9.3 and Figure 9.4 suggests that the empirical and bootstrapped theta histograms are not the same. It appears that the two histograms are significantly different and that the empirical histogram shows more points at the values ± 0.75 and ± 0.25. These are the values that correspond to the main diagonals of the compass rose.

The χ^2 test shows that Weyerhauser returns are not independent. The number of degrees of freedom, v, is equal to the number of bins, 201. Since v is large, we could rely on the asymptotic distribution to carry out our test. We have

$$P(\chi^2 > \chi^2_{obs}) \equiv Q(\chi^2_{obs}|v) \approx Q(x) \equiv 1/\sqrt{2\pi} \int_x^\infty e^{(-t^2/2)} dt \qquad (9.6)$$

where $x = \sqrt{2\chi^2_{obs}} - \sqrt{2v-1}$ (Abramovitz and Stegun 1972, formula 26.4.13). The χ^2 test is reported in Table 9.1. For this data, $\chi^2_{obs} = 5019.2$, which is much greater than the expected value of 201. The reduced normal variable $x = 80.2$. Thus, we can again use an asymptotic formula for large x (Abramovitz and Stegun 1972, formula 26.2.12), $Q(x) \approx 1/\sqrt{2\pi} e^{(-x^2/2)} / x$, which corresponds to an astronomically negligible value for $Q(x)$. Therefore we reject the null hypothesis of statistical independence.

This result of the χ^2 test is not entirely surprising. If the Weyerhauser data seem to exhibit ARCH phenomena, they are probably not statistically independent even if first-order autocorrelation is zero. The χ^2 test is not guaranteed to pick up all forms of statistical dependence. Information about the distance of a point from the origin, for instance, will not show up in the theta histogram. Nevertheless, if standard tests indicate that the data are autoregressive in conditional heteroskedasticity, it is not surprising that our χ^2 test should indicate statistical dependence.

We have seen that Figures 9.3 and 9.4 seemed to indicate a heavy accumulation of points at $\theta/\pi = \pm 0.75$ and ± 0.25. If these rays collect significantly more points than would be consistent with the null hypothesis of independence, then we have X-skewing in the Weyerhauser data. Results reported in Table 9.2 confirm the presence

Table 9.1 χ^2 hypothesis test for Weyerhauser data

Series	χ^2	x	$Q(x)$
Weyerhauser	5019.2	80.2	$\approx 10^{-1392}$

Note: The empirical series include $n = 7558$ observations histogrammed in $v = 201$ bins. $x = \sqrt{2\chi^2_{obs}} - \sqrt{2v-1}$ is the reduced variable which is asymptotically distributed normally, $Q(x)$ is the corresponding probability $P(x' \geq x)$.

Table 9.2 Bernoulli hypothesis test for Weyerhauser data, $\theta/\pi = \pm0.25$ (±0.005) and ±0.75 (±0.005)

Series	n	p	k	h	$\Delta k/\sigma$	$B(h)$
Weyerhauser	7558	0.02732 (±0.00013)	206.5 (±1.0)	872	665.5	??

Note: In this and the following Bernoulli tables, n is the number of points in the empirical distribution, p is the probability that θ/π belongs to the interval considered according to the bootstrapped histogram, $k = np$, h is the observed number of points in the interval considered, $\Delta k/\sigma = |h - k|/\sigma$ is the normalized fluctuation observed, and finally $B(h) = \Sigma_{k=h}^{n} P_k$ (where P_k is the Bernoulli probability of k observation in the bin) is the probability $P(k \geq h)$.

of such a pattern. The compound probability of a point being with the intervals ± 0.25 (± 0.005) and ± 0.75 (± 0.005) is $p = 0.0273$ under H_0. The expected number of points in those intervals is therefore $np = 206.5$. The observed number is $h = 872$. From (9.5), calculations using Numerical Recipes software (Press *et al.* 1992) give an astronomically small value for $P(k > h)$. The null should be rejected. It seems as if the main diagonals are accumulating "too many" points. Weyerhauser returns are X-skewed.

Crack and Ledoit (1996) repeat in a footnote their referee's comment that they have not shown "that there are no other predictable structures present" in the compass rose. X-skewing is an example of such a structure. The existence of this pattern shows that Crack and Ledoit were mistaken to claim that all of the information of the compass rose "is contained in decades-old studies on the time-series properties of stock returns" (1996, p. 755). These studies make distributional assumptions which may be false and may mask regularities easily detected by other techniques of analysis.

X-skewing is distinct from the ARCH behavior of standard models. But it induces standard tests to indicate ARCH behavior. The next section reports on a simulation that produces X-skewing and gives the (false) appearance of standard ARCH behavior.

A simple simulation of X-skewing

Weyerhauser returns exhibit X-skewing. X-skewing may be common. This pattern may explain the widespread phenomenon of ARCH behavior in return data. To test this possibility, Nardone and I ran a simple simulation. Our simulation was designed to see if X-skewing can cause standard procedures to indicate the presence of ARCH. It was not designed to model stock returns accurately. It seems that the

X-skewing we found in Weyerhauser data can indeed induce the false appearance of standard ARCH behavior.

Our simulation started with an initial price, $p(0)$, and return $r(0)$. It then drew from a normal distribution centered about $r(0)$. If the value drawn exceeded a pre-determined threshold level, it was discarded and a new value is drawn from the same distribution. (Without a cutoff value, the variance would grow without bound. Since our simulation is merely illustrative, we simply imposed a cutoff.) With a probability of 0.5, the sign of the value drawn was reversed. This value became a tentative return. The tentative return was added to the old price to get a new price. The new price was rounded up or down to simulate the existence of a postive tick size. From the new price a new return was calculated. The simulation then used these new values to calculate, in the same way, a price and return for the following period. And so on.

Each period's return was gotten by first drawing from a normal distribution centered about last period's return, then changing the sign with probability one-half, and, finally, adjusting to create discreteness in the associated price series. If the return in period t, $r(t)$, was large and positive, the absolute value of the return in period $t+1$, $|r(t + 1)|$, was likely to be large too. The return, $r(t + 1)$, was just as likely to be negative, however, as positive. The distribution of the $r(t + 1)$, given $r(t)$, is bimodal. One mode occurs at $r(t)$, the other at $-r(t)$. The distance between the modes is greater the larger $|r(t)|$. Only when $r(t) = 0$ is the conditional distribution of $r(t + 1)$, unimodal.

Since the sign of each period's return has an equal chance of being positive or negative, the expected value of $r(t)$ is zero for all t. The returns generated by this simulation have no autocorrelation in first moments. There is autoregression in conditional variance. But the series is not generated by the processes described in standard ARCH models, which assume a unimodal distribution. Figure 9.5 shows the compass rose for this simulated series.

The series generated by this simulation passes standard tests for the existence of ARCH behavior. Results of the Q and LM tests reject the null of no autocorrelation of conditional variance at the 0.0001 confidence level. John Broussard fit a GARCH(1,1) model to the data. The results, reported in Table 9.3, seem to indicate ARCH behavior. The SAS subroutine we ran indicated a statistically significant ARCH(1) coefficient and a statistically insignificant GARCH(1) coefficient. An unwary researcher might conclude that the series is an ARCH(1) process.

The purpose of this simulation was not to model stock returns, but to illustrate two points. First, X-skewing may be generated by a stochastic

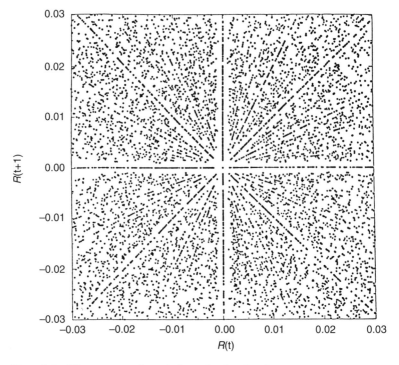

Figure 9.5 "Compass rose" graph for a simulated series

process which is not in the customary family of ARCH models. Second, X-skewing nevertheless causes standard tests to indicate ARCH behavior. The relationship between ARCH and X-skewing merits further study.

X-skewing is an unintended consequence of human action. The human actions which generate it are responses to the prevailing environment. If the regime governing the market process should change, the degree of X-skewing may change too.

Table 9.3   Results of SAS fit of simulation data to a GARCH (1,1) model

Variable	DF	B value	Std error	t ratio	Approx. prob.
Intercept	1	0.000256	0.000183	1.399	0.1618
ARC(0)	1	0.000224	0.000048	4.670	0.0001
ARCH(1)	1	0.128261	0.0283	4.537	0.0001
GARCH(1)	1	0.011617	0.1852	0.063	0.9500

Note: The results falsely suggest that the data follow an ARCH(1) process.

Big Players induce X-skewing

The results of this section suggest that X-skewing may result from the simultaneous presence of herding and contra-herding. From Yeager's ruble series, Nardone and I calculated empirical and bootstrapped theta histograms. The total number of samples in the bootstrapped histograms was 1000 times the length of the original series. The data points have been binned into 201 partitions with a resolution of $\theta/\pi = 0.01$. The probability associated with each bin is estimated to be $p = k/n$ with an error given by the corresponding (approximate) Bernoullian standard deviation $\sigma \approx \sqrt{np} = \sqrt{k}$.

Figures 9.6 and 9.7 show the empirical theta histograms from the Bunge and Vyshnegradsky periods. Figures 9.8 and 9.9 show their corresponding bootstrapped theta histograms. For the Bunge period, the empirical and bootstrapped histograms are almost identical. For the Vyshnegradsky period, they differ. The asymmetry in the Vyshnegradsky period is evident. Especially evident is the large number of points accumulated at $\theta/\pi = -0.5$. Days in which the ruble's exchange

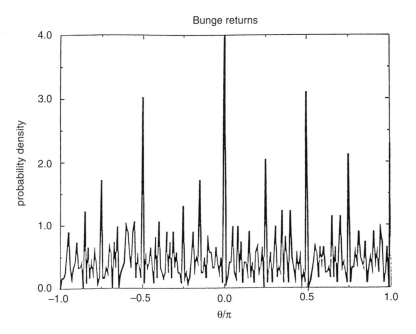

Figure 9.6   Empirical theta histogram, Bunge period

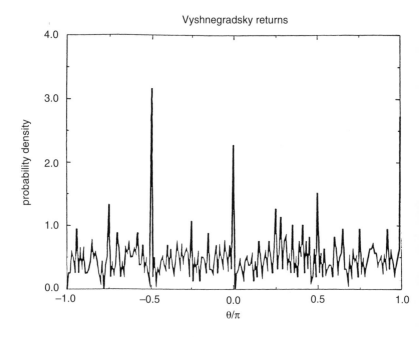

Figure 9.7 Empirical theta histogram, Vyshnegradsky period

rate did not change tended to be followed by days in which its value fell. I do not know why.

For each period, we tested the hypothesis that the probability of a point at $\theta/\pi = -0.5$ is equal to the relative frequency of such points when returns are independent. The results are reported in Table 9.4.

For the Bunge period, the number of points n in the sample was 1224. If returns were independent, the probability of a point at -0.5 (±0.005) would be $p = 0.0307$ and the expected value of the number of points would be $k = np = 37.6$. The actual number was $h = 37$, well within the standard deviation for a Bernoullian ($\sigma \approx \sqrt{np} = 6.1$). It is therefore inappropriate to reject the hypothesis of independence. In other words, for the Bunge period, we do not have so many points accumulating at -0.5 that we should reject the null hypothesis of independence in returns.

For the Vyshnegradsky period, the number of points in the sample was $n = 1581$. If returns were independent, the probability of a point at -0.5 (±0.005) would be $p = 0.0244$ and the expected value of the

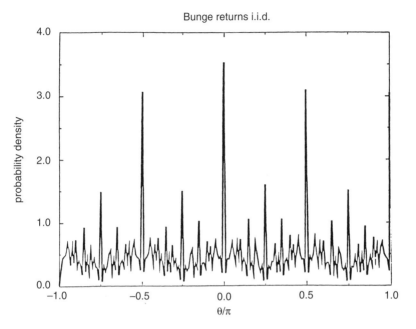

Figure 9.8 Bootstrapped theta histogram, Bunge period

number of points would be $k = 38.5$. The actual number was $h = 50$. From (9.5) one may calculate the probability to get such h or higher. This probability is 0.041. Since $P(k>h)$ is less than 0.05, our confidence level, the hypothesis of independence should be rejected. For the Vyshnegradsky period, under the assumption of independence, we have an improbably large number of points accumulating at –0.5. This formal hypothesis test supports the conclusion one is likely to draw from looking at Figure 9.7. Days in which the ruble's exchange rate did not change tended to be followed by days in which its value fell.

The Big Players' theory suggests we should find another difference between the Bunge and Vyshnegradsky periods. Under Vyshnegradsky, there should be X-skewing. There should be a greater tendency for points to accumulate at $\theta/\pi = \pm 0.25$ and $\theta/\pi = \pm 0.75$. These are the values corresponding to the two main diagonals of the compass rose pattern.

Figures 9.10 and 9.11 show the compass rose pattern for the absolute value of returns. Since absolute values are non-negative, all points appear in the positive quadrant. Under Bunge, no ray is obviously

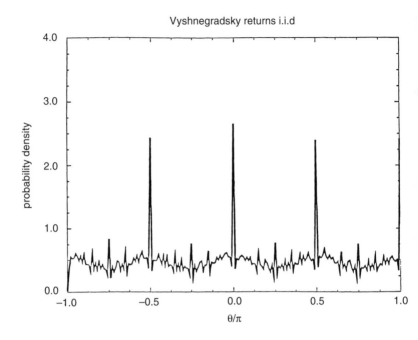

Figure 9.9   Bootstrapped theta histogram, Vyshnegradsky period

accumulating too many or too few points. Note that the graph shows something close to a grid, with little centrifugal smudging. This is because the ruble exchange rate did not vary widely during Bunge's tenure as finance minister. (This is exactly the result predicted by Crack and Ledoit 1996.) Under Vyshnegradsky, the 45-degree line seems to have collected more points than it would have if returns were independent. This difference between the Bunge and Vyshnegradsky periods is confirmed by hypothesis tests reported in Table 9.5.

In this case, in the Bunge period the compound probability for being within the intervals $\theta/\pi = \pm 0.25$ (± 0.005) and $\theta/\pi = \pm 0.75$ (± 0.005) is $p = 0.0610$, if returns were independent. Accordingly, the expected number of points is $k = 74.6$, while we observe $h = 88$. From (9.5) one can calculate the probability to get such an h or higher. This probability is 0.065. Since $P(k>h)$ is more than 0.05, it is inappropriate to reject the hypothesis of independence. For the Bunge period, under the assumption of independence, we do not have an improbably large or small number of points along the 45-degree line of Figure 9.10.

Table 9.4 Bernoulli hypothesis tests for ruble data, θ/π = 0.5 (±0.005)

Series	n	p	k	h	Δk/σ	B(h)
Bunge	1224	0.03072 (±0.00016)	37.60 (± 0.20)	37	0.10	> 0.5
Vyshnegradsky	1581	0.02436 (±0.00012)	38.51 (±0.19)	50	1.85	0.041

There is no X-skewing under Bunge. Broussard and I found statistically significant ARCH effects during this period. This pair of results is futher evidence that X-skewing and ARCH behavior are distinct even though they are related.

For the Vyshnegradsky period, $p = 0.0312$ and $k = 49.4$, while we observe $h = 73$. Again from (9.5) we obtain $P(k>h) = 0.0008$, a value much smaller than our level of confidence. We can therefore reject the hypothesis of independence. For the Vyshnegradsky period, under the

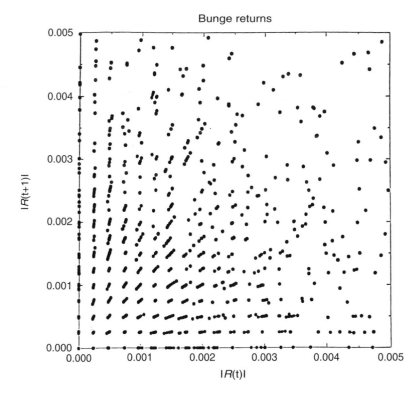

Figure 9.10 Compass rose in absolute values, Bunge period

Table 9.5   Bernoulli hypothesis tests for ruble data, θ/π = ±0.25 (±0.005) and ±0.75 (±0.005)

Series	n	p	k	h	Δk/σ	B(h)
Bunge	1224	0.06099 (±0.00022)	74.66 (± 0.27)	88	1.54	0.065
Vyshnegradsky	1581	0.03123 (±0.00014)	49.38 (±0.22)	73	1.85	0.0008

assumption of independence, we have an improbably large number of points accumulating at ±0.25 and ±0.75. Formal hypothesis testing supports the conclusion one is likely to draw from looking at Figure 9.11. Large changes in the exchange rate on one day tend to be followed by similarly large changes the next day, though not necessarily in the same direction. This tendency is consistent with the theory of Big Players.

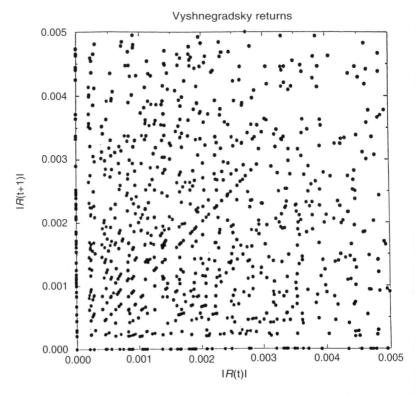

Figure 9.11   Compass rose in absolute values, Vyshnegradsky period

Table 9.6 χ^2 hypothesis tests for ruble data

Series	χ^2	x	$Q(x)$
Bunge	203.696	0.159	0.436
Vyshnegradsky	251.501	2.403	0.0082
mixed	291.102	4.104	0.00002

Note: The empirical series include $n = 988$ observations histogrammed in $v = 201$ bins. The reduced variable x^* corresponding to the 0.05 confidence level, i.e. $Q(x^*) = 0.05$, is 1.645.

Finally, for each period, Nardone and I tested the hypothesis of independence among returns using the χ^2 test. In order to avoid effects related to the number of points in the sample, we choose $n = 998$ for each series. A "mixed" series was studied, taking the end of the Bunge period and the beginning of the Vyshnegradsky period of tenure, in equal proportions. The number of degrees of freedom n coincides in our case with the number of bins, namely, 201. We again used the asymptotic formula (Abramovitz and Stegun 1972).

The χ^2 test results are reported in Table 9.6. The test is in agreement with the previous tests on specific θ/π values. For the Bunge period $\chi^2_{obs} = 203.7$, very close to the expected value of 201. Therefore $Q(x)$ is quite large and well within the confidence level. For the Vyshnegradsky period $\chi^2_{obs} = 251.5$ and $Q(x) = 0.008 < 0.05$. Therefore we can reject the hypothesis that Vyshnegradsky's empirical theta histogram is distributed as the corresponding i.i.d. returns histogram. This conclusion is even more probable for the "mixed" series, with $\chi^2_{obs} = 291.1$ and $Q(x) = 2 \times 10^{-5}$.

The angular distribution of credit-ruble returns in delay space shifted dramatically under the Big Player influence of Ivan Vyshnegradsky. There is no evidence of X-skewing under Bunge. X-skewing was clearly present under Vyshnegradsky. Thus, we have evidence that Big Players can induce or increase X-skewing by changing the interpretive environment of an asset market. This X-skewing, in turn, can induce the appearance of ARCH behavior.

10
Herding in Money Demand[1]

Money demand and the theory of Big Players

Big Players influence the demand for money in ways not easily captured by traditional monetary theory. Most monetary economists have been in search of a well-specified model that will allow them to track accurately the demand for money and predict its future movements. By the early 1970s, a general consensus had emerged among economists about the functional form of money demand. This form seemed highly stable in the period after the Second World War.[2] At about the same time the Federal Reserve System began a long series of changes in its policies and procedures. As argued below, these changes produced greater Fed activism and discretion. Shortly thereafter money demand estimates became unstable, and the emerging data began to expose shortcomings in the accepted models. Most economists came to believe these problems with tracking money demand were a product of misspecification of the models. Since the 1970s, the game has been one of discovering which measure of income or wealth to use, which measure of risk, and which measure of liquidity, as well as some way to account for advances in payment technologies and institutional change. Yet, no model to date has been robust over time.

The shortcomings of money demand specifications became clear about when the Fed adopted much more discretionary policies. The theory of Big Players suggests a causal connection. Gilanshah and I applied the theory to U.S. money demand from 1950s to 1980s. We found that after 1970, Fed policy grew more discretionary and that this increase in Big Player influence reduced the stability of money demand. We cannot exclude other factors. But the theory of Big Players does predict results that are consistent with the data.

The Fed began to undertake more discretionary policy actions begin-ning in 1970. Shortly thereafter, the estimates generated by the standard money demand specifications began to show sizable prediction errors. Despite considerable effort, no improved specification of money demand has emerged that can satisfactorily account for its seemingly aberrant behavior during the 1970s and 1980s. If the prediction errors were purely a product of misspecification, have economists been unable to produce a better model for money demand? Financial innovation, changes in definition of money, wage, and price controls, and other factors might have contributed to instabilities in money demand. The evidence reported below suggests that Big Players may also have played a role.

If the theory of the Big Players is correct, then the sort of instabilities generated by the discretionary actions of Federal Reserve policymakers cannot be explained by the addition of new variables. Instead of searching for such a variable, Gilanshah and I compared the behavior of money demand estimates over two periods, the 1950s–1960s and the 1970s–1980s. Using rescaled-range analysis, we tried to find out if the more discretionary monetary policy of the latter period was indeed a factor in the observed instabilities of money demand.

We found evidence that Fed activism did induce instability in money demand. If the result holds under scrutiny, it has important implications for monetary policy. The Fed should not abandon money supply targets, but should pursue them according to a fixed rule. This implication con-tradicts one common inference drawn from the literature on instability of money demand. Mishkin's undergraduate text (1995) is representative of this common view. Mishkin argues that "because the money demand function has become unstable, velocity is now harder to predict, and setting rigid money supply targets in order to control aggregate spending in the economy may not be an effective way to conduct monetary policy" (Mishkin 1995, p. 572). But if this instability of money demand is a product of Fed activism, Mishkin's conclusion does not follow. If discre-tion produces instability, we have an argument for less of it, not more.

Past chapters argued that Big Players induce "herding" or "band-wagon effects" in organized financial markets. Big Players also induce herding in the demand for money. The argument is similar to that of Chapter 7. Bandwagon effects enter money demand through the role of cash managers. A substantial portion of money demand is, of course, demand of business enterprises. The decision of how much money to hold is often made by a professional cash manager. Scharfstein and Stein (1990) have noted the importance of reputation for portfolio managers. We note that the same holds for cash managers.

Like the portfolio manager, the cash manager's job prospects depend mostly on his reputation. It is hard for cash manager's supervisors and potential employers to measure the quality of his decisions. One criterion they will employ is the cash manager's conformity to industry practice. This is a global criterion. Supervisors who use this global criterion will ask, for example, if their cash manager reduced money holdings when trade journals warned of the dangers of excess liquidity in the current macroeconomic climate. They will also want to know, however, if the cash manager's decisions were appropriate to the unique circumstances of their business situation. This is a local criterion.

Because the cash manager is judged partly on global criteria, he has an incentive to act as other cash managers act. If you act as others do and things go well, your reputation is ensured. If you act as others do and things go badly, you can share the blame with others. It is dangerous to act on one's own judgment. If you defy common wisdom and things go badly, your reputation is shot and job prospects diminished. As we have seen in Chapter 7, Scharfstein and Stein (who considered only portfolio managers) call this incentive to imitate the "sharing-the-blame effect" (1990, p. 466).

Cash managers are not judged on global criteria only. They are also judged on local criteria. A cash manager who can consistently make good decisions in defiance of common wisdom will earn a strongly favorable reputation and enjoy improved job prospects. There is therefore a counter-incentive discouraging bandwagon effects.

Money demand is influenced by the sharing-the-blame effect, which creates herding, and by counter-incentives to act on local information. At any one time we can expect some herding to occur without imagining cash managers to be perfect sheep. Some will herd, others will not. Big Players influence the fraction that herds.

A Big Player monetary authority weakens the counter-incentives to sharing-the-blame and thus encourages herding. The Big Player's discretionary actions influence the opportunity cost of holding money. It is thus important for cash managers to pay attention to the actions and prospective actions of the Big Player. Fed watching is necessitated by discretionary monetary policy. Fed watching, however, diverts attention from local factors. Moreover, a Big Player Fed is difficult to fathom. As I have argued earlier, the actions of a discretionary agent cannot be predicted. Thus, cash managers' attention is diverted from what is relatively easy to predict to what is relatively hard to predict. In this greater state of ignorance, the cash manager has a stronger incentive to share the blame. Each cash manager has a stronger incentive to

act as other cash managers do. The advice promulgated in trade journals will be more universally adhered to, less frequently ignored. There
will be more herding in money demand.

Fed policy went from one of little Big Player discretion in the 1950s
and 1960s to one of greater Big Player discretion in the 1970s and
1980s. We chronicle this change and provide evidence that it induced
increased herding in money demand.

The Federal Reserve as a Big Player

In the 1950s and 60s, the primary operational guide for Federal Reserve
policymakers was free reserves (excess reserves less borrowed reserves),
with bank credit (commercial loans and investments) serving as an
intermediate guide (Meulendyke 1989, p. 34). Free reserve targets did
not constitute a strict and binding rule; nonetheless, throughout this
period, the Federal Reserve would respond to changes in the level of
free reserves in a predictable manner. Equally importantly, throughout
this period, the assumptions underlying monetary policy procedures
were relatively stable. This meant that private actors could form expectations of what the Federal Reserve was going to do or how it was
going to react to a given change with reasonable certainty. In other
words, the element of discretion in Federal Reserve policymaking was
relatively low. As a number of studies showed, money demand
behaved in a predictable manner over this period such that, by 1970,
there was general agreement among economists over its long-term
functional form – which seemed to exhibit stability over time.

The basic model utilized in such studies as Laidler (1977) and
Goldfeld (1973) took the following form:

$$\ln (M_t/P_t) = \beta_0 + \beta_1 \ln Y_t + \beta_2 \ln R_t^s + \beta_3 \ln R_t^m + \beta_4 \ln (M_{t-1}/P_{t-1})$$

where Y_t = some measure of wealth or income, such as GNP

R_t^s = interest rate on savings deposits
R_t^m = some market interest rate, such as the rate on T-bills
M_{t-1}/P_{t-1} = real money balances, lagged one period.

The inflationary pressure of the late 1960s prompted many economists
to question the assumed relationships underlying current monetary
policy (Meulendyke 1989, p. 38). This led to a number of policy initia-
tives in the early 1970s that resulted in much more discretionary and

activist policies. Indeed, 1970 marked the beginning of a new era in Federal Reserve policy in which there would be greater discretion not only as to the appropriate range for a given Federal Reserve target, but discretion as to which targets were appropriate. In other words, what had previously been a system of relatively modest discretion within the rules now turned into a series of discretionary and unpredictable changes in the rules themselves. The Federal Reserve had truly become a Big Player.

There were three identifiable regime shifts in the 1970s and1980s: 1970–2, 1979, and 1983.[3] Following each shift to a new regime, there was a significant period of experimentation and modification on the part of the Federal Reserve policymakers as they sought the best way to implement their new objectives. During these periods, the market was characterized by greater uncertainty, as small players could not clearly distinguish signals reflecting discretionary interventions from those reflecting shifts in underlying economic fundamentals. Furthermore, following a shift, the market would reward entrepreneurs who could correctly anticipate the actions of the Big Player, resulting in a realloca-tion of resources toward "Fed watching".[4] At the same time, the Federal Reserve, uncertain of how its new technique would affect the market, responded to every jitter and jump, basing each move on how it expected the market to react. Likewise, private actors' market expecta-tions would now have to be based not only on their theories of what the market would do in the absence of intervention, but also on their theories of what the Fed would do. Meulendyke (1989, p. 188) describes the market's response to the changes in the following way:

> Decisions about the management of money and credit were influenced by estimates of how rapidly the monetary authorities would raise or lower the funds rate; the judgment often depended as much on assessing policymakers' willingness to allow interest rates to change as on observing the behavior of money growth and the economy. Most forecasting focused on the factors believed to affect the timing and magnitude of funds rate changes.

The result, as the Big Players theory suggests, was a separation of expectations formation from underlying economic fundamentals; the Federal Reserve had created a "Keynesian beauty contest."

Discretion becomes the rule: the 1970s[5]

In an attempt to bring down inflation, the Federal Reserve formally adopted monetary targets in 1970.[6] The new operational guides required new techniques, however, for setting targets and pursuing monetary policy, and this process involved much experimentation and modification during the early years of the decade. At various stages, the Fed attempted to control money through the demand side, at others, through the supply side, and at others still, by manipulating both. For instance, in 1972, the Federal Reserve briefly experimented with targeting reserves on private deposits (RPD). Fearing unacceptable volatility in interest rates, however, it also attempted to constrain the federal funds rate. The Federal Open Market Committee (FOMC) was always reluctant to change the Fed funds rate by more than incremental steps, even when larger movements were deemed necessary to hit monetary targets. Thus, despite the stated policy of RPD targeting, the narrow range set for the federal funds rate was typically the binding constraint, and the reserve targets were frequently missed. The result, of course, was inflation. By 1973, the targets on RPD were already widely perceived to be unachievable, and they were downgraded to an intermediate target.[7] (Meulendyke 1989, pp. 38–43).

By the mid-1970s, the federal funds rate had essentially become the *de facto* operational target.[8] Once this shift had taken place, the FOMC's desk became increasingly reluctant to permit the Fed funds rate to deviate from its target. Thus, by the late 1970s, the desk was promptly and predictably responding "to even small wiggles in the federal funds rate."[9] This again created an environment in which private actors could form expectations of Federal Reserve behavior with some degree of certainty. But the inability of this regime to contain the runaway inflation indicated that a new technique or target was just around the corner.

The Volcker experiment: 1979–82

The federal funds targeting regime clearly had not brought inflation under control. Many critics of the fed-funds regime, influenced by the monetarists, argued that what was needed was a rule-based operating technique in which the Federal Reserve would control money from the supply side. Driven by pressures on all sides, in October 1979, Paul Volcker, the new Chairman of the Board of Governors, implemented sweeping changes in the Federal Reserve's operating technique. Although the new regime appeared to be rule-based, it was actually a convoluted scheme of multiple targets and derived estimates. As described in Meulendyke (1989, pp. 43–44), operationally, the FOMC would choose a desired quarterly growth rate for one of the monetary aggregates. Then, the Federal Reserve staff would estimate a level of total reserves consistent with that growth rate, as well as deposit and currency mixes to derive average reserve ratios and currency-deposit ratios. Finally, the desk would derive a target for non-borrowed reserves, which at the same time would determine the level of borrowed reserves ($TR - NBR = BR$), given the FOMC's total reserve target. Thus, what was called "M1 targeting", was based on an estimation technique that involved the analyst's discretion at nearly every one of the four steps.

Even under this "supply-side" regime, the federal funds rate was not ignored. It was recognized that this key rate, along with all other interest rates, would be both higher and more volatile; yet, its level was considered, and could result in the acceleration or delay of an operation necessary for a reserve adjustment.[10] In addition, it was occasionally deemed that the pace of adjustment implied by the FOMC's orders was proceeding either too slow or too fast, in which case, discretion entered the equation again as the desk was granted permission to make alterations in the borrowing objective between official meetings.

Under this regime, non-borrowed reserve growth targets were derived for inter-meeting average periods. As Meulendyke (1989, pp. 44–45) describes it, this technique meant that if a reserve target were missed in the early part of the period, as it often was, it had to be offset by large swings in borrowing at the end of the period. Thus, "informal adjustments" were sometimes implemented "to smooth temporary spikes and drops that were deemed inconsistent with the longer term patterns. Although [these] adjustments were considered necessary to avoid severe short-term swings in reserve availability and interest rates, they gave the appearance of 'fiddling' and caused considerable confusion for outside observers."[11]

Only three years after its introduction, in late 1982, the Federal Reserve abandoned M1 targeting. New data indicated that the relationship between M1 and economic activity was not a stable one – a prerequisite for monetary targeting. The FOMC briefly experimented with M2 targeting in the final quarter of 1982, but the introduction of money-market deposit accounts (MMDAs) in December strongly affected the demand for M2, and this scheme, too, proved unsuccessful.[12]

The Volcker years, while successful in moderating inflation, generated further unpredictable swings in money demand. In 1980–82, the demand for M1 rose sharply in a way that no model predicted. Though the theory of the Big Player doesn't speak to the direction of changes in key variables, it does suggest that the unpredictable movements in money demand were, at least in part, a consequence of the unpredictable and discretionary actions of the Federal Reserve.

The guise of borrowed reserve targeting: 1983–87

Beginning in the last weeks of 1982, the Federal Reserve shifted its focus from the indirect method of non-borrowed reserve targeting to targeting borrowed reserves directly. This, however, was essentially a move back toward targeting interest rates. The FOMC would choose the desired level of borrowed reserves, but the way to attain that level was through the interest rate. Then, if interest rates threatened to rise, the Fed would supply non-borrowed reserves to the market to bring the interest rate back down. Operationally, in addition to weighing economic activity and inflation, the FOMC would consider a number of "supplemental indicators" such as foreign exchange movements and financial market conditions in formulating its policy decisions. In essence, the FOMC considered whatever variables it deemed important at that time, and often even gave the desk further discretionary powers within the targeted ranges.[13]

The borrowed-reserve targeting regime was no different than the previous regimes in that it relied heavily on the discretion of a few individuals. "Fed watchers" tried, as they had in previous monetary regimes, to estimate reaction functions for the Big Player. Yet, policies that rely on the discretion of individuals are by their nature impervious to such quantification. Thus, small players had to form expectations of both what the market would do, and how the Federal Reserve would react. Meulendyke (1989, p. 189) describes the process in the following way:

> In observing the behavior of the funds rate, market participants had to decide whether a move in the rate occurred for policy or for other reasons. Since the Federal Reserve was basing its borrowed reserve objectives on a variety of indicators, including the outlook for economic activity and inflation as well as the behavior of the monetary aggregates, participants [had to] forecast those variables in order to estimate the next move in the policy stance.

But often, the Fed didn't even know how it would react; it was frequently uncertain of how its policies would affect the market, and thus, had to react to every jump and jitter, even if those volatilities were in response to its own prior actions. The uncertainty associated with the FOMC's reactions only increased as the policymakers expanded their number of "supplemental indicators" during this 1983–7 regime. As predicted by the theory of the Big Player, money demand estimates throughout this period continued to behave in an unpredictable and volatile manner.

If money demand is subject to increased herding because of increased discretion in Fed policy, there should be increased persistence in the residuals of money demand equations. Herding among cash managers will create a tendency of money demand to swing up and down in irregular pseudo-cycles about its trend line. If the regression line from a money demand equation is a reasonable measure of that trend, the residuals from it will swing up and down in irregular pseudo-cycles about zero. Moreover, these pseudo-cycles will be greater after 1970 than before. Increased Big Player influence will cause an increase in persistent dependence after 1970 in the residuals from money demand equations. This prediction is confirmed by the statistical analysis reported below.

Gilanshah and I ran six versions of a standard money demand equation. In each case M1 was the dependent variable. Our quarterly data cover the period from 1960 to 1987. In each case the equation was of the following form:

$$\ln (M_t/P_t) = \beta_0 + \beta_1 \ln Y_t + \beta_2 \ln R_t^s + \beta_3 \ln R_t^m + \beta_4 \ln (M_{t-1}/P_{t-1})$$

where Y_t = some measure of wealth or income, such as GNP

R_t^s = interest rate on savings deposits
R_t^m = some market interest rate, such as the rate on T-bills
M_{t-1}/P_{t-1} = real money balances, lagged one period.

What differed from one equation to the next was the choice of variables used to measure the various right-hand-side items.

We took the residuals from these six money-demand equations and applied R/S analysis to them. We divided the residuals into an initial period running through 1969 and a final period beginning in 1971. We omitted 1970 as a transition year. For each equation and each period we calculated the Hurst coefficient, h. Our results are presented in Table 10.1.

The results should be viewed as tentative and preliminary. Nevertheless, they are remarkably consistent. In each case our measure of persistent dependence grows for the period after 1970. In all but one case, the difference is statistically significant. Thus our evidence supports (though it does not "prove") the following claims:

(1) There was less stability of money demand after 1970 than before
(2) This reduction in stability was caused by increased Big Player influence
(3) Increased Big Player influence reduced the stability of money demand by inducing herding in the behavior of cash managers.

Table 10.1 Hurst coefficients

Version	Hurst coefficient for initial period	Hurst coefficient for final period
1)	0.865	0.898
	(0.028)	(0.013)
2)	0.361	0.722
	(0.027)	(0.021)
3)	0.784	0.926
	(0.025)	(0.011)
4)	0.186	0.619
	(0.019)	(0.015)
5)	0.540	0.647
	(0.025)	(0.017)
6)	0.168	0.686
	(0.018)	(0.029)

Note: The column labeled "Initial period" reports the Hurst coefficient for period up to and including the fourth quarter of 1969. The column labeled "Final period" reports the Hurst coefficient for the period beginning the first quarter of 1971. Standard errors are reported in parentheses.

Discussion and conclusion

If the analysis of this chapter is about right, there is something missing from standard money-demand regressions, namely, the degree of Big Player influence. This influence cannot be accounted for, however, by adding in one or more new regressors. To have such a regressor (or group of regressors) we would need a measurable variable that rises when cash managers herd in one direction and falls when they herd in the opposite direction. This variable would have to track the microeconomic dynamics of cash managers' environment. The relevant events it would have to track, however, occur below our threshold of observation. No macroeconomic variable tracks the underlying dynamics. Nor does any measurable microeconomic variable. One might say, if one wishes, that Gilanshah and I have identified a missing variable causing misspecification of money-demand equations. The misspecification, however, cannot be put right by adding in any measurable variable.

In his famous restatement of the quantity theory, Milton Friedman (1956) seems to be reacting to critics of the quantity theory from the 1930s. According to these critics, Friedman explained, "[t]he demand for money ... is a will-o'-the wisp, shifting erratically and unpredictably with every rumor and expectation; one cannot, it was asserted, reliably specify a limited number of variables on which it depends" (1956,

p. 16). Chicago's oral tradition, by contrast, "accepts the empirical hypothesis that the demand for money is highly stable." Indeed, it is a stable function of a few known variables. "For to expand the number of variables regarded as significant is to empty the hypothesis of its empirical content" (1956, p. 16).

This view of things, however, neglects the possibility that the stability of money demand may itself be a function of institutional particulars. Old and new monetarists alike have neglected the possibility of identifying empirical circumstances governing stability of money demand. We need not choose between "stability always" and "stability never." We have "stability sometimes." Moreover, we can identify the conditions that increase stability and those that reduce it. "Stability sometimes" is thus an empirically viable program. This chapter has identified one empirical factor that influences the stability of money demand, namely, Big Players. Others probably exist.

Coda

How this book relates to the emerging new orthodoxy in economics

Standard economic theory models human action as rational maximizing. Most economists are dissatisfied with this "neoclassical" model. But no clear replacement has come along. Most economists recognize that rational maximizing is a reasonable assumption in certain cases. But they also recognize that these special cases, though important, are only some of the cases of interest to economists. The argument of this book, including the language-games framework of Chapter 5, may be useful to modern economists dissatisfied with the standard model.

Although no one model of action has emerged as a successor to rational maximizing, there are similarities among the many different models being used or discussed by leading theorists. The similarities can be grouped under several headings, namely, bounded rationality, rule following, evolution, institutions, and cognition. Together they suggest, though only in vague outline, an emerging new orthodoxy. Important examples or precursors of the emerging new orthodoxy are the New Institutional Economics, Post Walrasian Economics, Constitutional Political Economy, Complexity Economics, and Austrian economics. (See Anderson *et al.* 1988, Buchanan 1990, Colander 1996a, Hayek 1967 and Langlois 1986b.)

Perhaps I should refer to the *converging* new orthodoxy. Each of the schools I have identified as contributors has a long history. The ideas of the new orthodoxy were never fully banished from the old orthodoxy. But developments since 1980 have led to a convergence among these schools. They are not converging on one uniform theory shared by all, but on a broad theoretical framework within which narrower theoretical, empirical, and policy disputes will continue. The framework they are converging on is very different from the "neoclassical" theories of Walras (1874–1877), and Debreu (1959).

Bounded rationality

The great majority of economists agree that agents should be modeled as having, in some sense, only "bounded rationality." Neoclassical models assume (implicitly sometimes) that no bounds limit the agents' ability to figure out the best action in any situation. Objecting to this assumption, Herbert Simon (1955) coined the term "bounded rationality." The decision by Sargent (1993) to adopt the assumption of bounded rationality is a signal of the widespread acceptance of it. Simon's work has led to a very large literature within economics, including the organizational economics of March and others (Cyert and March 1963) and the transaction-cost economics of Oliver Williamson (1975) and others. Bounded rationality is a characteristic assumption of "New Institutional" economics (Langlois 1986a). It is a characteristic feature of complexity models as well (Arthur 1994b). A large experimental literature has identified several behavioral regularities that are consistent with bounded rationality, but not with complete rationality (Allais 1953, Ellsberg 1961, Kahneman and Tversky 1979, Thaler 1992). A growing literature on computability suggests that some form of bounded rationality may be logically necessary (Albin 1998, Anderlini and Sabourian 1995, Binmore 1987, Koppl and Rosser 2001, Prasad 1991, Rabin 1957, Spear 1989, and Velupillai 1996).

Rule following

The appeal of rule following is less universal than that of bounded rationality. Nevertheless, a rule-following framework has been suggested by many economists including Heiner, Buchanan, Vanberg, Nelson and Winter, Frank, and Herbert Simon. Hayek viewed action as rule following. "Man is as much a rule-following animal as a purpose-seeking one" (Hayek 1973, p. 11). I believe Victor Vanberg drew the right inference from this remark. We need a theory of action that "would allow us systematically to account for both features of human behaviour, its responsiveness to incentives *and* its rule-following nature" (1994, p. 16 emphasis in original). Indeed, one of the central difficulties of implementing a rule-following framework is squaring it with the economic principle that individuals tend to seek out their interests cunningly.

Evolution.

One of the standard defenses of rational maximizing relies on evolution (Friedman 1953). The solution of the maximization model describes what the agent must do if it is to survive market competition. This defense is widely recognized to have considerable merit. But it leaves unexamined the evolutionary mechanisms at work in economic life (Langlois 1986a, pp. 241–247, Nelson and Winter 1982, pp. 139–141). Besides, although evolution sometimes approximates an optimal solution, it does not always do so (Whitman 1998). Many economists today are interested in analyzing evolutionary mechanisms in the economy. The popularity of evolutionary game theory illustrates this interest. Defenders of evolution include Nelson and Winter, Buchanan, Hayek, Langlois, Witt, Alchian, Heiner, Hirschleifer, and Hodgson.

Institutions

The appeal to evolution necessitates an attention to institutions. On the microeconomic side, New Institutional Economists want theory with institutions and a theory of institutions. On the macroeconomic side, Post Walrasian Economists want theory with institutions and macroeconomic foundations of microeconomics. Economists who have emphasized institutions include O'Driscoll and Rizzo (1985), North, Horwitz, Coase, Williamson, Leijonhufvud, Clower, Langlois, Loasby, and Boettke.

Cognition

Once the assumption of bounded rationality is introduced, it is hard to avoid entering into cognitive psychology. Several economists have taken cognitive psychology seriously. These include F. A. Hayek, Vernon Smith, Douglass North, and Brian Arthur. Like floodwaters, the level of interest in cognitive psychology is high and rising. One important source is Holland *et al.* (1986). Hayek (1952a) is a still neglected source that should be of special interest to economists. Economists should construe "cognition" broadly so that Schutz's phenomenological psychology would fit under this heading.

Hayek's view of cognition is strikingly similar to views expressed by Holland and by Kauffman. For Kauffman (1993), "adaptive systems" make piecemeal adjustments to their environments. To do so successfully, they must respond to their environments; they must engage in "computation and adaptation" (1993, p. 232). Adaptive systems must "*interact* with and *represent* other entities of their environment" (p. 232, emphasis in original):

> In other words, complex living systems must "know" their worlds. Whether we consider *E. coli* swimming upstream in a glucose gradient, a tree manufacturing a toxin against a herbivore insect, or a hawk diving to catch a chick, organisms sense, classify, and act upon their worlds. In a phrase, organisms have internal models of their worlds which compress information and allow action. (Kauffman 1993, p. 232)

This view of cognition as classification seems to be identical to that of Hayek. Like Hayek, Kauffman find the classification in the response patterns of the organism. In the case of *E. coli*, for example, Kauffman says, "I permit myself the word 'classified' because we may imagine that the bacterium responds more or less identically to any ligand binding the receptor, be it glucose or some other molecule" (1993, p. 233).

Holland (1992) too, uses the example of bacteria. A "bacterium moves in the direction of a chemical gradient, implicitly predicting that food lies in that direction" (1992, p. 197). He also uses Hebb's connectionist model to describe the central nervous system (1992, pp. 58–65). As we have seen, Hebb's (1949) model is very close to that of Hayek. Like Hayek, Holland notes that the operations of the central nervous system are too complex to be captured in a simple stimulus–response framework.

In the emerging new orthodoxy, agents with bounded rationality are guided by general rules and rules of thumb. They have, nevertheless, some cunning and the disposition to seek out and follow their incentives. Natural selection can turn this cunning disposition into a good approximation of rational maximizing, but only in the right institutional setting. No economic explanation can be accepted until its cognitive foundations are clarified. The actions imputed to the agents must make sense given our knowledge of how people sift information and structure knowledge.

The language-games framework satisfies the requirements of the emerging new orthodoxy. The framework is not a theory of economics. It is only a convention regarding the description of individual action. The framework is not *true*; it is *useful*. It is useful because it provides a unifying and integrative framework with which to organize the otherwise scattered writings of the emerging new orthodoxy in economic theory. It is also a useful foundation for the theory of expectations.

Expectations are a characteristic theme of the emerging new orthodoxy. Expectations are a central theme of Post Walrasian, Austrian, and complexity economics. The word "expectations" appears less often in works of Constitutional political economists and New Institutional economists. But their interest in knowledge and learning point to very similar issues and problems. If the theory of this book has merit, then it is a contribution to the emerging new orthodoxy in economic theory.

Some suggestions for further work

If the argument of this book is sound, several areas of research may be worth pursuing. The problem of expectations raises many issues, only a few of which have been addressed here. I am not attempting a complete survey of any set of issues. I wish only to suggest that the ideas of this book can be developed in several different directions. I will not discuss international finance, but see Yeager (1998) for a discussion of Big Players and international financial crises.

Financial markets

If the theory of Big Players is empirically well grounded, as I believe it to be, then it is a contribution to the theory of financial markets. Some authors have focused on whether bubbles and herding exist at all. I prefer to ask when they are more important and when less. I believe that that approach helps us to formulate empirical hypotheses that are more readily testable.

If we ask only if bubbles exist or not, we may easily descend into arid arguments. Clever researchers can square the data with either hypothesis. The questions then become "metaphysical" in the pejorative sense. The theory my co-authors and I have developed identifies testable differences across markets. In the language of Imre Lakatos, it identifies "excess empirical content." While this "excess" is not the only criterion of theory choice (Hands 1993), it has value. Excess empirical content should count in favor of a theory or "research program."

Several questions seem worthy of pursuit. I will mention four. First, I have looked at only one thing that reduces market efficiency, namely, Big Players. A more complete list of causes would be very desirable. Second, the relationship between X-skewing and GARCH should be refined and clarified. Third, a more complete treatment of contra-herding is called for. Finally, institutional investors provide an area for research on Big Player effects. Institutional investors have some of the characteristics of Big Players. But they face competition and they are sensitive to profit and loss. They may cause something like a Big Player effect. But it is not likely to be as straightforward as the pure Big Player effects studied in this book.

Entrepreneurship

The Kirznerian theory of entrepreneurship sketched in Chapter 6 may be worth developing. The emerging discipline of entrepreneurship seems to be in need of further work on its most basic foundations. Further work in this area would be welcome. The theory I sketched out in Chapter 6 may be of some use. The theory is essentially that of Israel Kirzner (1973). But Kirzner's Misesian framework makes it hard to draw empirical content from the theory. The modifications I have suggested may help researchers to draw empirical conclusions from the theory.

Fiscal policy

The theory of Big Players has not been applied to fiscal policy. Frequent changes in tax rules, for example, should have Big Player effects. But they also have direct effects that may dominate the Big Player effect. In other cases, the direct effects – even if salutary – will be dominated by Big Player effects. Sorting these issues out is an important task as yet unfinished.

Money demand

I have argued that the stability of money demand is a function of the stability of money supply. This claim needs further study. Chapter 10 reports on the results of Gilanshah and Koppl (2001). Their study should be viewed as preliminary. More generally, the theory of expectations I have proposed suggests the need to re-examine the theory of money demand.

I believe that the theory of money demand would be improved by bringing a subjectivist perspective to it. But such an effort will probably not add to our knowledge and understanding unless it generates the sort of empirical implications I have discussed in Chapter 10. In this area too, the subjectivism of a broadly "Austrian" perspective can produce excess empirical content.

Non-parametric statisitics

The techniques described in Chapter 9 may be worth developing. They do not require any specific *ex ante* assumption about the distribution of any random variable. Today's low costs of calculation permits the use of such non-parametric techniques. Their essential advantage is simple. They let us get along with fewer assumptions. They give us fewer excuses should the data fail to display the patterns predicted by theory.

William Brock (2000) has commented on the advantages of boot-strapping techniques. Brock notes that if cars had advanced as rapidly as computers, "You would have something like a ten cent Ferrari that could accelerate from zero to sixty in, perhaps, a tenth of a second" (2000, p. 43). He explains that "in the age of dirt-cheap computing" we can "get rid of constraints on econometric practice that were formed in the days of expensive computer power and before advances such as bootstrapping theory." He enjoins us to "design an econometrics that is tailor-made for finance, where the statistical quantities used are financially relevant" (2000, p. 44). Brock favors "tailoring your statistical quantities to be directly relevant to the application at hand" and "using quantities that closely capture the purposive behavior of the agents you are studying" (2000, p. 45).

Complexity theory

The argument of this book has drawn some inspiration from the complexity theory of the Santa Fe Institute. For instance, the horizon principle of Chapter 6 owes something to Kauffman (1993, 1994). Colander (2000) may be the best of several useful introductions to complexity economics. Austrian economics is close to complexity theory (Koppl 2000b, 2000c, Vaughn 1999).

The connections between complexity theory and Austrian economics may be worth exploring. It seems reasonable to guess that complexity theory may provide Austrian economists with some useful tools of analysis. The literature on complexity economics is by now quite large. Arthur (2000) contains some useful references, as do other contributions to Colander (2000). It seems likely that at least some tools and arguments from literature will have enduring value. One especially suggestive link may be that between the combinatorial reasoning found in Hayek and the combinatorial models of Kauffman (1993, 1994). Menger's theory of the evolution of money describes a non-linear Polya process. Such processes were pioneered by Arthur (1994a).

The Austrian tradition may have something to offer complexity theory as well. In Chapter 6, my discussion of reflexivity was informed by the *Verstehen* tradition as represented by Alfred Schutz. It may be worth examining other ways in which the *Verstehen* tradition can inform complexity economics. Hayek's *The Sensory Order* (1952a) describes the mind as a complex adaptive system, though it does not use that exact phrase. The book contains an elaborate defense of methodological dualism. Thus, it seems a likely source book for scholars wishing to bring insights from the *Verstehen* tradition to the complexity vision in economics.

New Institutional Economics

Richard Langlois identifies the three defining characteristics of the New Institutional Economics as (1) bounded rationality, (2) evolutionary reasoning, and (3) institutional analysis (1986a, pp. 5–6). Chapter 5 offered a theoretical framework for bounded rationality. Its further development may be of use in New Institutional analyses of the firm and of ideology, and other issues. The idea of the natural selection of language games may help us to unite the three themes of New Institutionalism under one framework. Institutions are the results of evolutionary processes; they shape the actions of boundedly rational agents. The natural selection of language games is a process of institutional evolution. It is a process that shapes both agent-practices and agent-theories. In developing these connections, scholars should probably draw on Max Weber's ideas about the peculiar rationality of Western capitalism. Unique events in European history produced a social and economic system in which the "rationality" of daily life has reached unprecedented levels of intensity and extension (Weber 1927).

Constitutional Political Economy

The Virginia School of Political Economy takes a constitutional perspective. The theoretical arguments of economists should be based on comparative institutional analyses. According to this Virginia view, what people do depends on the constitutional regime. It depends on the "choice of constraints." Economists should gear their arguments and models to the assumed choice of constraints. Surprisingly, members of the Virginia School have not taken this constitutional perspective toward questions of economic expectations. The Virginia School of Political Economy has tended to emphasize the effects of institutions on the incentives. It has neglected what is, perhaps, a more "Austrian" role of institutions, namely, the effect of institutions on the production and distribution of knowledge. Further work in this direction may be worthwhile.

I have taken such a constitutional approach to expectations. I have argued, in effect, that the nature of economic expectations depends on the constitutional regime under which they are formed. There are epistemic consequences of the choice of constraints. Some members of both the Virginia and Austrian schools have long felt the desire for a synthesis of the two traditions. This book is a contribution to just such a synthesis.

Post Walrasian macroeconomics

Most Post Walrasian macroeconomists are at least somewhat "Keynesian." While I have drawn on Keynes, I have also criticized fundamental aspects of his system. But the definition of "Post Walrasian" is broad enough to include Austrians and other non-Keynesians. (And we must not fuss too much over labels.) Post Walrasians seek "macrofoundations of microeconomics" (Colander 1996b). I believe the theory of Big Players is a good, relatively concrete example of how the macroeconomic environment influences microeconomic behavior. I hope I may also have added something to our understanding of coordination and equilibrium. I have argued that coordination does not imply common expectations. This insight about coordination is rather broad. It may be desirable to develop a richer, Post Walrasian theory of coordination, in which coordination does not require common expectations.

Austrian economics

This book comes out of the Austrian tradition. But trying to solve the Lachmann problem has also driven me to something of a reinterpretation of that tradition. (My reinterpretation owes much to other scholars, of course.) The key to this interpretation is Mises' desire to unite the *Vestehen* tradition with old-fashioned neoclassical economics. Many advocates of *Verstehen* neglect or disparage the "mechanistic" models of more traditional economics. Many of those who value such "mechanistic" models reject the "fuzzy thinking" of the *Verstehen* tradition. I believe progress would be made within the Austrian tradition by a return to Mises' original vision.

Appendixes

Appendix 1: What is *Verstehen*?

Verstehen is understanding

"*Verstehen*" is simply the German word for "understanding." As a technical term in the social sciences, the word identifies the human ability to grasp human meanings. This ability is remarkable because the data for any inference about human meanings never single out only one interpretation. For example, "Can you open the window?" may mean, "Please open the window," or "Are you able to open the window?" or something else, depending on context. While our guesses about such things are fallible, we have a remarkable ability to hone in on the intended meaning.

Utterances are not the only meanings we can guess. Any purposeful human action has a meaning to the actor. It has a "meant meaning." Observers can guess the meaning. A certain gesture may be meant as a threat, as a greeting, or as a mock-threat. A given act may be a theft or a purchase depending on the intentions of the actors.

Wilhelm Dilthey (1833–1911) was the progenitor of the *Verstehen* tradition of social theory. He defined "understanding" as "the process of recognizing a mental state from a sense-given sign by which it is expressed" (Dilthey 1900). "Understanding" is achieved through "interpretation." Dilthey used the term "hermeneutics" for the methodology of "interpretation" (Rickman 1976, p. 10).

Verstehen is clever guessing

When we understand a human meaning, we interpret an act or utterance. The interpretation refers to the thoughts of others, which cannot be observed. Only the external signs can be observed. The interpretation is a guess.

On the one hand, the evidence for any guess is always inadequate to logically isolate one interpretation. On the other hand, we consistently hit upon the right interpretation, or something close to it. Mistakes are common. But they are not as common as they should be given the inadequacy of the evidence supporting most interpretations. This puzzle is the problem of understanding.

The problem of understanding is similar to the problem of induction as analyzed by Hume and Popper. In both cases, you have a finite data set that is inadequate to isolate one hypothesis. In the case of induction, the hypothesis is a general rule; in the case of *Verstehen*, it is a human meaning. In both cases, our "inferences" are not strictly logical. They are leaps. Popper called these leaps "conjectures." Pierce coined the term "abduction." In social life, we are able to make the right abductive leap more consistently than chance alone would imply. We are curiously good guessers of human meanings.

Verstehen uses intuition

Etymologically, "intuition" means "looking in." It is direct perception or immediate apprehension. Intuition contrasts with deliberation and logical reasoning. An intuition is not thought through; it is just seen. When observing human action, we often "just see" the intended meaning. We use our intuition. Sometimes, we deliberate. We weigh evidence and compare competing hypotheses. But even in these cases, we use our intuition. There is a gap between the evidence and our guess. Intuition closes the gap.

We can (partially) explain our intuitions

The intuitions through which we understand human meanings can be given a scientific explanation. We can do something more than just point to them and acknowledge their existence. To do that something more, it is useful to compare the intuitions of *Verstehen* with our intuitions about nature. I will argue that the intuitions through which we understand human meanings are similar to the intuitions through which we understand nature, and that both types of intuitions are made possible by special mental functions put in place by biological evolution.

This evolutionary explanation of intuition is incomplete for two reasons. First, there are practical and logical limits to the scientific explanation of mental phenomena. I briefly discuss them below under the heading, "We cannot eliminate the intuitions of *Verstehen*." Second, in addition to the special mental functions, I will highlight some general mental functions that help our intuitions. The next paragraph briefly develops the point.

We are curiously good guessers about many things. Some of the reasons for our skill in guessing do not relate to the special mental functions I mentioned above. Regardless of the object of mental activity, however, our abductive leaps are almost never purely random. We use tricks such as analogy to narrow down the set of plausible guesses. Holland *et al.* (1986) call this "inductive constraint." The conjectures we entertain in any field are constrained. The constraints let us come to good guesses more quickly and surely than we could if our guesses were unconstrained. Holland *et al.* (1986) discuss general cognitive strategies that help us to constrain our guesses cleverly. In addition to these general features of human reasoning, however, we are programmed with special inductive constraints "designed" by evolution for special circumstances. I turn to these now.

Our understanding of nature of uses intuition

There is a sense in which we are pre-programmed to be right about nature. Biological evolution has given us a cognitive system adapted (imperfectly) to the environment of our ancestors. We are born with theories of the physical world. Some of these theories are embodied in structures such as our eyes and ears. Shepard (1992), for example, explains the structure of our color vision by certain regularities in the spectral properties of the light hitting the Earth's surface. The structure of the eye and the pre-programmed psychology of color vision are the evolved reflection of certain regularities of the biological environment in which our species developed. They enable us to make good guesses about the meaning of what we see. If our ancestors did not quickly infer that certain movements in the visual field meant a charging beast, they would not have survived long enough to reproduce.

Landscape preference is another useful example. When shown different scenes of nature, experimental subjects quickly and easily express preferences among them. Their preferences have some common features. We tend to prefer landscapes with "coherence," "complexity," "legibility," and "mystery" (Kaplan 1992). But we are not conscious of these factors. Most experimental subjects cannot explain their preferences. They do not know the variables that predict their choices. The subject completes a complicated task of information processing, but is not conscious of it. Kaplan explains the intuitive nature of the subjects' experience of landscape preference. "The way preference feels to the perceiver stands in sharp contrast to the process that underlies it. Preference is experienced as direct and immediate. There is no hint in consciousness of the complex, inferential process that appears to underlie the judgment of preference. Given the range of variables that are being assessed, the underlying process must be carried out with remarkable speed and efficiency" (1992 p. 595).

Our intuitions about people and things are similar

The inferences governing landscape preference or color perception are not strictly logical. They are fallible conclusions derived from a kind of biologically programmed algorithm acting on sense data. Color perception and landscape preference are processes of inference whose particulars are hidden from us. They seem "direct" and "immediate" to us. Similar processes of inference operate in the realm of human meanings. We "just see" that a certain action is meant as a threat, or a gift, or an offer of exchange. We grasp the meanings of the actions of others through "direct" and "immediate" acts of "intuition." These acts of "intuition" are inferences whose particulars are hidden from us.

Evolution pre-programmed us to make good guesses about the physical world. It also pre-programmed us to make good guesses about the social world. Tooby and Cosmides (1992, p. 39) list several "specialized mechanisms" of human psychology: Chomsky's language acquisition device, a mate preference device, sexual jealousy mechanisms, mother–infant emotion communication signals, and social contract algorithms. We are born with these mechanisms. They are like scripts for social exchanges. The scripts are programmed into us; we know them already.

Chomsky's language acquisition device, for example, lets us know in advance the general grammatical structure of the particular languages we learn as young children. The examples of speech to which we are exposed are filled with errors and interruptions. And yet, we are able to infer the underlying rules of grammar with few errors. This achievement is not some magnificent feat of induction or abduction. It is the consequence of the language acquisition device. Similarly, social contract algorithms are programmed into us from birth. (Such algorithms may develop after birth, however, in much the way the body grows during youth.) We are pre-programmed to understand reciprocity and cheating, sharing and taking, offers and agreement (Cosmides and Tooby 1992).

We cannot eliminate the intuitions of *Verstehen*

We cannot fully reveal the inferential processes that lie behind the intuitive understanding of others. To do so, one would have to identify the physical signals that are interpreted as meaningful acts. If the signals were not described in purely physical terms, some of the processes of inference would remain hidden. Second, one would have to identify the all the particular inferential mechanisms applied to those signals. Either step is probably too much for current science. If Hayek is right, it is logically impossible to eliminate reference to mental states in our descriptions of human action. Thus, the method of *Verstehen* is a practical necessity for us. This claim is the doctrine of methodological dualism. Chapter 4 examines Hayek's defense of methodological dualism at greater length.

Verstehen is not mysterious

Some critics of *Verstehen* have seen it as rather mysterious. Brunswik (1955) blasts Dilthey and others for being "arbitrary" and "sloppy" (1955, p. 719). Many economists have expressed to me attitudes similar to Brunswik's. They think *Verstehen* is mysterious and incoherent.

The *Verstehen* tradition gets some of the blame for the mystery surrounding the idea. Dilthey's work contains obscure passages. For example, the "turn toward reflection" in human studies, "does not depend on looking at life from the outside, but is based on life itself" (1910). Many examples of obscurity can be found in the works of the *Verstehen* tradition. But *Verstehen* is not mysterious.

Verstehen is the human ability to understand human meanings. The ability may seem strange or mysterious because it is based on intuitions that we cannot fully reduce to explicit inferences. But similar intuitions guide our interpretations of the physical world, too. Both kinds of intuition are the result of hidden processes of inference. Both kinds of intuition are fallible. And in both cases, the hidden processes were shaped by biological evolution.

Appendix 2: What did Wittgenstein really mean?

I have decided to use the term "language game" in spite of the difficulties occasioned by the allusion to Wittgenstein. I now believe that it would be an evasion to stick with the term originally use by Langlois and myself, namely, "social game." But it is a doubtful case. My use of the term raises the question of what Wittgenstein "really" meant. But my arguments do not depend on any particular interpretation of Wittgenstein. They stand or fall without him. Nevertheless, it may be appropriate to consider a few issues.

Three specific objections to my use of the term have been raised by discussants in seminars and private conversations. Some critics have objected that economics is about action and not language. As I have defined the term, a language game is a set of rules governing our actions, not just our rhetoric. Moreover, I believe the same may be said of Wittgenstein's concept. Baker and Hacker (1983) define a language game as a "complex consisting of activity and language-use" (1983, p. 33). Wittgenstein says, "And to imagine a language is to imagine a form of life" (1958b, p. 8e). And, "Here the term 'language-*game*' is meant to bring into prominence the fact that the *speaking* of language is part of an activity, or of a form of life" (1958b, p. 11e, emphasis in original).

It is true, however, that language itself gets more attention in Wittgenstein's use of the concept than in my own. Pitkin (1972), for instance, identifies three kinds of "language game" in Wittgenstein (1958b, pp. 39–41). First, there are the games we use to teach children language. Second, there are primitive language games we invent in order to illustrate or understand something about, say, meaning. Third, there are "our many verbal activities, the things we actually do by or with the use of language" (1958b, p. 41). This taxonomy suggests that Wittgenstein did not apply the concept of language games as broadly as I have.

Some critics have objected that language games are "incommensurable" in Wittgenstein, but not in my use of the idea. It probably is true that language games are incommensurable in Wittgenstein. Wittgenstein says, for example, "What has to be accepted, the given, is – so one could say – *forms of life*" (1958b, p. 226e, emphasis in original). If language games are subject to natural selection, then there is at least some commensurability among them. Moreover, in Chapter 5 I appeal to "evolutionary psychology" to argue that there are some universal features of our very different sets of language games. Thus, my use of the idea is far more "modernist" than that of others. (The modernism I appeal to, however, is the anti-Cartesian modernism of the Scottish Enlightenment.)

Related to the last criticism is the charge that Wittgenstein is a relativist and that I am not, or should not be. The term "relativism" is highly charged and probably only an obstruction to clear communication. My preference for Hayek and for Scottish Enlightenment philosophy over "post modernism" probably implies that I am not a relativist. In that case, perhaps, there is a further difference between my use of the concept of "language games" and that of Wittgenstein. Wittgenstein more easily sustains a postmodernist interpretation than do Mises, Hayek, and Schutz. But I doubt that the term "relativism" has a clear meaning. Some truths are relatively "absolute" because we cannot hope to identify limiting conditions beyond which the truth in question does not apply. But these absolutes remain only relatively absolute because they are always open to criticism and revision.

I believe my concept of "language games" is indeed that of Wittgenstein. (As I have noted, it is also the concept of "social games" originally developed by Koppl and Langlois 1994.) I have put it to use, however, in ways that he probably would not have.

Appendix 3: An elementary set-theoretic model of language games

To sort out a few of the complexities in the structure of language games let us assume that there is some primitive or basic set of actions out of which all actions are composed. (I am not invoking the philosophical notions of "primitive action" [Davidson 1971, p. 49] and "basic action" [Danto 1965, p. 44]. They were developed for a different context, namely an analysis of causality and action.) Assume further that we have a complete set of rules governing these elementary actions. These two assumptions let us construct an elementary set theoretic model of the structure of language games. The model below is not meant to be complete. It does not represent, for example, the signals that agents rely upon to know what language game to apply. Nor does it represent the rich networks of meanings connecting rules with one another. But the simple model presented here may help sort our a few issues.

Let $R^{(0)}$ be the set of all rules governing elementary actions in a given society.

$R^{(0)} = \{r_i^{(0)}\}$, where $i \in I$ and I is an index set. If I is countable, $R^{(0)} = \{r_0^{(0)}, r_1^{(0)}, r_2^{(0)}, ...\}$. Let $P(R^{(0)})$ be the power set of $R^{(0)}$. $P(R^{(0)})$ is the set of all subsets of $R^{(0)}$. The set of "first-order elementary language games," $E_0^{(0)}$, is a strict subset of $P(R^{(0)})$. $E_0^{(0)} \subset P(R^{(0)})$. Not all members of $P(R^{(0)})$ are in $E_0^{(0)}$. The empty set is in $P(R^{(0)})$, but not $E_0^{(0)}$. (The empty set does not represent "do nothing." It represents action unconstrained by any rule, an absurdity.) $R^{(0)}$ is not in $E_0^{(0)}$; no elementary action is subject to all existing rules governing such actions. If $R^{(0)}$ has more than one pair of incompatible rules, each of the sets $R^{(0)} - \{r_i^{(0)}\}$ is in $P(R^{(0)})$ but not $E_0^{(0)}$. Some members of $E_0^{(0)}$ will be subsets of other members of $E_0^{(0)}$. Because of the nesting structure of first-order elementary language games, there are cases in which the same action can be described as governed by elementary language game A or by elementary language game B, where $A \subset B$.

Let $P(E_0^{(0)})$ be the power set of $E_0^{(0)}$. The set of "second-order elementary language games," $E_1^{(0)}$, is a strict subset of $P(E_0^{(0)})$. $E_1^{(0)} \subset P(E_0^{(0)})$. We can define in the same way $E_2^{(0)}$, $E_3^{(0)}$, $E_4^{(0)}$, and so on. After some finite number of iterations we reach the highest relevant level, $E_n^{(0)}$. No action is guided by the rules of an elementary language game of order higher than n+1.

Let $E^{(0)}$ be the union of the $E_i^{(0)}$. $E^{(0)} = \bigcup_{i=0}^{n} E_i^{(0)}$. $E^{(0)}$ is the set of elementary language games.

Let $R^{(1)}$ be the set of rules governing choice among elementary language games plus $R^{(0)}$. $P(R^{(1)})$ is the set of all subsets of $R^{(1)}$. The set of "first-order secondary language games," $E_0^{(1)}$, is a strict subset of $P(R^{(1)})$. Including $R^{(0)}$ in $R^{(1)}$ lets $E_0^{(1)}$ include members with both kinds of rule sets so far considered. It is stipulated that $E_0^{(1)}$ exclude all members of $E^{(0)}$. We can define the sets $E_1^{(1)}$, $E_2^{(1)}$, $E_3^{(1)}$, and so on up to $E_m^{(1)}$. $E^{(1)} = \bigcup_{i=0}^{m} E_i^{(1)}$. $E^{(1)}$ is the set of secondary language games.

We may define $E^{(2)}$, $E^{(3)}$, $E^{(4)}$, ... $E^{(N)}$. N is our highest level. No actions are governed by $(N + 1)$-ary language games. The set of language games, S, is the union of the $E^{(i)}$

$$S = \bigcup_{i=0}^{N} E^{(i)}$$

.

Any action can be correctly described as falling under the rules of any of several language games, depending on the purposes of the analyst. A give action might be described as falling under, say, the third member of the set $E_7^{(0)}$, the eighth member of the set $E_4^{(7)}$, or the fourth member of the set $E^{(12)}$. Using lower case letters to indicate the members of these sets, we may say of a given action that $e^3{}_7{}^{(0)}$, $e^8{}_4{}^{(7)}$, or $e^{4(12)}$ is the language game whose rules govern the action. Which description to use is a function of the scientific purpose at hand.

Any action taken has a meaning to the actor. The actor's intention determines the meaning. The intention, in fact, determines a complex structure of meanings. The observing social scientist has no choice about this. The meant meaning is that of the actor, not the scientist. This meant meaning, together with the total social situation, determines which language games govern the action. In terms of our set theoretic model, it is the actor's meant meaning that makes $e^3{}_7{}^{(0)}$, $e^8{}_4{}^{(7)}$, and $e^{4(12)}$ apply.

But the scientist has some freedom to choose. The actor will not generally be aware of the full structure of the set, S, of language games. He might recognize, in some sense, that his meant meaning corresponds to, say, $e^8{}_4{}^{(7)}$. He might not. It is the scientist who chooses which of the language games $e^3{}_7{}^{(0)}$, $e^8{}_4{}^{(7)}$, or $e^{4(12)}$ he will use in describing the action. Moreover, he will use scientific language. He will use Schutz's "second-order constructs." He will not try to import the actor's interpretations "directly" into his theory. He cannot do so. He can only offer (fallible) interpretations of the actor's interpretations. Thus he is obliged to make his scientific interpretations conform to the Schutzian postulates discussed in Chapter 3.

The actor, then, does not decide for the scientist what language game the scientist should invoke to describe or explain the action. But the actor's action, his "meant meaning," does constrain the scientist's choice. It decides which language games are at work and which are not.

The set of language games contains first-order language games and higher-order language games. Choice from within a higher-order language game can be modeled as choice among lower-order language games. With some exceptions, then, the distinction I have drawn between these two kinds of choice is not a distinction between two different kinds of choices existing in the world. It is a distinction between two ways of describing a given choice.

Appendix 4: Notes on reflexivity

Introduction

Any theory of expectations must address reflexivity. I have done so in Chapter 6, where I discuss closed and open reflexivity. That discussion may suggest something of the potential of the *Verstehen* tradition to help sort out the logic paradoxes produced by reflexivity. I discussed the biology of *Verstehen* earlier. That discussion may suggest that we are biologically adapted to cope with the problems of reflexivity that arise in small groups. Some further comments on reflexivity may be in order.

Holmes and Moriarty: some logical difficulties of reflexivity[1]

Oskar Morgenstern's essay "Perfect Foresight and Economic Equilibrium" (1935) contains a classic and, I believe, fundamental treatment of reflexivity. In that classic article which led to his collaboration with John von Neumann, Morgenstern argued that perfect foresight is inconsistent with economic equilibrium. Perfect foresight requires that I know perfectly well what you will do and vice versa. I have a complete and correct model of you and all of your thoughts. Your have an equally perfect model of me and all of my thoughts. My model of you contains your model of me, which, in turn, contains again my model of you, and so on.

I think that you think that I think that you think that I think ... Morgenstern argued that this infinite chain of perfect reflections creates inescapable paradoxes. In making his argument, Morgenstern repeated an analysis he had made in an earlier paper (1928). His analysis describes the Holmes–Moriarty problem.

> Sherlock Holmes, pursued by his opponent, Moriarty, leaves London for Dover. The train stops at a station on the way, and he alights there rather than travelling on to Dover. He has seen Moriarty at the railway station, recognizes that he is very clever and expects that Moriarity will take a faster special train in order to catch him in Dover. Holmes' anticipations turns out to be correct. But what if Moriarity had been still more clever, had estimated Holmes' mental abilities better and had foreseen his actions accordingly? Then, obviously, he would have travelled to the intermediate station. Holmes again would have had to calculate that, and he himself would have decided to go on to Dover. Whereupon, Moriarity would again have "reacted" differently. Because of so much thinking they might not have been able act at all or the intellectually weaker of the two would have surrendered to the other in the Victoria Station, since the whole flight would have become unnecessary. Examples of this kind can be drawn from everywhere. However, chess, strategy, etc. presuppose expert knowledge, which encumbers the example unnecessarily. (1935, p. 174)

In this passage, Morgenstern describes the two-person zero-sum game represented in Figure A4.1. Morgenstern drew his example from "The Final Problem." In this story Conan Doyle pits Holmes against an equally rational enemy. The two are perfectly matched and in the end can only destroy each other. It is impossible that one should win and the other loose. In the middle of the story, Moriarty comes to Holmes' home to confront him.

		Moriarity: Dover	Moriarity: Intermediate Station
Holmes	Dover	0,1	1,0
	Intermediate Station	1,0	0,1

Each player must choose whether to get off in Dover or at the intermediate station. If both choose the same location, Moriarity wins. If they choose different stations, Holmeswins. The first number in each box is the payoff to Holmes, who chooses the row. The second number is the payoff to Moriarty, who chooses the column. A Nash equilibrium in mixedstrategies exists if each player assigns a probability weight of 0.5 to each of his pure strategies.

Figure A4.1 Morgenstern's two-person zero-sum game

Holmes relates the event to Watson as follows.

> '"All that I have to say has already crossed your mind," said he.
> '"Then possibly my answer has crossed yours," I replied.
> '"You stand fast?"
> '"Absolutely."'

This exchange represents perfectly the situation that would have to exist if each of two perfectly rational players possessed a complete model of the other.

In the Holmes–Moriarity game and in similar cases, as Morgenstern argued, "there is exhibited an endless chain of reciprocally conjectural reactions and counter-reactions." Morgenstern notes, in an anticipation of Keynes' "animal spirits," that "[t]his chain can never be broken by an act of knowledge but always only through an arbitrary act – a resolution." He concludes that "[t]he paradox still remains no matter how one attempts to twist or turn things around" (1935 p. 174). There is a long lecture-hall tradition of using the Holmes–Moriarty problem as an exemplar to demonstrate the power of game-theoretic reasoning. The lecturer imagines that standard game-theoretic solutions disperse all paradox. Rosser and I (Koppl and Rosser 2001) argue that this lecture-hall tradition has been mistaken. The paradoxes Morgenstern identified are not dispersed by a game-theoretic analysis.

First, we show that a best reply is not computable in the Holmes–Moriarty game. We imagine the parts of Holmes and Moriarty to be played by "Turing machines." A Turing machine is a mathematical model of a calculating machine. There are infinitely many such machines. Any Turing machine can perform some calculations, but not others. There are some calculations that cannot be performed by any machine. These impossible calculations correspond to problems and functions that are not "computable." (This fact is related to Kurt Gödel's famous theorem to the effect that some true propositions of mathematics have no formal proof.)

Mathematicians have been able to find an order among these machines that lets them list them and assign a whole number to any Turing machine. (Thus, the set of Turing machines is "countable.") If you know the numbering scheme, a Turing machine's number tells you everything about the machine. Rosser and I let each machine learn the number of its opponent. We show that under this set up each player's best-reply strategy is non-computable. "The value of our proof," we say, "lies in showing that the problem of mutually interlocking expectations does not admit of a purely logical solution, at least in some cases." Holmes and Moriarty must remain ciphers to one another at least in some degree. They cannot be perfectly transparent to one another.

Rosser and I go on to show that Bayesian updating does not necessarily solve the problem. We assume each player a flawless Bayesian updater and they let each player observe the other's thinking about himself. "In this context," we argue, "the two may be unable to hit on a mutually consistent set of prior beliefs that would allow convergence." We reproduce a theorem from Diaconis and Freedman (1986) showing that in such cases Bayesian updating may not lead to convergence. "The infinite regress of total mutual awareness undermines the convergence as Holmes and Moriarty endlessly cycle after each other."

Finally, Rosser and I show that "econometricians cannot always process information faster than the economy." We imagine a computer that has been programmed with all the laws of economics. Certain questions about the economy at moment $t + \delta$ can be inferred from the initial conditions given at moment t and the laws of economics. The computer can "predict" the state of the economy. We show, however, that no computer can always spit out such predictions ahead of time. The computer will spit out some "predictions" only after the fact. The proof (adapted from Wolpert 1996) builds on the idea that the economy may contain computers similar to the ones we are asking predictions from. Such a computer could be programmed, in essence, to falsify the prediction. We conclude, "limits to rationality exist no matter what model of rationality we adopt. They exist even if we assume the relevant problems are all solvable in a finite amount of time."

The problem of reflexivity admits of no "eductive" solution. When you think that I think that you think, there is no purely logical solution to the problem of predicting outcomes. Expectations are necessarily determined at least in part by something other than ratiocination.

The Keynesian beauty contest: some economic aspects of reflexivity[2]

Atomistic reflexivity

In Chapter 12 of *The General Theory*, Keynes described a competition in which contestants try to select the six most beautiful women from a large group of photographs reproduced in a newspaper. The prize goes to the contestant whose choices most perfectly reflect the average choice computed from all entries sent to the paper. In such a contest, Keynes explained, each player picks "not those faces which he himself finds prettiest, but those which he thinks likeliest to catch the fancy of the other competitors, all of whom are looking at the problem from the same point of view" (Keynes 1936, p. 156). In this contest, the contestants do not make their choices on the basis of any opinions of their own concerning the beauty of the women in the photographs. They do not even necessarily concern themselves with what average opinion might really be. "We have reached the third degree where we devote our intelligences to anticipating what average opinion expects the average opinion to be. And there are some, I believe, who practice the fourth, fifth, and higher degree" (1936 p. 156).

We may express the peculiar situation created by the Keynesian beauty contest as one of "atomistic reflexivity." The reflexivity is *atomistic* because no coordination mechanism exists to fit expectations together in a self-consistent pattern.

In the beauty contest, each contestant's choices are based on expectations about the decisions of the other players. Because this is true for all players, their expectations are expectations about the expectations of others.

Often, it is possible for individual action to bring about a coordination of expectations. In the beauty contest it is not. Here, even though expectations are interdependent they are not coordinated because there is no underlying harmony of interests propelling the contestants toward an equilibrium position, and, second, there is no mechanism for contestants to establish a coordination of expectations.

In a market setting it is possible to speak of tendencies toward a harmony of interests.[3] Institutional arrangements require the mutual adaptation of individual actions in ways that promote the attainment of individual plans. Prices act as signals guiding us to actions conforming to the actions taken by other market participants, each of whom is guided by these same price signals (Hayek 1937). Each of us has an interest in coordinating his actions with the actions of all other market participants. In this sense, there is a long-run harmony of interests propelling us toward a coordination of expectations. I want your plans to succeed because I want my plans to succeed. In the Keynesian beauty contest, there is no long-run harmony of interests propelling us toward a coordination of expectations because no contestant wants to improve the guesses of any other contestant. Your good guess is my bad luck; if your plans succeed, mine fail.

Second, there is no mechanism to establish a coordination of expectations in the Keynesian beauty contest. The market, on the other hand, does provide a mechanism for traders to establish a coordination of expectations. When suppliers sell less than expected, they lower prices in an effort to draw business away from their competitors. When prices fall in the wake of such plan revisions, sales improve and expectations are more fully coordinated. Similarly, when suppliers sell more than expected, they raise prices in an effort to extract transient profits or maintain desired inventory levels. When prices rise in the wake of such plan revisions, sales fall off and expectations are more fully coordinated. In the standard Marshallian diagram of supply and demand, the plans of demanders and suppliers are perfectly coordinated in equilibrium and nowhere else. Through this mechanism, a sequence of piecemeal adjustments coordinates the expectations of market participants. No such mechanisms are at work in the Keynesian beauty contest. Contestants do not write contracts with each other that make mutual promises about what beauties will be selected. Contestants cannot make piecemeal adjustments to their entries in the wake of disappointed expectations.

As Keynes (1936, p. 156) constructed his example, there is no link between the contestants' decisions and the underlying reality, the beauty of the faces being judged. Because "we have reached the third degree" in which each contestant acts on his guess about "what average opinion expects average opinion to be," any connecting threads running between the beauty of a face and the votes it receives have been cut. By construction, no decision maker in the model cares who really has the prettiest face. Any concern one might have had over such matters is mitigated and ultimately swamped by the way expectations are interdependent in the contest. The design of the contest ensures a weak link between what contestants think about this reality and what they do.

The market is not a Keynesian beauty contest

Keynes used his beauty contest as a parable of the stock exchange. There is reason to question this application. Whether we consider the stock market or the market for shoes, the expectations formed in the market tend to be neither atomistically determined nor unmoored to the underlying economic reality. There are at least three reasons economic expectations tend to be more coherent and better moored to reality than Keynes' metaphor implies. First, there is an (imperfect) long-run harmony of interests propelling participants toward an equilibrium pattern of expectations. Second, the market has an equilibration process. Third, market participants have a direct concern for the underlying realities.

There is a long-run harmony of interests in the market. I have already mentioned the long-run harmony of interests. In the stock market, as in any market, deviations from the equilibrium pattern of prices induce plan inconsistency. If stock prices are wrong, the plans of producers and consumers will not fit, nor will the plans of borrowers and lenders, or of different producers. Such inconsistency means, for at least some persons, plan failure and revision. Such inconsistencies will also be reflected, sooner or later, in changes in stock prices. Alert entrepreneurs will detect such inconsistencies and act to profit from them. In so doing, however, they tend to eliminate these inconsistencies.

In the beauty contest, each player wishes to out-guess the other players. Incentives that could work to establish a mutually consistent pattern of action and expectation, and hence promote a long-run harmony of interests, are perfectly absent. The situation is quite different in markets. Market participants have, in general, an incentive to avoid discoordination and painful re-equilibration processes. Though it is imperfect in that some persons profit from market failures, there is a very real long-run harmony of interests in the market that helps to co-ordinate expectations. Each participant in the market has an incentive to adapt his actions and expectations to the overall pattern of action and expectation around him.

Markets have equilibration mechanisms. The second factor absent from the Keynesian beauty contest but present in the market is an equilibration process. In the market an equilibrium pattern of action and expectation tends to emerge out of a sequence of mutual adaptations of each participant to all other participants. This process of "adaptive, sequential decision making" (Williamson 1976, p. 83) has a built-in tendency toward equilibrium. The equilibrating agent is the entrepreneur.

In the beauty contest there are many "levels" of play, but there is no sequence of actions. Each actor makes his choice in splendid isolation, independently and alone. The results of his choice give him no opportunity to revise his plans. In the market, there is give and take, profit and loss. At least within the "corridor" (Leijonhufvud 1973), this give and take creates a tendency toward equilibrium.

Market participants are directly concerned with the underlying realities. The third and final factor at work in the market but absent from the beauty contest is a direct concern for the underlying realities. In the beauty contest, reflexivity is everything; underlying realities are nothing. As we have seen, the underlying beauty of the faces may be of no interest to contestants in the beauty contest. Market participants cannot so easily ignore the underlying realities. For them, the fundamentals determine profit and loss. Thus, there is a kind of "objective" reality for entrepreneurs to discover. The market process is not purely self-referential.

In the market, any deviation between the underlying scarcities and economic action brings losses to someone. When plans and expectations are out of line with the underlying economic reality, plan failure is sure to hit someone. Those plan failures will bring losses and regret. In order to avoid such losses and regret, economic actors take an interest in the fundamentals. Alert entrepreneurs seize upon past failures to grasp adequately these fundamentals.

The market process is decidedly imperfect. Ignorance and uncertainty lead to herding. But there are important differences between the market process and the Keynesian beauty contest. The market process contains mechanisms and inducements to coordination that are not present in the Keynesian beauty contest. The market process contains mechanisms and incentive to transform open reflexivity into closed reflexivity.

Notes

1   Introduction and Summary

1. Much of this chapter draws on Koppl (1998).
2. The literature on Schutz and the Austrian school is growing. See the symposium in volume 14 (2001) of the *Review of Austrian Economics* for an introduction to this literature as well as a substantial contribution to it. Prendergast (1986) is the crucial article in this group. See also Helling (1984) and Augier (1999).
3. Appendix 2 (p. 208) discusses the similarities and differences between my use of the idea and that of its originator, Ludwig Wittgenstein. I have probably used the idea in ways Wittgenstein would not have done.
4. This section reproduces portions of Koppl (1998).
5. have been ignoring the difference between the thoughts of agents and our representations of those thoughts. This difference can matter. As far as I can tell, however, it does not matter for the points being made in this chapter.

2   The Misesian Context

1. Husserl claimed that all natural science, including psychology, is "naïve" because it assumes uncritically that a natural world exists (1911, p. 85). In this sense, Hayek's naturalistic psychology is probably not naïve.
2. Apparently, Husserl never gave the term a proper definition. See Quentin Lauer's note to this passage.
3. The phrase "scientific subjectivism" is due to Caldwell (1994) who used it to describe the methodology of F. A. Hayek.
4. As far as I know, O'Driscoll and Rizzo (1985) were the first authors to recognize the importance of Bergson to Mises' thought.
5. The evolutionary psychology represented by Barkow *et al.* and Tooby 1992 challenges this traditional philosophical view.
6. In this passage Mises refers to "the kind of psychology" Dilthey "was referring to." But Mises has already equated this "psychology" with "understanding." (See Mises 1957, p. 265.)
7. Mises quotes the original French, citing the 4th edition of Bergson's *La Pensee et le mouvant*, p. 205. I've quoted p. 6 of Bergson (1903a), which is an exact translation of the passage in Mises.
8. Concepts such as "purpose" and "preference" have application, however, in behavioral biology. Even the concept of "voluntary exchange" applies as in the case of vampire bats (Cosmides and Tooby 1992, McGrew and Feistner 1992). Thus, methodological dualism may be a matter of degree just as the distinction between theory and history is a matter of degree.

9. Mises' treatment of methodological individualism is more sophisticated in *Human Action* than in *Epistemological Problems of Economics*.

3   Schutz

1. Parts of this chapter draw on Koppl (1997) and Koppl (2001).
2. The term "sense-contents" comes from Ayers (1952).
3. In this book I will stick to acting man and his "stock of knowledge at hand." I will not discuss the "constitution" of "typifications" from the flow of "pre-predicative" experience. On the role of reflection and remembrance in constituting meanings see Schutz (1932, pp. 45–53).
4. "It is as Husserl has shown, a universal prinicple of consciousness that in my conscious acts I 'live' attentive to their intentional Objects, not to the acts themselves. Thus, in order to grasp these acts I must attend to them reflectively; that is, of necessity *post hoc*" (Schutz and Luckmann 1973, p. 53).
5. Schutz (1932b) is a fragment of Schutz's 1932 book, *Der sinnhafte Aufbau der sozialen Welt*, translated by Thomas Luckmann.
6. Social science is "never" based on "prepredicative Acts of laying hold on" (1932a, p. 223).
7. In Schutz's view of choice, there is no "moment" of choice. Choosing is a process that unrolls through inner-time. See Schutz (1951).
8. The quote from Mises can be found in Mises (1933, p. 85).
9. Husserl's comments on the "Interdependence of the Sciences of Fact and of Essence" (1913, p. 57) bear a striking resemblance to later remarks by Mises on the relation of "praxeology" and history. Too little research has been done on the similarities and differences between Mises and Husserl.

4   Hayek

1. Parts of this chapter draw on Koppl (1999), and Butos and Koppl (1993).
2. This account of Hutchison's views simplifies, but not much. I will not address the question of Popper's influence on Hayek.
3. The footnotes on p. 36 and 37 are particularly revealing.
4. William Butos first drew my attention to the close connection between these two books.

5   Language Games and Economic Theory

1. My argument is probably similar to Wittgenstein's argument that there can be no private language (1958b).
2. Most of this paragraph is taken from Koppl (2000a).
3. Clower and Howitt (1996) have severely criticized Menger's model. They argue that the evolution of money necessarily coincided with the evolution of firms and markets. I believe they are right. But I do not believe their

argument contradicts Menger at all. (It does contradict some modern search-theoretic models such as Jones 1976.) Their argument extends and complements that of Menger; it does not replace it.

4. Kreiner cites Offe (1976) for his use of the term "achievement principle."

6 Expectations

1. Butos and Koppl (1999) propose viewing Kirznerian entrepreneurs as Hayekian learners. Credit for the idea goes entirely to Butos.
2. As far as I know, it does not matter if this equilibrium position can be modeled as one in which the system moves "to the edge of chaos."
3. This section is reproduced from Butos and Koppl (2001).
4. Butos and Koppl (2001) criticize the Post Keynesian use of the term "nonergodic." Davidson (1989) seems to be the first to use the term in its Post Keynesian sense.
5. The imaginary trader could not devise a trading strategy whose expected return exceeded the risk premium by more than the risk-free rate of interest.

7 Big Players

1. Parts of this chapter draw on Koppl (1996) and Koppl and Yeager (1996).
2. The argument of this section is adapted from Hayek (1952a, 1967). The "counting argument" of this section is also discussed in Butos and Koppl (1997b) and in Koppl (2000b).
3. This argument is essentially the same as Hayek's argument that the mind cannot explain itself. Hayek's argument was discussed in Chapter 4.
4. This and the following four paragraphs are taken from Broussard and Koppl (1999).
5. Let r and w have the meanings Heiner gives them, but applied to Scharfstein and Stein's "smart" managers. Let r' and w' be the corresponding probabilities for "dumb" managers. Then Scharfstein and Stein's p is equivalent to r, while their q is equivalent to w. Their z is equivalent to r' which equals w'. Scharfstein and Stein's α is Heiner's π. Their x_H is Heiner's g and, finally, their x_L is Heiner's l.
6. Parke (1999) uses his model to represent persistence in the volatility of asset prices.
7. In this case, the several errors of a period would all endure for the same number of periods. Dropping this assumption would complicate Parke's error-duration model. I conjecture that it would not alter any of the conclusions I have drawn in this chapter.

8 Big Players in Czarist Russia

1. This chapter is based on Koppl and Yeager (1996) and Broussard and Koppl (1999). Credit for the discovery of the historical episode in question goes entirely to Leland Yeager. Yeager is the principal author of the section of this chapter describing the episode. I am responsible for the R/S test. Broussard

ran the GARCH analyses. The data examined in this chapter were collected from contemporary newspapers by Yeager.

2. These are the approximately complete calendar years. Actually, Bunge served from 18 May 1881 to 13 January 1887, Vyshnegradsky from then until 11 September 1892 (Western calendar). However, Vyshnegradsky suffered a stroke on 7 April 1892 and was pretty much out of action thereafter.

3. The story is told in Witte (1923, pp. 200, 207–216). Gindin (1960, pp. 320, 321n.) retells the story in some detail. He cites unpublished documents as well as Witte's memoirs. See also the editorial commentary in Polovtsov (1966, II, p. 517).

4. Thanks to Dr. Edelbert F. Brand for photocopies of the relevant *Börsen-Courier* articles of August and September 1890. On the great influence of the gold-standard rumors, compare Schulze-Gävernitz (1899, pp. 476, 476n, 517), Ratner (1898, pp. 56–57), Raffalovich (1892, p. 20), and Witte (1923, p. 127). See also *Aktionär*, February 5, 1893, p. 71, and February 12, 1893, p. 79.

5. For other statistical analyses of the same and related data, see Yeager (1969). Yeager (1984) further describes the state of public and professional opinion at the time.

6. The literature on GARCH modeling is quite extensive. Representative works include Akgiray (1989), Akgiray and Booth (1990), Akgiray *et al.* (1991), Baillie and Bollerslev (1990), Koutmos and Theodossiou (1994), and Theodossiou (1994).

7. There is a qualification to this remark. Short-term autocorrelation may create the false impression of persistence when a researcher gives too much weight to measurements on short intervals.

9 The Angular Distribution of Asset Returns in Delay Space

1. This chapter is a modified version of Koppl and Nardone (2001).

10 Herding in Money Demand

1. This chapter is based on Gilanshah and Koppl (2001).

2. See Goldfeld (1973), Laidler (1993, p. 171).

3. The period since 1987 appears to be a regime of discretion with no ostensible target. This period may be an appropriate subject for another study.

4. See Meulendyke (1989, pp. 197–198). See also Jones (1989) and Melton (1985).

5. The historical account of monetary policy regimes in the following sections draws heavily from Meulendyke (1989).

6. Also of significance, the inflation of the previous years was causing large gold outflows by 1970. This prompted Nixon, in 1971, to close the gold window and allow the official price of gold to rise significantly. By 1973, the Treasury had terminated all purchases and sales of gold, thereby eliminating the constraining force its price had been in the growth of money.

7. Further modifications of monetary targeting practices were implemented in 1975 and 1978 in response to congressional legislation.

8. See Roley (1990).

9. Meulendyke (1989, p. 43).
10. Meulendyke (1989, p. 45).
11. To further confuse the already dizzying system, the Federal Reserve redefined monetary aggregates in 1980, and introduced "shift aggregates" in 1981, in an attempt to account for new liquid assets and other financial innovations.
12. Meulendyke (1989, p. 46).
13. Meulendyke (1989, p. 47).

Appendix 4: Notes on Reflexivity

1. This section reproduces some passages from Koppl and Rosser (2000)
2. This section draws on Butos and Koppl (1999)
3. A traditional source for the "principle of self-interest rightly understood" is Tocqueville (1835, 1840, II, pp. 128–132): "The principle of self-interest rightly understood is not a lofty one, but it is clear and sure ... By its admirable conformity to human weakness it easily obtains great dominion; nor is that dominion precarious, since the principle checks one personal interest by another, and uses, to direct the passions, the very same instrument that excites them" (1835, 1840, p. 131). On this and related doctrines see Hirschman (1977), Mises (1966, pp. 673–82), Hayek (1973, p. 97), and Elster (1999).

Bibliography

Abramowitz, Milton, and Irene A. Stegun (eds.) 1972. *Handbook of Mathematical Functions*, New York: Dover Publishers.

Ahmed, Ehsan, Roger Koppl, J. Barkley Rosser, and Mark V. White 1997. "Complex Bubble Persistence in Closed-End Country Funds," *Journal of Economic Behavior and Organization*, 32(1): 19–37.

Akgiray, V. 1989. "Conditional Heteroskedasticity in Time Series of Stock Returns: Evidence and Forecasts," *Journal of Business*, 62(1): 55–80.

Akgiray, V. and G. Geoffrey Booth 1990. "Modeling the Stochastic Behavior of Canadian Foreign Exchange Rates," *Journal of Multinational Financial Management*, 1: 43–71.

Akgiray, V., G. Geoffrey Booth, John J. Hatem, and Chowdhury Mustafa 1991. "Conditional Dependence in Precious Metal Prices," *The Financial Review*, 26: 367–86.

Albin, P.S. 1998. *Barriers and Bounds to Rationality: Essays on Economic Complexity and Dynamics in Interactive Systems*, ed. Duncan K. Foley, Princeton: Princeton University Press.

Alchian, Armen A. 1950. "Uncertainty, Evolution and Economic Theory," *Journal of Political Economy*, 58: 211–21.

Allais, M. 1953. "Le comportement de l'homme rationnel devant le risque, critique des postulats et axiomes de l'ecole americaine," *Econometrica*, 21: 503–26.

Anderlini, L. and H. Sabourian 1995. "Cooperation and Effective Computability," *Econometrica*, 63, 1337–69.

Anderson, Philip W., Kenneth J. Arrow, and David Pines (eds.) 1988. *The Economy as an Evolving Complex System*, Redwood, Cal: Addison-Wesley.

Arthur, Brian 1994a. *Increasing Returns and Path Dependence in the Economy*, Ann Arbor: The University of Michigan Press.

Arthur, Brian 1994b. "Inductive Reasoning and Bounded Rationality," *American Economic Review*, 84(2): 406–11.

Arthur, Brian W. 2000. "Complexity and the Economy," in David Colander ed. *The Complexity Vision and the Teaching of Economics*, Cheltenham, UK: Edward Elgar.

Augier, Mie 1999. "Some Notes on Alfred Schütz and the Austrian School of Economics: Review of Alfred Schutz's Collected Papers, Vol. IV. Edited by H. Wagner, G. Psathas and F. Kersten," *Review of Austrian Economics*, 11(1/2): 145–62.

Ayers, Alfred J. 1952. *Language, Truth and Logic*, New York: Dover Publications Inc.

Baillie, Richard. T. and Tim Bollerslev 1990. "Intra-Day and Intra-Market Volatility in Foreign Exchange Rates," *Review of Economic Statistics*, 58: 565–85.

Baker, G. P. and P. M. S. Hacker 1983. *An Analytical Commentary on Wittgenstein's Philosophical Investigations*, (vol. 1) Chicago: The University of Chicago Press.

Barkow, Jerome, Leda Cosmides, and John Tooby (eds.) 1992 *The Adapted Mind: Evalutionary Pschology and the Generation of Culture*, New York and Oxford: Oxford University Press.

Baumol, William 1990. "Entrepreneurship: Productive, Unproductive, and Destructive," *Journal of Political Economy*, 98(5): 893–21.

Begg, David K. H. 1982. *The Rational Expectations Revolution in Macroeconomics: Theory and Findings*, Baltimore: Johns Hopkins University Press.

Bergson, Henri [1903a] 1961. "Introduction to Metaphysics," trans. Mabelle L. Andison, New York: Wisdom Library.

Bergson, Henri [1903b] 1946. "Introduction to Metaphysics," in Henri Bergson, *The Creative Mind: An Introduction to Metaphysics*, trans. Mabelle L. Andison, New York: Wisdom Library.

Bikhchandani, S., D. Hirshleifer, and I. Welch 1992. "A Theory of Fads, Fashions, Custom, and Cultural Change as Informational Cascades," *Journal of Political Economy*, 100: 612–43.

Binmore, K. 1987. "Modeling Rational Players I," *Economics and Philosophy*, 3: 9–55.

Black, Fisher 1986. "Noise," *The Journal of Finance*, 41(3): 529–43.

Boettke, Peter J. 1990. "Interpretive Reasoning and the Study of Social Life," *Methodus* 2(2): 35–45, reprinted in David L. Prychitko (ed.), *Individuals, Institutions, Interpretations*, Brookfield, VT: Avebury 1995.

Bollerslev, T. 1986. "Generalized Autoregressive Conditional Heteroskedasticity," *Journal of Econometrics*, 31: 307–27.

Booth, G. Geoffrey and Fred R. Kaen 1979. "Gold and Silver Spot Prices and Market Information Efficiency," *Financial Review*, 14: 21–6.

Booth, G. Geoffrey, Fred R. Kaen, and Peter F. Koveos 1981. "Foreign Exchange Market Behavior: 1975–1978," *Rivista Internazionale di Scienze Economiche e Commerciali*, April: 311–25.

Booth, G. Geoffrey, Fred R. Kaen, and Peter F. Koveos 1982. "R/S Analysis of Foreign Exchange Rates Under Two International Monetary Regimes," *Journal of Monetary Economics*, 10: 407–15.

Brealy, Richard A. and Stewart C. Meyers 1991. *Principles of Corporate Finance*, New York: McGraw-Hill, 4th edn.

Brealy, Richard A. and Stewart C. Meyers 1996. *Principles of Corporate Finance*, New York: McGraw-Hill, 5th edn.

Brock, William A. 2000. "Some Santa Fe Scenery," in David Colander (ed.), *The Complexity Vision and the Teaching of Economics*, Cheltenham, UK: Edward Elgar.

Brockwell, Peter J. and Richard A. Davis 1991. *Time Series: Theory and Methods*, New York and Berlin: Springer-Verlag, 2nd edn.

Broussard, John and Roger Koppl 1999. "Explaining Volatility Dynamics: The Case of the Russian Ruble," *Managerial Finance*, 25(1): 49–63.

Brunswik, Egon 1955. "The Conceptual Framework of Psychology," in Otto Neurath, Rudolf Carnap, and Charles Morris (eds.), *International Encyclopedia of Unified Science, Volume I, Nos. 6-10*, Chicago: University of Chicago Press.

Buchanan, James 1990. "The Domain of Constitutional Economics," *Constitutional Political Economy*, 1(1): 1–18.

Bunge, Nikolai 1880. "Zametki o nastojashchem polozhenii nashej denezhnoj sistemy i sredstvakh k eja uluchsheniju," *Sbornik Gosudarstvennykh Znanij VIII*, quoted at length in Gurjev 1896.

Burczak, Theodore A. 2001. "Profit Expectations and Confidence: Some Unresolved Issues in the Austrian/Post Keynesian Debate," *Review of Political Economy*, 13(1): 59–80.

Butos, William 1997. "Toward an Austrian Theory of Expectations," *Advances in Austrian Economics*, 4: 75–94.

Butos, William and Roger Koppl 1993. "Hayekian Expectations: Theory and Empirical Applications," *Constitutional Political Economy*, 4(3): 303–29.

Butos, William and Roger Koppl 1997a. "Science as a Spontaneous Order," manuscript, Fairleigh Dickinson University.

Butos, William and Roger Koppl 1997b. "The Varieties of Subjectivism: Keynes and Hayek on Expectations," *History of Political Economy*, 29(2): 327–59.

Butos, William and Roger Koppl 1999. "Hayek and Kirzner at the Keynesian Beauty Contest," *Journal des Etudes Humaines et des Etudes Humaines*, 9(2/3): 257–75.

Butos, William and Roger Koppl 2001. "Confidence in Keynes and Hayek: Reply to Buczak," *Review of Political Economy*, 13(1): 81–6.

Caldwell, Bruce 1982. *Beyond Positivism: Economic Methodology in the Twentieth Century*, London: George Allen & Unwin.

Caldwell, Bruce 1984. "Praxeology and its Critics: An Appraisal," *History of Political Economy*, 16: 363–79.

Caldwell, Bruce 1988. "Hayek's Transformation," *History of Political Economy*, 20: 513–41.

Caldwell, Bruce 1992a." Hayek the Falsificationist? A Refutation," *Research in the History of Economic Thought and Methodology*, 10: 1–15.

Caldwell, Bruce 1992b. "Hayek the Falsificationist: Reply to Hutchison," *Research in the History of Economic Thought and Methodology*, 10: 33–42.

Caldwell, Bruce 1994. "Hayek's Scientific Subjectivism," *Economics and Philosophy*, 10(2): 305–13.

Carnap, Rudolf 1958. *Introduction to Symbolic Logic and its Applications*, New York: Dover.

Chen, An-Sing 1997. "The Square Compass Rose: the Evidence From Taiwan," *Journal of Multinational Financial Management*, 7(2): 127–44.

Choi, Young Back 1993. *Paradigms and Conventions: Uncertainty, Decision Making, and Entrepreneurship*, Ann Arbor: University of Michigan Press.

Clower, Robert and Peter Howitt 1996. "Taking Markets Seriously," in David Colander (ed.) *Beyond Microfoundations: Post-Walrasian Macroeconomics*, Cambridge: Cambridge University Press: 21–37.

Cochrane, John H. 1991. "Volatility Tests and Efficient Markets: A Review Essay," *Journal of Monetary Economics*, 27(3): 463–85.

Colander David (ed.) 1996a. *Beyond Microfoundations: Post-Walrasian Macroeconomics*, Cambridge: Cambridge University Press.

Colander, David 1996b. "The Macrofoundations of Micro," in David Colander (ed.), *Beyond Microfoundations: Post-Walrasian Macroeconomics*, Cambridge: Cambridge University Press: 57–68.

Colander, David (ed.) 2000. *The Complexity Vision and the Teaching of Economics*, Cheltenham, UK: Edward Elgar.

Cosmides, Leda and John Tooby 1992. "Cognitive Adaptations for Social Exchange," in Jerome H. Barkow, Leda Cosmides, and John Tooby (eds) *The Adapted Mind: Evolutionary Psychology and the Generation of Culture*, New York and Oxford: Oxford University Press.

Crack, Timothy F. and Olivier Ledoit 1996. "Robust Structure Without Predictability: The 'Compass Rose' Pattern of the Stock Market," *Journal of Finance*, 51: 751–62.

Cyert, Richard and James G. March. (1963). *A Behavioral Theory of the Firm*, Englewood Cliffs, New Jersey: Prentice-Hall.

Danto, Arthur C. [1965] 1968. "Basic Actions," in Alan R. White (ed.), *The Philosophy of Action*, Oxford: Oxford University Press.

Davidson, Donald [1971] 1980. "Agency," in Donald Davidson, *Essays on Actions and Events*, Oxford: Clarendon Press.

Davidson, Paul 1989. "The Economics of Ignorance or Ignorance of Economics?," *Critical Review*, 3: 467–87.

Day, R. H. and W. Huang 1990. "Bulls, Bears, and Market Sheep," *Journal of Economic Behavior and Organization*, 14: 299–329.

Debreu, Gerard 1959. *Theory of Value*, New Haven and London: Yale University Press.

DeLong, J. Bradford, Andrei Shleifer, Lawrence H. Summers, and Robert J. Waldmann 1990. "Noise Trader Risk in Financial Markets,"*Journal of Political Economy*, 98(4): 703–38.

Denzau, Arthur T. and Douglass C. North 1994. "Shared Mental Models: Ideologies and Institutions," *Kyklos*, 47(1): 1–13.

Diaconis, Persi and David Freedman 1986. "On the Consistency of Bayes Estimates," *The Annals of Statistics*, 14(1): 1–26.

Dickey, D. A. and W. A. Fuller 1979. "Distribution of the Estimates for Autoregressive Time Series with Unit Root," *Journal of the American Statistical Association*, 74: 427–32.

Dickey, D. A. and W. A. Fuller 1981. "Likelihood Ratio Statistics for Autoregressive Time Series with a Unit Root," *Econometrica*, 49: 1057–72.

Diebold, Francis and Jose A. Lopez 1995. "Modeling Volatility Dynamics," *Federal Reserve Bank of New York Research Paper*, 9522.

Diebold, Francis and Mark Nerlove 1989. "The Dynamics of Exchange Rate Volatility: A Multivariate Latent-Factor ARCH Model," *Journal of Applied Econometrics*, 4: 1–22.

Dilthey, W. [1900] 1976. "The Development of Hermeneutics," in H.P. Rickman (ed.), *W. Dilthey: Selected Writings*, London: Cambridge University Press.

Dilthey, W. [1910] 1976. "The Construction of the Historical World," in H. P. Rickman (ed.), *W. Dilthey: Selected Writings*, London: Cambridge University Press.

Ellsberg, D. 1961. "Risk, Ambiguity and the Savage Axioms," *Quarterly Journal of Economics*, 75: 643–79.

Elster, Jon 1999. *Alchemies of the Mind: Rationality and the Emotions*. New York: Cambridge University Press.

Engle, R. F. 1982. "Autoregressive Conditional Heteroskedasticity with Estimates of the Variance of U.K. Inflation," *Econometrica*, 50: 987–1008.

Engle, R, F. (ed.) 1995. *ARCH: Selected Readings*, Oxford: Oxford University Press.

Fajans, W. 1909. *Die russische Goldwährung*, Leipzig: Duncker & Humblot.

Fogel, Robert W. 1989. *Without Consent or Contract: The Rise and Fall of American Slavery*, New York: W. W. Norton.

Friedman, Milton 1953. "The Methodology of Positive Economics," in Milton Friedman, *Essays in Positive Economics*, Chicago: University of Chicago Press.

Friedman, Milton 1956. "The Quantity Theory of Money – A Restatement," in Milton Friedman, (ed.), *Studies in the Quantity Theory of Money*, Chicago: University of Chicago Press.

Gifford, S. 1998. *The Allocation of Limited Entrepreneurial Attention*, Dordrecht: Kluwer Academic.

Gilad, Benjamin 1981. *An Interdisciplinary Approach to Entrepreneurship: Locus of Control and Alertness*, PhD dissertation, New York University.

Gilanshah, Catherine Beckett and Roger Koppl 2001. "Big Players and Money Demand," in Jürgen Backhouse (ed.), *Modern Applications of Austrian Economics*, New York: Routledge, forthcoming.

Gindin, Iosif Frolovich 1960. *Gosudarstvennyj Bank i .Ekonomicheskaja Politika Tsarskogo Praviteljstva* (1861–1892 gody), Moscow: Gosfinizdat.

Gode, Dhananjay K. and Shyam Sunder 1993. "Allocative Efficiency of Markets with Zero Intelligence Traders: Market as a Partial Substitute for Individual Rationality," *The Journal of Political Economy*, 101(1): 119–37.

Goetzmann, W. N. 1993. "Patterns in Three Centuries of Stock Market Prices," *Journal of Business*, 66: 249–70.

Goldfeld, S. M. 1973. "The Demand for Money Revisited," *Brookings Papers on Economic Activity*, 3: 577–638.

Greene, Myron T. and Bruce Fielitz 1977. "Long-Term Dependence in Common Stock Returns," *Journal of Financial Economics*, 4: 339–49.

Gurjev, Aleksandr Nikolaevich 1896. *Reforma Denezhnago Obrashchenija*, St. Petersburg: Kirshbaum.

Hall, R. L. and C. J. Hitch 1939. "Price Theory and Business Behavior," *Oxford Economic Papers*, 2.

Hands, D. Wade 1993. "Popper and Lakatos in Economic Methodology," in Uskali Mäki, Bo Gustafsson, and Christian Knudsen (eds.), *Rationality, Institutions and Economic Methodology*, London and New York: Routledge.

Hardouvelis, Gikas A., Rafael La Porta, and Thierry A. Wizman 1993. "What Moves the Discount on Country Equity Funds?," *NBER Working Paper* 4571.

Harrison, Paul 1996. "Are All Financial Time-Series Alike? Evidence from 18th Century Stock Markets," manuscript, Brandeis University.

Hayek, F. A. 1935. "The Nature and History of the Problem," in F. A. Hayek, (ed.), *Collectivist Economic Planning*, London: George Routledge & Sons, Ltd.

Hayek, F. A. [1937] 1948. "Economics and Knowledge," in F. A. Hayek, *Individualism and Economic Order*, Chicago: University of Chicago Press.

Hayek, F. A. 1952a. *The Sensory Order*, Chicago: University of Chicago Press.

Hayek, F. A. 1952b. *The Counter Revolution of Science: Studies in the Abuse of Reason*, Chicago: University of Chicago Press.

Hayek, F. A. 1967. *Studies in Philosophy, Politics and Economics*, Chicago: University of Chicago Press.

Hayek, F. A. 1967a. "The Theory of Complex Phenomena," in F. A. Hayek, *Studies in Philosophy, Politics and Economics*, Chicago: University of Chicago Press.

Hayek, F. A. 1967b. "Rules, Perception and Intelligibility," in F. A. Hayek, *Studies in Philosophy, Politics and Economics*, Chicago: University of Chicago Press.

Hayek, F. A. [1969] 1978. "The Primacy of the Abstract," in F. A. Hayek, *New Studies in Philosophy, Politics, Economics and the History of Ideas*, Chicago: University of Chicago Press.

Hayek, F. A. 1973. *Law, Legislation and Liberty, Volume I: Rules and Order*. Chicago: University of Chicago Press.

Hayek, F. A. 1981. "Foreword," to Ludwig von Mises, *Socialism: An Economic and Sociological Analysis*, trans. J. Kahane, Indianapolis, Ind.: Liberty Classics.

Hayek, F. A. 1988. *The Fatal Conceit: The Errors of Socialism*, Chicago: University of Chicago Press.

Hayek, F. A. 1994. *Hayek on Hayek: An Autobiographical Dialogue*, eds. Stephe Kresge and Leif Wenar, Chicago: University of Chicago Press.

Hebb, D. O. 1949. *The Organization of Behavior*, New York: Wiley.

Heiner, Ronald A. 1983. "The Origin of Predictable Behavior," *American Economic Review*, 73: 560–95.

Helling, Ingeborg K. 1984. "A. Schutz and F. Kaufmann: Sociology Between Science and Interpretation," *Human Studies*, 7(2): 141–61.

Helms, Billy P., Fred R. Kaen, and Robert E. Rosenman 1984. "Memory in Commodity Futures Contracts," *Journal of Futures Markets*, 4: 559–67.

Hiemstra, Craig 1993. "An Application of the Modified Rescaled Range Test to the Daily Returns of Individual-Firm Stocks," mimeo, Loyola College.

Hirschman Albert O. 1977. *The Passions and the Interests: Political Arguments for Capitalism before Triumph* Princeton: Princeton University Press.

Holland, John H. 1992. *Adaptation in Natural and Artificial Systems: An Introductory Analysis with Applications to Biology, Control, and Artificial Intelligence*, Cambridge, Mass: MIT Press.

Holland, John H., K. J. Holyoak, R. E. Nisbett, and P. R. Thagard 1986. *Induction: Processes of Inference, Learning, and Discovery*, Cambridge, Mass.: MIT Press.

Horwitz, Steven 1999. "From Smith to Menger to Hayek: Liberalism in the Tradition of the Scottish Enlightenment," Paper presented to the History of Economics Society, June.

Horwitz, Steven 2000. *Microfoundations and Macroeconomics: An Austrian Perspective*, New York: Routledge.

Horwitz, Steven 2002. "The Costs of Inflation Revisited," *Review of Austrian Economics*, forthcoming.

Howitt, Peter and Robert Clower 2000. "The Emergence of Economic Organization," *Journal of Economic Behavior and Organization*, 41: 55–84.

Huang, Roger D. and Hans R. Stoll 1994. "Market Microstructure and Stock Return Predictions," *Review of Financial Studies*, 7: 179–213.

Hurst, H. E. *et al.* 1965. *Long-Term Storage, An Experimental Study*, London: Constable.

Husserl, Edmund [1911] 1965. "Philosophy as Rigorous Science," in Edmund Husserl, *Phenomenology and the Crisis of Philosophy*, trans. and ed. Quentin Lauer, New York: Harper Torchbooks.

Husserl, Edmund [1913] 1962. *Ideas: General Introduction to Pure Phenomenology*, trans. W. R. Boyce Gibson, New York: Collier Books.

Hutchison, T. W. 1984. *The Politics and Philosophy of Economics*, New York and London: New York University Press.

Jones, David M. 1989. *Fed Watching and Interest Rate Projections: A Practical Guide*, New York Institute of Finance, New York: Simon and Schuster.

Jones, R. A. 1976. "The Origin and Development of Media of Exchange," *Journal of Political Economy*, 84: 757–75.

Kaen, Fred R. and Robert E. Rosenman 1986. "Predictable Behavior in Financial Markets: Some Evidence in Support of Heiner's Hypothesis," *American Economic Review*, 76: 212–20.

Kahneman, D. and A. Tversky (1979). "Prospect Theory: An Analysis of Decision Under Risk," *Econometrica*, 47 March: 263–91.

Kant, Immanuel 1787 [1934]. *Critique of Pure Reason*, New York: E. P. Dutton & Co.

Kaplan, Stephen 1992. "Environmental Preference in a Knowledge-Seeking, Knowledge-Using Organism," in Jerome Barkow, Leda Cosmides, and John Tooby (eds.), *The Adapted Mind: Evolutionary Psychology and the Generation of Culture*, New York and Oxford: Oxford University Press.

Kauffman, Stuart A. 1993. *The Origins of Order: Self-Organization and Selection in Evolution*, New York and Oxford: Oxford University Press.

Kauffman, Stuart A. 1994. "Whispers from Carnot: The Origins of Order and Prinicples of Adaptation in Complex Nonequilibrium Systems," in George A. Cowan, David Pines, and David Meltzer (eds.), *Complexity: Metaphors, Models, and Reality*, Reading, Mass.: Addison-Wesley.

Keynes, John Maynard [1936] 1973. "The General Theory of Employment, Interest, and Money," *The Collected Writings of John Maynard Keynes*, Vol. VII, London: Macmillan.

Keynes, John Maynard [1937] 1973. "The General Theory of Employment," in *Collected Writings*, Vol. XIV, New York: St. Martin's Press.

Kirzner, I. M. 1973. *Competition and Entrepreneurship*, Chicago: University of Chicago Press.

Kirzner, I. M. 1979. *Perception, Opportunity, and Profit: Studies in the Theory of Entrepreneurship* Chicago: University of Chicago Press.

Knudsen, Christian 1993. "Equilibrium, Perfect Rationality and the Problem of Self-Reference in Economics," in Uskali Mäki, Bo Gustafsson, and Christian Knudsen (eds.), *Rationality, Institutions, and Economic Methodology*, London: Routledge.

Koppl, Roger 1992. "Invisible-Hand Explanations and Neoclassical Economics: Toward a Post Marginalist Economics," *Journal of Institutional and Theoretical Economics*, 148(2): 292–313.

Koppl, Roger 1994. "Lachmann on Schutz and Shackle," *Advances in Austrian Economics*, 1: 289–301.

Koppl, Roger 1996. "It is High Time We Take Our Ignorance More Seriously," *International Review of Financial Analysis*, 5(3): 259–72.

Koppl, Roger 1997. "Mises and Schutz on Ideal Types," *Cultural Dynamics*, 9(1): 67–76.

Koppl, Roger 1998. "Lachmann on the Subjectivism of Active Minds," in Roger Koppl and Gary Mongiovi (eds.), *Subjectivism and Economic Analysis: Essays in Memory of Ludwig Lachmann*, New York and London: Routledge.

Koppl, Roger 1999. "Apriorism and Dualism," *Advances in Austrian Economics*, 5: 159–79.

Koppl, Roger 2000a. "Machlup and Behavioralism," *Industrial and Corporate Change*, 9(4): 595–622.

Koppl, Roger 2000b. "Policy Implications of Complexity: An Austrian Perspective," in David Colander (ed.), *The Complexity Vision and the Teaching of Economics*, Cheltenham, UK: Edward Elgar.

Koppl, Roger 2000c. "Teaching Complexity: An Austrian Approach," in David Colander (ed.), *The Complexity Vision and the Teaching of Economics*, Cheltenham, UK: Edward Elgar.

Koppl, Roger 2001. "Schutz and Shackle: Two Views of Choice," *Review of Austrian Economics*, 14(2/3): 181–91.

Koppl, Roger and Richard N. Langlois 1994. "When Do Ideas Matter? A Study in the Natural Selection of Social Games," *Advances in Austrian Economics*, 1: 81–104.

Koppl, Roger and Dusan Mramor 2000. "Big Players in Slovenia," manuscript, Fairleigh Dickinson University.

Koppl, Roger and Carlo Nardone 2001. "The Angular Distribution of Asset Returns in Delay Space," *Discrete Dynamics in Nature and Society*, 6: 101–20.

Koppl, Roger and Leland B. Yeager 1996. "Big Players and Herding in Asset Markets: The Case of the Russian Ruble," *Explorations in Economic History*, 33(3): 367–83

Koppl, Roger and J. Barkley Rosser 2001. "All That I Have to Say Has Already Crossed Your Mind," manuscript, Fairleigh Dickinson University.

Koutmos, G. and P. Theodossiou 1994. "Time-Series Properties and Predictability of Greek Exchange Rates," *Managerial and Decision Economics*, 14, 159–67.

Kramer, Walter and Ralf Runde 1997. "Chaos and the Compass Rose," *Economics Letters*, 54(2): 113–18.

Kreiner, Kristian 1989. "Culture and Meaning: Making Sense of Conflicting Realities in the Workplace," *International Studies of Management and Organization*,19(3): 64–81.

Kurrild-Klitgaard, Peter 2001. "On Rationality, Ideal Types and Economics: Alfred Schutz and the Austrian School," *Review of Austrian Economics*, 14(2/3): 119–43.

Kydland, Finn E. and Edward C. Prescott 1977. "Rules Rather than Discretion: The Inconsistency of Optimal Plans," *Journal of Political Economy*, 85(3): 473–91.

Lachmann, Ludwig 1943 [1977]. "The Role of Expectations in Economics as a Social Science," in Ludwig Lachmann and Walter E. Grinder (eds), *Capital, Expectations, and the Market Process*, Kansas City, Missouri: Sheed Andrews & McMeel: 149–165.

Lachmann, Ludwig 1976. "From Mises to Shackle: An Essay on Austrian Economics and the Kaleidic Society," *Journal of Economic Literature*, 14(1): 54–62.

Lachmann, Ludwig 1981. "Forward" to Ludwig von Mises, *Epistemological Problems of Economics*, trans. George Reisman, New York and London: New York University Press.

Lachmann, Ludwig 1990. "G. L. S. Shackle's Place in the History of Subjectivist Thought," in S.F. Fowen (ed.), *Unknowledge and Choice: Proceedings of a Conference in Honour of G. L. S. Shackle*, New York: St. Martin's Press.

Laidler, D. E. W. 1977. *The Demand for Money: Theories and Evidence,* New York: Dun-Donnelley.

Laidler, D. E. W. 1993. *The Demand for Money: Theories, Evidence, and Problems*, New York: HarperCollins, 4th edn.

Lamoreaux, C. G. and W. D. Lastrapes 1993. "Forecasting Stock Return Variance: Toward an Understanding of Stochastic Implied Volitilities," *Review of Financial Studies*, 6: 293–326.

Langlois, Richard N. 1986a. "Rationality, Institutions, and Explanation," in Richard Langlois (ed.), *Economics as a Process: Essays in the New Institutional Economics*, Chicago: University of Chicago Press.

Langlois, Richard N. (ed.), 1986b. *Economics as a Process: Essays in the New Institutional Economics*, Chicago: University of Chicago Press.

Langlois, Richard N. 1989. "What Was Wrong with the 'Old' Institutional Economics? (And What Is Still Wrong with the 'New'?)," *Review of Political Economy*, 1(3): 272–300.

Langlois, Richard N. 1998. "Rule-Following, Expertise, and Rationality: A New Behavioral Economics?," in Kenneth Dennis (ed.), *Rationality in Economics: Alternative Perspectives*, Dordrecht: Kluwer Academic.

Langlois, Richard N. and Roger Koppl. 1991. "Fritz Machlup and Marginalism: A Reevaluation," *Methodus*, 3(2): 86–102.

Lavoie, Don 1986. "Euclideanism versus Hermeneutics: A Reinterpretation of Misesian Apriorism," in Israel Kirzner, *Subjectivism, Intelligibility and Economic*

Understanding: Essays in Honor of Ludwig M. Lachmann on his Eightieth Birthday, New York: New York University Press.

Lavoie, Don 1994. "The Interpretive Turn," in Peter J. Boettke (ed.), *The Elgar Companion to Austrian Economics,* Cheltenham, UK: Edward Elgar.

Law, John 1705 [1966]. *Money and Trade Considered, With a Proposal For Supplying The Nation With Money,* New York: Augustus M. Kelley.

Leijonhufvud, Axel. [1973] 1981. "Effective Demand Failures," in Leijonhufvud, A. *Information and Coordination.* New York and Oxford: Oxford University Press.

Leijonhufvud, Axel 1986. "Inflation and Economic Performance," in Barry N. Siegel (ed.), *Money in Crisis,* Cambridge, Mass.: Ballinger.

LeRoy, Stephen F. 1989. "Efficient Capital Markets and Martingales," *Journal of Economic Literature,* 23(4): 1583–621.

Ljung, G. M. and G. E. P. Box 1978. "On a Measure of Lack of Fit in Time Series Models," *Biometrika,* 65, 297–303.

Lo, Andrew 1991. "Long-Term Memory in Stock Market Prices," *Econometrica,* 59: 1279–313.

Loretan, M. and P. C. B. Phillips 1994. "Testing the Covariance Stationarity of Heavy-Tailed Time Series: An Overview of the Theory With Applications to Several Financial Datasets," *Journal of Empirical Finance,* 1: 211–48.

Lucas, Robert E. 1980. "Methods and Problems in Business Cycle Theory," in Robert E. Lucas, *Studies in Business Cycle Theory,* Cambridge, Mass.: MIT Press.

Luo, Guo Ying 1999. "Evolution of Money as a Medium of Exchange," *Journal of Economic Dynamics & Control,* 23: 415–58.

Machlup, Fritz [1936] 1978. "Why Bother With Methodology?," in Firtz Machlup, *Methodology of Economics and Other Social Sciences,* New York: Academic Press.

Machlup, Fritz 1946 [1975]. "Marginal Analysis and Empirical Research," in Firtz Machlup, *Essays in Economic Semantics,* New York: New York University Press.

Machlup, Fritz 1952. *The Economics of Sellers' Competition: Model Analysis of Sellers' Conduct,* Baltimore: Johns Hopkins University Press.

Machlup, Fritz 1967 [1978]. "Theories of the Firm: Marginalist, Behavioral, Managerial," in Firtz Machlup *Methodology of Economics and Other Social Sciences,* New York: Academic Press.

Machlup, Fritz 1978. *Methodology of Economics and Other Social Sciences,* New York: Academic Press.

Machlup, Fritz 1980, "An Interview with Professor Machlup," *Austrian Economics Newsletter,* 3, 1, 9–12.

Mandelbrot, Benoit 1971. "When Can Price be Arbitraged Efficiently? A Limit to the Validity of the Random Walk and Martingale Models," *Review of Economics and Statistics,* 53(3): 225–36.

Mandelbrot, Benoit 1972. "Statistical Methodology for Nonperiodic Cycles: From the Covariance to R/S Analysis," *Annals of Economic and Social Measurement,* 1(3): 259–90.

Mandelbrot, Benoit 1997. *Fractals and Scaling in Finance: Discontinuity, Concentration, Risk,* New York: Springer.

Mandelbrot, Benoit and J.R. Wallis 1968. "Noah, Joseph, and Operational Hydrology," *Water Resources Research,* 4: 909–17.

Mandelbrot, Benoit and J.R. Wallis 1969a. "Some Long-Run Properties of Geophysical Records," *Water Resources Research,* 5: 321–40.

Mandelbrot, Benoit and J. R. Wallis, 1969b. "Robustness of the Rescaled Range R/S in the Measurement of Noncyclic Long Run Statistical Dependence," *Water Resources Research,* 5(5): 967–88.

McCloskey, Donald and Arjo Klamer 1995. "One Quarter of GDP is Persuasion," *American Economic Review,* 85(2): 191–95.

McGrew, W. C. and Anna T. C. Feistner 1992. "Two Nonhuman Primate Models for the Evolution of Human Food Sharing: Chimpanzees and Callitrichids," in Jerome Barkow, Leda Cosmides, and John Tooby (eds.), *The Adapted Mind: Evolutionary Psychology and the Generation of Culture,* New York and Oxford: Oxford University Press.

Meese, R. 1990. "Currency Fluctuations in the Post-Bretton Woods Era," *Journal of Economic Perspectives,* 4(1): 117–34.

Melton, William W. 1985. *Inside the Fed: Making Monetary Policy,* Homewood, Ill.: Dow Jones-Irwin.

Menger, C. [1871] 1981. *Principles of Economics,* trans. James Dingwell and Bert F. Hoselitz, New York: New York University Press.

Menger, C. [1883] 1963. *Problems of Economics and Sociology,* trans. Francis J. Nock, ed. Louis Scheider, Urbana, Ill.: University of Illinois Press.

Menger, Karl [1934] 1974. *Morality, Decision and Social Organization,* Dordrecht, Holland and Boston: D. Reidel Publishing company.

Meulendyke, Ann-Marie 1989. *U.S. Monetary Policy and Financial Markets,* Federal Reserve Bank of New York.

Migulin, P. P. 1899–1904. *Russkij Gosudarstvennyj Kredit (1769–1899),* several volumes and supplements, Kharkov: Tipo-Litografija "Pechatnoe Delo."

Minniti, Maria 1999. "Entrepreneurial Activity and Economic Growth," *Global Business and Economics Review,* 11(1): 31–42.

Minniti, Maria and William Bygrave 1999. "The Microfoundations of Entrepreneurship," *Entrepreneurship Theory and Practice,* 23(4): 1–12.

Minniti, Maria and William Bygrave 2000. "The Social Dynamics of Entrepreneurship," *Entrepreneurship Theory and Practice,* 24(3): 25–36.

Minniti, Maria and Roger Koppl 1999. "The Unintended Consequences of Entrepreneurship," *Journal des Economistes et des Etudes Humaines,* 9(4): 567–86.

Minniti, Maria and Lidja Polutnik 1999. "No Name Money," manuscript, Babson College.

Mirowski, Philip 1990. "From Mandelbrot to Chaos in Economic Theory," *Southern Economic Journal,* 57(2): 289–307.

Mises, Ludwig [1933] 1981. *Epistemological Problems of Economics,* trans. by George Reisman, New York and London: New York University Press.

Mises, Ludwig [1929] 1981. "Sociology and History," in *Epistemological Problems of Economics,* New York and London: New York University Press.

Mises, Ludwig [1930] 1981. "Conception and Understanding," in *Epistemological Problems of Economics,* New York and London: New York University Press.

Mises, Ludwig [1933a] 1981. "Preface to the German Edition," of Ludwig Mises, *Epistemological Problems of Economics,* New York and London: New York University Press.

Mises, Ludwig [1933b] 1981. "The Task and Scope of the Science of Human Action," in *Epistemological Problems of Economics,* New York and London: New York University Press.

Mises, Ludwig [1957] 1969. *Theory and History: An Interpretation of Social and Economic Evolution*, Westport, Conn.: Arlington House.

Mises, Ludwig 1962. *The Ultimate Foundations of Economic Science: An Essay on Method*, Princeton: D. Van Nostrand.

Mises, Ludwig 1966. *Human Action: A Treatise on Economics*, Chicago: Henry Regnery Company, 3rd rev. edn.

Mishkin, Frederic S. 1995. *The Economics of Money, Banking, and Financial Markets*, New York: HarperCollins, 4th edn.

Morgenstern, Oskar [1935] 1976. "Perfect Foresight and Economic Equilibrium" (Frank Knight's translation of "Vollkommene Voraussicht und wirtschaftliches Gleichgewicht," *Zeitschrift für Nationalökonomie*, 6(3):337–57), reprinted in Andrew Schotter (ed.), *Selected Writings of Oskar Morgenstern*, New York: New York University Press.

Natanson, Maurice 1973. *Edmund Husserl: Philosopher of Infinite Tasks*, Evanston, Ill.: Northwestern University Press.

Nelson, Richard R. and Sidney G. Winter 1982. *An Evolutionary Theory of Economic Change*, Cambridge, Mas: Harvard University Press.

Oakley, Allen 1997. *The Foundations of Austria Economics from Menger and Mises: A Critico-Historical Retrospective of Subjectivism*, Cheltenham, UK: Edward Elgar.

O'Driscoll, Gerald 1977. *Economics as a Coordination Problem*, Mission, Kansas: Sheed Andrews and McMeel.

O'Driscoll, Gerald and Mario Rizzo 1985. *The Economics of Time and Ignorance*, Oxford: Basil Blackwell.

O'Driscoll, Gerald and Mario Rizzo 1996. *The Economics of Time and Ignorance*, London and New York: Routledge, reprint with a new introduction of the original 1985 edn.

Offe, Claus 1976. *Industry and Inequality: The Achievement Principle in Work and Social Status*, London: Edward Arnold, Ltd.

Parke, William R. 1999. "What is Fractional Integration?," *Review of Economics and Statistics*, 81(4): 632–38.

Peters, Edgar E. 1989. "Fractal Structure in the Capital Markets," *Financial Analysts Journal*, July–August: 32–7.

Phillips, P. C. B. and P. Perron 1988. "Testing for a Unit Root in Time Series Regression," *Biometrika*, 75, 335–46.

Pitkin Hanna F. 1972. *Wittgenstein and Justice: On the Significance of Ludwig Wittgenstein for Social and Political Thought*, Berkeley: University of California Press.

Piron, Robert 1991. "Correspondence: Keynes as Noise Trader," *Journal of Economic Perspectives*, 5(2): 215–17.

Polovtsov, Aleksandr Aleksandrovich 1966. *Dnevnik Gosudarstvennogo Sekretarja A. A. Polovtsova,* 2 vols., Moscow: Izdateljstvo "Nauka."

Prasad, Kislaya 1991. "Computability and Randomness of Nash Equilibrium in Infinite Games" Journal of Mathematical Economics 20(5): 429–42.

Prendergast, Christopher 1986. "Alfred Schutz and the Austrian School of Economics," *American Journal of Sociology*, 92: 1–26.

Press, W. H., B. P. Flannery, S. A. Teukolski, and W. T. Vetterling 1992. *Numerical Recipes*, Cambridge: Cambridge University Press, 2nd edn.

Propper, Stanislav Maksimilianovich v. 1929. *Was nicht in die Zeitung kam*, Frankfurt a/M: Frankfurter Societäts-Druckerei.

Prychitko, David L. 1994. "Praxeology," in Peter J. Boettke (ed.), *Elgar Companion to Austrian Economics*, Aldershot, UK: Edward Elgar.

Rabin, M. O. 1957. "Effective Computability of Winning Strategies," in M. Dresher, A. W. Tucker, and P. Wolfe (eds), *Annals of Mathematical Studies*, 3 (39), Princeton: Princeton University Press: 147–57.

Radner, Roy 1975. "A Behavioral Model of Cost Reduction," *The Bell Journal of Economics*, 6(1): 196–215.

Radner, Roy and Michael Rothschild 1975. "On the Allocation of Effort," *Journal of Economic Theory*, 10: 358–76.

Raffalovich, Arthur 1892. *Le marché financier en 1891*, Paris: Guillaumin.

Ratner, David 1898. *Rubel- und -Wechselkurse 1885–1895*, Munich: Kastner & Lossen.

Rickman H. P. (ed.) 1976. *W. Dilthey: Selected Writings*, London: Cambridge University Press.

Robbins, Lionel. 1932. *An Essay on the Nature and Significance of Economic Science*. London: Macmillan & Co., Ltd.

Roley, Vance 1990. "Market Perceptions of U.S. Policy Since 1982," in Thomas Davis (ed.), *Financial Market Volatility and the Economy*, Federal Reserve Bank of Kansas: 39–40.

Rosser, J. Barkley, Jr. 2001. "Uncertainty and Expectations," in Richard P. F. Holt and Steven Pressman (eds), *A New Guide to Post Keynesian Economics*, London: Routledge.

Sargent, Thomas J. 1993. *Bounded Rationality in Macroeconomics*, Oxford: Oxford University Press.

Scharfstein, David S. and Jeremy C. Stein 1990. "Herd Behavior and Investment," *American Economic Review*, 80(3): 465–79.

Schulze-Gävernitz, Gerhart v. 1899. *Volkswirtschaftliche Studien aus Russland*, Leipzig: Dunker & Humblot.

Schumpeter, Joseph A. 1934. *The Theory of Economic Development*, Oxford: Oxford University Press.

Schumpeter, Joseph A. 1939. *Business Cycles*, 2 vols, New York: McGraw-Hill.

Schutz, Alfred [1932a] 1967. *The Phenomenology of the Social World*, trans. George Walsh and Frederick Lehnert, Evanston, Ill.: Northwestern University Press.

Schutz, Alfred [1932b] 1976. "The Dimensions of the Social World," in Alfred Schutz, *Collected Papers II: Studies in Social Theory*, ed. Arvid Brodersen, The Hague: Martinus Nijhoff.

Schutz, Alfred 1934. "Staat-Gesellschaft-Recht-Wirtschaft," review of Mises 'Grundprobleme der Nationalökonomie', *Deutsche Literaturzeitung*, 1 (January): 36–42, translated as: "Basic Problems of Political Economy," in Alfred Schutz, *Collected Papers, Vol. IV*. eds. Helmut Wagner, George Psathas, and Fred Kersten, Dordrecht: Kluwer Academic, 1996: 88–92.

Schutz, Alfred 1943[1964]. "The Problem of Rationality in the Social World," in Alfred Schutz, *Collected Papers II: Studies in Social Theory*, ed. Arvid Brodersen, The Hague: Martinus Nijhoff.

Schutz, Alfred 1946 [1964]. "The Well-Informed Citizen," in *Collected Papers II: Studies in Social Theory*, ed. Arvid Brodersen, The Hague: Martinus Nijhoff.

Schutz, Alfred 1951 [1962]. "Choosing Among Projects of Action," in Alfred Schutz, *Collected Papers I: The Problem of Social Reality*, ed. Maurue Natanson The Hague: Martinus Nijhoff.

Schutz, Alfred [1953] 1962. "Common-Sense and Scientific Interpretation of Human Action," in Alfred Schutz, *Collected Papers I: The Problem of Social Reality*, ed. Maurice Natanson, The Hague: Martinus Nijhoff.

Schutz, Alfred [1954] 1962. "Concept and Theory Formation in the Social Sciences," in Alfred Schutz, *Collected Papers I: The Problem of Social Reality*, ed. Maurice Natanson, The Hague: Martinus Nijhoff.

Schutz, Alfred [1959] 1964. "Tiresias, or our Knowledge of Future Events," in Alfred Schutz *Collected Papers II: Studies in Social Theory*, ed. Arved Brodersen, The Hague: Martinus Nijhoff.

Schutz, Alfred 1967. *The Phenomenology of the Social World*, trans. George Walsh and Frederick Lehnert, Evanston, Ill: Northwestern University Press.

Schutz, Alfred and Thomas Luckmann 1973. *The Structures of the Life-World* (Volume I), Evanston, Ill: Northwestern University Press.

Selgin, George n.d. "Network Effects, Adaptive Learning, and the Transition to Fiat Money," manuscript, University of Georgia

Shackle, George L. S. 1949. *Expectations in Economics*, Cambrige: Cambridge University Press.

Shackle, George L. S. 1972. *Epistemics and Economics*, Cambridge: Cambridge University Press.

Shepard, Roger 1992. "The Perceptual Organization of Colors: An Adaptation to Regularities of the Terrestial World?," in Jerome H. Barkow, Leda Cosmides, and John Tooby (eds) *The Adapted Mind: Evolutionary Psychology and the Generation of Culture*, New York and Oxford: Oxford University Press.

Shiller, Robert. 1989. *Market Volatility*, Cambridge, Mass.: MIT Press.

Shleifer, Andrei and Lawrence Summers 1990. "The Noise Trader Approach to Finance," *Journal of Economic Perspectives*, 4(2): 19–33.

Simon, Herbert A. 1955. "A Behavioral Model of Rational Choice," *Quarterly Journal of Economics*, 69: 99-118.

Smith, Adam 1937. *An Inquiry into the Nature and Causes of the Wealth of Nations*, ed. Edwin Canaan, New York: Modern Library.

Spear, S.E. 1989. "Learning Rational Expectations Under Computability Constraints," *Econometrica*, 57: 889–910.

Symons, Donald 1992. "On the Use and Misuse of Darwinism in the Study of Human Behavior," in Jerome H. Barkow, Leda Cosmides, and John Tooby (eds) *The Adapted Mind: Evolutionary Psychology and the Generation of Culture*, New York and Oxford: Oxford University Press.

Tauchen, George and Mark Pitts 1983. "The Price Variability–Volume Relationship on Speculative Markets," *Econometrica*, 51(2): 485–506.

Thaler, Richard H. 1992. *The Winner's Curse: Paradoxes and Anomalies of Economic Life*, Princeton: Princeton University Press.

Theodossiou, P. 1994. "The Stochastic Properties of Major Canadian Exchange Rates," *The Financial Review*, 29: 193–221.

Tocqueville, Alexis [1835 as 1840] 1945 *Democracy in America: The Henry Reeve Text*, edited by Philips Bradley, New York: Vintage Books.

Tooby, John and Leda Cosmides 1992. "The Psychological Foundations of Culture," in Jerome H. Barkow, Leda Cosmides, and John Tooby (eds), *The Adapted Mind: Evolutionary Psychology and the Generation of Culture*, New York and Oxford: Oxford University Press.

Topol, R. 1991. "Bubbles and Volatility of Stock Prices: Effect of Mimetic Contagion," *Economic Journal*, 101(407): 786–800.

Tsion, I. F. 1892. *Itogi Finansovago Upravlenija g. Vyshnegradskago po Ofitsijaljnym Dokumentam*, Paris: Chamerot & Renouard; lausanne: Benda.

Vanberg, Victor 1994. *Rules and Choice in Economics*, London and New York: Routledge.

Vaughn, Karen I. 1999. "Hayek's Theory of the Market Order as an Instance of the Theory of Complex, Adaptive Systems," *Journal des Economistes et des Etudes Humaines*, 9(2/3): 241–56.

Velupillai, Kumaraswamy 1996. "The Computable Alternative in the Formalization of Economics: A Counterfactual Essay," *Kyklos*, 49(3): 251–72.

Wallis, James R. and Nicholas C. Matalas 1970. "Small Sample Properties of H and K-Estimators of the Hurst Coefficient h," *Water Resources Research*, 6(6): 1583–94.

Walras, Léon 1874-1877 [1954]. *Elements of Pure Economics*, trans. from the Edition Définitive of 1926 by William Jaffé, Homewood, Ill.: Richard D. Irwin.

Weber, Max 1927 [1980]. *General Economic History*, New Brunswick: Transaction Books.

Weber, Max 1962. *Basic Concepts in Sociology*, Secaucus, New Jersey: Citadel Press.

West, Kenneth D. 1988. "Bubbles, Fads and Stock Price Volatility Tests: A Partial Evaluation," *Journal of Finance*, 43(3): 639–56.

Westie, Frank R. 1965. "The American Dilemma: An Empirical Test," *American Sociological Review*, 30: 527–38.

Whitman, Douglas Glen 1998. "Hayek contra Pangloss on Evolutionary Systems," *Constitutional Political Economy*, 9: 45–66.

Williamson, Oliver E. 1975. *Markets and Hierarchies: Analysis and Antitrust Implications*, New York: Free Press.

Williamson, Oliver E, 1976. "Franchise Bidding for Natural Monopolies – in General and with Respect to CATV," *Bell Journal of Economics*, 7(1): 73–104.

Witte, Sergej Juljevich 1923. *Vospominanija. Detstvo. Tsarstvovanija Aleksandra II i Aleksandra III (1849-1894)*, Berlin: Slovo.

Wittgenstein, Ludwig 1958a. *The Blue and Brown Books*, New York: Harper & Row.

Wittgenstein, Ludwig 1958b. *Philosophical Investigations*, New York: Macmillan Publishing, 3rd edn.

Wolpert, David H. 1996. "An Incompleteness Theorem for Calculating the Future," Santa Fe Institute, *Working Paper*, 96-03-008.

Yeager, Leland B. 1969. "Fluctuating Exchange Rates in the Nineteenth Century: The Experiences of Austria and Russia," in R. A. Mundell and A. K. Swoboda, (eds.), *Monetary Problems of the International Economy*, Chicago: University of Chicago Press.

Yeager, Leland B. 1981. "Rules Versus Authorities Revisited," *Atlantic Economic Journal*, 9(3): 1–10.

Yeager, Leland B. 1984. "The Image of the Gold Standard," in Michael D. Bordo and Anna J. Schwartz (eds.), *A Retrospective on the Classical Gold Standard, 1821–1931*, Chicago: University of Chicago Press.

Yeager, Leland B. 1998. "How to Avoid International Financial Crises," *Cato Journal*, 17(3).

Zacharakis, Andrew, Paul D. Reynolds, and William D. Bygrave 1999. *Global Entrepreneurship Monitor: 1999 Executive Report*, Kansas City, Mo.: Kaufman Center for Entrepreneurial Leadership.

Name Index

Subject Index